FORGIVE
for
GOOD

**A PROVEN PRESCRIPTION FOR
HEALTH AND HAPPINESS**

DR. FRED LUSKIN

HarperOne
An Imprint of HarperCollinsPublishers

HarperOne

HarperCollins books may be purchased for educational, business, or
sales promotional use. For information please write: Special Markets
Department, HarperCollins Publishers, 10 East 53rd Street, New York,
NY 10022.

HarperCollins Web site: http://www.harpercollins.com

HarperCollins®, ▥®, and HarperOne™ are trademarks of HarperCollins
Publishers.

FIRST HARPERCOLLINS PAPERBACK EDITION PUBLISHED IN 2003

Library of Congress Cataloging-in-Publication Data
Luskin, Fred.
Forgive for good : a proven prescription for health and happiness /
Fred Luskin. — 1st ed.
p. cm.
ISBN: 978–0–06–251721–0
1. Forgiveness. I. Title.
BF637.F67 L87 2001
158.2—dc21   2001047030

10 11 RRD(H) 30 29 28 27 26 25 24

Praise for *Forgive for Good*

"Dr. Luskin lifts forgiveness out of the purely psychological and religious domains and anchors it in science, medicine, and health. This book is vitally needed."

—Larry Dossey, M.D., author of *Healing Words*

"Simply the best book on the subject, adding sophistication and depth to our instinctive but sometimes uncertain understanding of how forgiveness heals both those forgiven and those who forgive. Luskin's research also shows how modern psychology can enrich traditional moral teachings. His book will stand as a modern classic in psychology."

—Michael Murphy, cofounder of the Esalen Institute and author of *Future of the Body*

"Combining groundbreaking research with a proven methodology, *Forgive for Good* is an accessible and practical guide to learning the power of forgiveness."

—John Gray, Ph.D., author of *Men Are from Mars, Women Are from Venus*

"Straightforward, sincere, and essential."

—Dave Pelzer, author of *A Child Called It* and *Help Yourself*

"A rare and marvelous book—warm, loving, solidly researched, and wise. It could change your life."

—George Leonard, author of *Mastery* and president of the Esalen Institute

"Dr. Luskin's wise and clinically astute methods for finding forgiveness could not be more timely . . . a sure-handed guide through the painful emotions of hurt, sadness and anger towards a resolution that makes peace with the past, soothes the present, and liberates the future."

—David Spiegel, M.D., professor and associate chair of Psychiatry & Behavioral Sciences, Stanford University

"Good practical advice for a very difficult task."

—*Booklist*

"Luskin shows why forgiveness is important for mental and physical health, explains how to form a grievance and suggests practical steps for healing . . . solidly researched and convincing."

—*Publishers Weekly*

*This book is dedicated to my parents Barbara and Philip Luskin
who loved me to the best of their ability, forgave me tirelessly and
without complaint, and modeled the virtue of trying
to make the world a better place.*

Contents

Introduction

Picture the crowded screen in front of a harried air traffic controller. Picture the chaos in the room and the jumble of planes on the screen. Now imagine that your unresolved grievances are the planes on that screen that have been circling for days and weeks on end. Most of the other planes have landed, but your unresolved grievances continue to take up precious air space, draining resources that may be needed in an emergency. Having them on the screen forces you to work harder and increases the chance for accidents. The grievance planes become a source of stress and burnout is often the result.

HOW DID THE PLANES GET UP THERE IN THE FIRST PLACE?

You took something too personally.

You continued to blame the person who hurt you for how bad you felt.

You created a grievance story.

WHAT IS FORGIVENESS?

- Forgiveness is the peace you learn to feel when you allow these circling planes to land.
- Forgiveness is for you and not the offender.
- Forgiveness is taking back your power.
- Forgiveness is taking responsibility for how you feel.
- Forgiveness is about your healing and not about the people who hurt you.
- Forgiveness is a trainable skill just like learning to throw a baseball.

- Forgiveness helps you get control over your feelings.
- Forgiveness can improve your mental and physical health.
- Forgiveness is becoming a hero instead of a victim.
- Forgiveness is a choice.
- Everyone can learn to forgive.

WHAT FORGIVENESS IS NOT

- Forgiveness is not condoning unkindness.
- Forgiveness is not forgetting that something painful happened.
- Forgiveness is not excusing poor behavior.
- Forgiveness does not have to be an otherworldly or religious experience.
- Forgiveness is not denying or minimizing your hurt.
- Forgiveness does not mean reconciling with the offender.
- Forgiveness does not mean you give up having feelings.

I do not suggest that forgiveness means we give up our right to be angry when we have been hurt or mistreated. My forgiveness research shows that people retain their ability to be angry but simply use that ability more wisely. I am not suggesting that forgiveness means we condone the hurtful things that people have done to us. I have seen that forgiveness helps people control their emotions so they maintain good judgment. They do not waste precious energy trapped in anger and hurt over things they can do nothing about. Forgiveness acknowledges we can't change the past. Forgiveness allows us not to stay stuck in the past. Forgiveness allows us to land our planes and then make any repairs that may be necessary. Forgiveness gives us a well deserved break.

Some of you may have doubts that forgiveness will help you as much as I claim. You may think that by forgiving you are somehow letting the other person get away with their actions. Or that forgiveness means reconciling with someone who hurt you. You might be still searching to understand why someone was so cruel to you, and you don't believe learning to forgive is going to help you find the reason. Or you have suffered for a long time and are just plain suspicious of anything that sounds like a cure. If this is you in any way, you are not alone. I confront it every time I teach a new class.

Recently, I had a man in my forgiveness seminar who voiced the concerns that many were feeling. Jeremy attended because his boss at work had lied to him and he was anxious to know how to deal with that betrayal. His boss had lied repeatedly about something important, and two months ago Jeremy finally discovered the truth. He was so furious as he talked that it seemed as if he just uncovered the lie the day before. He questioned me immediately about the value of forgiveness.

Jeremy had the following concerns.

1. If I forgive my boss, am I condoning his lying?
2. How can I trust my boss again?
3. Should I confront my boss?
4. How do I stop obsessing over this?

I told Jeremy what I will tell all of you. Just because someone hurt you does not mean you have to suffer indefinitely. Jeremy's boss lied, and that is clearly wrong. In order to forgive, you have to know that lying is wrong. Forgiveness does not mean condoning lying. Forgiveness helps Jeremy become able to answer the question of what he can do about his lying boss. Forgiveness shows Jeremy that he can still enjoy his life, his family, and his friends and not invite this lying boss along everywhere he goes.

I asked Jeremy if his boss was really worth the ruining of so many days in the last eight weeks. Jeremy said he was not. I responded that the solution, then, is to learn a new skill so that he does not ruin the next two months. That skill is forgiveness.

I told Jeremy that he might not be able to trust his boss again and that he may never respect him again. He might choose to remain at work with a boss he does not respect, or he might get a new job. He might choose to confront his boss, or he might not. Clearly, Jeremy had some hard choices to make. I finally told him that as long as he was trapped in his anger, he would not be able to clear his mind enough to make the best possible decisions. As long as he was angry and hurt, the decisions he was contemplating were more about his lying boss than they were about his own well-being. Learning to forgive allows Jeremy and us to make the best possible life decisions. And whether Jeremy was calm or miserable, he still had to decide what to do about working for a boss who lies.

I added one more point. Sometimes there are lying bosses in our life, and we wish we could just go back in time and pretend it never happened. Unfortunately, there are no "do overs." We can't change the past. I asked Jeremy if being upset for two months changed what happened. I asked him if being upset for another two months would change what happened. Jeremy, of course, knew the answers. So I asked him to take a couple of slow deep breaths to calm down and then create a story that has him surviving his boss's actions and being happy in his life. As he invented the story, I saw him relax and noticed that his breathing became more normal. Finally, I told him that forgiveness is the first and most important step in living out his new story.

Sarah's story is another example of how learning to forgive helps us move away from the past so that we can live in the present and future. Sarah married Jim after they had gone on only a few dates. Most of her friends and family cautioned her to wait, but she knew better. Unfortunately, it took only a few months before Sarah found herself mistreated and with an empty checking account.

Notices of overdue bills starting showing up at the same time that Jim began staying out late every night. Soon Sarah found herself carrying a new life at the very moment her own was collapsing. She crashed when she discovered Jim's secret. Almost all the money from their business was feeding his cocaine and alcohol addictions. When their son was born, Jim disappeared for a week. One day he called from another state to say he would not be home for a while.

After this phone call, Sarah lost it. Her life deteriorated to the point that her parents had to come and take her to live with them. When Jim eventually returned from his wanderings he began stalking her and even threatened her life. She was scared, vulnerable, and, despite the help of her parents, dependent on welfare.

Slowly she began to rebuild her life. She started graduate school and became a hospital-based nurse. She moved into an apartment with a close friend. In addition, she took my forgiveness class at Stanford University called "Forgive for Good." Through this class Sarah let go of her resentment toward Jim and put her time and energy into rebuilding her life and caring for her child.

While forgiveness may feel like a trivial matter in light of her crushing problems, Sarah believes that learning to forgive—not forget—Jim for his awful behavior made her reawakening possible. Sarah found that forgiveness allowed her to feel less anger. She did not give up her ability to get angry, only her sense of being trapped by an excessive amount of anger. Sarah found that as her obsession with Jim lessened, she was able to make better life choices. She was thinking more of herself and less of him. Sarah also found that learning how to forgive gave her greater appreciation for her child, for the help her parents gave her, and for her friends and her fresh start. Sarah also vowed to teach her son how to forgive so that he would not have to suffer in the same way.

Like Sarah, many of us have a story to tell about how we were mistreated by someone to whom we were close. Unfortunately, too many of us have parents who were unable to provide the care, guidance, or love we needed. Or we have spouses who lied to us or had affairs. Or we had friends who disappointed us. Many of us have been victims of random acts of cruelty.

When these things happen it is normal to feel hurt and angry, even for a long time. However, hurt and anger are meant to be fleeting emotions, not permanent fixtures. Too many of us never get over the bad things that happened, towing grudges from the past that hinder our lives, harm our health, and shorten our horizons.

I was one of them. I almost did not get over the unexpected abandonment that happened to me and led to my interest in forgiveness. Many years ago my longtime best friend, Sam, met a woman destined to become his wife. For whatever reason, this woman did not like me, and so shortly and unexpectedly Sam cut himself off. When I would ask him what happened, the only thing he would tell me was that I had been unkind to his new partner. At that time, I had spent only a minimal amount of time with her.

It got worse. Sometime later I found out that Sam was to be married. You can imagine my dismay as I discovered I was not invited to the wedding. If that was not bad enough, I found out about Sam's wedding through a mutual friend. Sam neither called nor wrote to tell me he was getting married. I was deeply hurt and confused, and the abandonment pained me for years.

One reason the loss of this friendship hurt so much was that I am an only child. I grew up without brothers and sisters and considered my close friends to be a part of my family. I never expected this could happen, and I was ill prepared to deal with my loss. I needed to learn how to Forgive for Good. It took me years to learn how to get over my hurt, and now I can teach you how to get over yours.

While this may seem minor compared to an unfaithful spouse, it too was devastating. Sam and I had been like brothers, and this abandonment left me hurt for years. My confidence in my ability to attract and keep friends was shattered; my sense of trust was broken. My wife told me that I sounded bitter and that I judged everybody's motives. Aching with bitterness, resentment, and sadness, I decided this had to end. I knew I had to forgive Sam if I were to get my life back. And so *Forgive for Good* was born.

In developing it I learned that much of my suffering and that of the people I worked with is unnecessary. No matter the hurt, to forgive brings an almost divine peace. But if you are anything like I was, you have no idea how to bring forgiveness into your own life. You need these tools as badly as I did.

I can attest firsthand to the power of forgiveness. Through working through my forgiveness methods and making strong decisions along the way, I have again become good friends with Sam. I feel lucky that he is in my life. When we get together I appreciate his company, and the confidence I feel when I see him reminds me of the healing power of forgiveness. Through forgiveness, you too can gain the confidence to bounce back when life is tough.

I define forgiveness as the experience of peace and understanding that can be felt in the present moment. You forgive by challenging the rigid rules you have for other people's behavior and by focusing your attention on the good things in your life as opposed to the bad. Forgiveness does not mean forgetting or denying that painful things occurred. Forgiveness is the powerful assertion that bad things will not ruin your today even though they may have spoiled your past.

One of the central messages of my forgiveness training is that only three core components underlie the creation of any long-standing hurt and grievance:

- The exaggerated taking of personal offense
- The blaming of the offender for how you feel
- The creation of a grievance story

Careful feeding and dedicated nurturing of these grievance components can keep a hurt alive forever. That is exactly what we do when we refuse to forgive. Debbie is a case in point. The grievance story she was telling about her ex-husband kept her stuck and in the hurts of the past. The facts did not change: Debbie's husband cheated on her. She would confront him when she found out what he was up to, and each time he would swear he would never do it again. One time she came home and found another woman with her husband on the couch. Debbie threw her husband out, but that wasn't the end of it. Debbie told everyone she met what a louse she had been married to. She blamed him for how she felt (rather than for what he did), and she had a doozy of a grievance story.

Every time she complained about her ex-husband, her stomach would hurt and her body would tense. Debbie did not know how to deal with her loss and pain in a productive manner. It was crucial to her that everyone realize what a louse he was, that what he did was wrong, and that what happened was not her fault. The temporary glee she felt when recounting her travails was dwarfed by the power it gave to her ex. Rather than moving on, Debbie remained fully in her husband's thrall, feeling no more healed than when she found him in the act.

Through forgiveness training, however, she recognized that reciting her grievance story only highlighted the power her ex-husband still had over her. If she wanted her life back she had to take it back from him, and that meant she had to forgive. Debbie was so thankful when she was able to see things differently. And as a result, she was able to move on to a new and better relationship.

Though there may be an infinite number of ways people can be unkind to you, the mechanisms by which a deep hurt is created are the same. No matter what caused the pain, the three steps of the grievance process can be clearly dissected. Understanding this process will lead to the wonderful experience of forgiveness.

Jill entered my forgiveness classes when she was in her late forties. Her mother had been dead for a decade, but Jill still complained about her mother's inability to love her. She talked about events that had happened thirty-five years ago with a freshness that belied the fact that she had whined about her mother her whole adult life. Jill resented the power her mother held over her and hated her life.

I worked with Jill until she saw that if she continued to blame her mother for how she felt, her mother would retain power over her indefinitely. Until she took my forgiveness training Jill had not considered that her complaining had no effect on her dead mother but had hurt her a great deal. She practiced my techniques and forgave her mother. Jill is now able to look to her female friends for the support she never got from her mother.

Over the years I have seen many people who have trouble forgiving, and most tell me that the major problem was that no one showed them how. After working with thousands of people who have been hurt and have struggled to forgive, I am convinced that the ability to get over these wounds is crucial to health, both emotional and physical.

The forgiveness classes that I teach usually last for six sessions. I am always a little nervous before starting because of the burdens the people in my classes carry. Many of the people have been in therapy for years, while others have tried time and again through various means to help themselves, often exhausting the patience of their family and friends as they struggle to make sense of their suffering.

While each person's story is unique, all of the students share one thing: they have been unsuccessful in their quest for healing and still feel hurt or angry. I share with each group my story to let them know I have experienced many of the feelings they have. I tell you, the reader, what I tell the people in my classes: that if you can learn to forgive (and in these pages you'll learn how), you will feel better and gain a power over your life that might have seemed impossible.

If you learn to forgive you will find your life to have possibilities you could only dream of. You will gain a sense of control over your feelings and discover that you have more energy available to make good decisions. You will find that your decisions are based less on hurt feelings and more on what is best for you and those you love.

In this book you will learn how a grievance is formed, how carrying one is destructive, how to forgive, and how to keep from getting hurt again. You will learn to employ these proven forgiveness techniques to move beyond past hurts so you can greet each day with confidence and create better relationships. In these pages you will find a prescription for how to recover from life's slings and arrows to gain a state of peace and well-being.

Fascinating research has emerged in the past ten years that documents the healing power of forgiveness. In careful scientific studies, forgiveness training has been shown to reduce depression, increase hopefulness, decrease anger, improve spiritual connection, increase emotional self-confidence, and help heal relationships. Learning to forgive is good for both your mental and physical well-being and your relationships.

Studies reveal:

- People who are more forgiving report fewer health problems.
- Forgiveness leads to less stress.
- Forgiveness leads to fewer physical symptoms of stress.
- Failure to forgive may be more important than hostility as a risk factor for heart disease.
- People who blame other people for their troubles have higher incidences of illnesses such as cardiovascular disease and cancers.
- People who imagine not forgiving someone show negative changes in blood pressure, muscle tension, and immune response.
- People who imagine forgiving their offender note immediate improvement in their cardiovascular, muscular, and nervous systems.
- Even people with devastating losses can learn to forgive and feel better psychologically and emotionally.

I recently offered two rounds of forgiveness training to groups of Catholic and Protestant people from Northern Ireland who had lost family members to the thirty years of political violence. In both of these projects I conducted research on the outcomes, and each project was successful. In the first session I worked only with women who had lost a son to the violence. After the week-long forgiveness training, the women showed less hurt, depression, stress, and anger. They also showed more optimism and forgiveness. The women returned to Northern Ireland

and six months later still reported all of the positive changes in mood and outlook.

On one standard psychological test, the women reported that the hurt they felt went from more than 8 on a scale of 1 to 10 at the beginning of the week to less than 4 at the end of the week. On a different psychological test their rate of depression was reduced by 40 percent from the beginning of their forgiveness training to the end. Each of these women has agreed to go back to Northern Ireland with the goal of helping others in their country to learn to forgive. With this act they demonstrate the incredible power of forgiveness to help both others and ourselves.

In the second round of training with people from Northern Ireland, I worked with Catholic and Protestant men and women who had lost a family member in the violence. Some people's parents had been murdered; others had lost brothers or sisters, and still others had lost a child. Seventeen people had suffered the loss of a loved one to murder. Each of these people had a right, if anyone does, to be bitter, angry, and victimized. Yet at the end of this week of forgiveness training the victims were less depressed, felt more physically healthy and energetic, and were less hurt by their loss.

Clearly, the loss of a child or other family member is a devastating experience. Nothing can fully replace that loss. Yet if these men and women can improve their emotional and psychological functioning, then there is no question that each of us as well can heal.

As a pioneer in this forgiveness research, I will integrate the findings from this emerging science with my developed art of helping people to make *Forgive for Good* an indispensable tool for anyone wanting to forgive.

For me, forgiveness means much more than the end of a grievance. Forgiveness has become my life's work. I am the director and cofounder of the Stanford University Forgiveness Project, the largest interpersonal forgiveness training research project ever conducted. The Forgiveness Project replicates on a larger scale an earlier study that established the effectiveness of my forgiveness training.

In the Forgiveness Project we recruited people from the San Francisco Bay Area who said they could not get over an interpersonal hurt.

Participants learned to forgive, and our research team measured the effectiveness of the training both right after the workshop and up to four and a half months afterward. The people who took my forgiveness training became less hurt, stressed, and angry and more forgiving and optimistic, and they even reported slightly improved physical health.

Forgive for Good distills the essential elements of my forgiveness training into a program that can be of great value to many. In my work I have heard untold stories of pain and mistreatment, but here are techniques that can help you feel less hurt and angry. My forgiveness work has shown that to forgive now also can help you limit the degree to which you get hurt in the future.

When I initiated my first research project on the training of interpersonal forgiveness in 1996, I was completing my Ph.D. in counseling and health psychology. I was excited for the opportunity to scientifically test the forgiveness methods I had used to help myself and occasionally others. At the time only four studies had been published in the field, the earliest from 1993. I am one of the pioneers in the emerging field of integrating the training of forgiveness with the science of demonstrating which techniques actually work. Through my teaching I continue to refine my processes, resulting in what I know to be the strongest forgiveness training the field has to offer. For the first time, this Forgive for Good method is available to everyone.

I know what it's like to keep grievance planes circling in my mind for years. I have seen the benefits in my life and the lives of countless others of the peace that comes when your grievance planes are allowed to land. So, fellow seeker, if you are looking to learn how to Forgive for Good—for the good of your health, for the good of your relationships, for the good of the world and, possibly, forever—please join me and read on.

PART ONE

Creating a Grievance

CHAPTER 1

Renting Too Much Space to Disappointment

Man can preserve a vestige of spiritual freedom, of independence of mind, even in such terrible conditions of psychic and physical stress.

VIKTOR FRANKL, *Man's Search for Meaning*

Thank you for joining me on this journey to well-being through forgiveness. Together we will see how a grievance is formed, how to forgive, and how to create a meaningful story of what happened. Remember that the process I teach has been proven to work in four careful research studies. In those studies people with hurts big and small made positive changes in their physical and emotional health. I have countless testimonials of how forgiveness has changed lives, and I will share with you many of those stories. I am convinced that when you learn these methods and practice what I teach, you too can Forgive for Good.

In order to understand the process of forgiveness, it helps to see how a grievance begins. In the early chapters, I will explain how a grievance is formed, examine the parts of a grievance that make your life difficult, and help you test for the signs that a grievance has taken hold. I have seen that when people understand how a grievance is formed they emerge ready to heal.

HOW A GRIEVANCE FORMS

A grievance emerges when two things coincide. The first is that something happens in our lives that we did not want to happen. Then, second, we deal with this problem by thinking about it too much, or what I call renting too much space in our minds. In this chapter I will explain these two ideas and show you how each occurs.

The difficulty at the core of being hurt is how to remain peaceful when someone hurts or disappoints you. Another way of stating this is to ask, how can we be hurt but not end up with a smoldering grievance? Each of us has at some point in our lives been hurt or mistreated. But some people adapt better than others. Some talk about their wounds for a long time and some let them go. If you are one of those who have not let go of what has hurt you, then this book is for you.

It is not easy to recover a state of peace when we are mistreated. Everyone to a greater or lesser degree struggles when facing injury, abandonment, cheating, or lying. At the heart of the myriad of wounds is the simple fact that a grievance results because some event or thing we really hoped would happen simply did not occur.

While I may sound repetitious, I want to stress the importance of this concept. At the very core of creating a grievance or grudge is that something happened that we did not want to happen. Alternatively, something we really wanted did not happen. In either case, a grievance begins when part of our life turns out radically different from what we expected. Faced with the unexpected, we lacked the skills to manage our feelings. Here are two examples.

Dana is an account executive at a large software company in Silicon Valley. She has worked for this company for almost ten years and has a successful career. Often she stayed late and toiled for long hours, missing precious time with her two children. Recently she was passed over for a promotion. Dana was told her job performance was excellent but that her company had instituted a new policy to hire some executives from the outside. Yet even with this information, she was furious at being passed over and talked about how her continued dedication to work was causing her health to suffer.

When I met her, Dana was bitterly complaining about her bosses, life's unfairness, and the wasted time she had spent at her office. She clearly stated that she was owed this promotion and that it was unfair she did not get it. Dana was now reappraising her ten years with the company and finding slights she had previously ignored. The story she told was of many years of unfairness, not just of a missed promotion. What I saw was a woman who did not get a promotion she felt was owed her and in response created a whopper of a grievance.

Mike works at an Internet start-up company. He works all of the time at a place where everyone else works all of the time. It is common in this work culture for employees to do whatever is needed to make the company successful. Mike was originally hired to help with Web design, and because he enjoyed this work, the seventy-hour weeks did not bother him. However, as the company grew, managers hired more Web designers and found they now needed technical writers. Mike was asked to take this on, and soon his days at work became a drag. While he is good at technical writing, he does not enjoy it. He wanted to be a design person and now complains to everyone that he is wasting his time.

When Mike came to my forgiveness class he was disgruntled and bitter. He had invested a great deal of time and energy in his company and did not feel ready to leave because of the chance he could make a lot of money if the company went public. Mike felt trapped in a job he did not like. He complained that he had been cheated out of the opportunity to do work he enjoyed and was forced to do work he hated.

Both Dana and Mike had to cope with disappointment. Dana did not get promoted, a perfect example of not getting something she wanted. Mike had to do work he disliked, an example of getting something unwanted. The problem is the same either way.

Dana and Mike's stories show how difficult it is to deal with things not working out. However, it is not only at work that we struggle to make peace. Not getting what we want occurs in a host of situations from the ridiculous to the horrendous. See if any of these stories rings true with you:

- You drive into the parking lot at work and notice someone has taken your parking space. The result is you have to go to a spot at the other end of the lot. You did not get the parking space that you wanted.
- Your partner announces they want to end your relationship when you want it to continue. You are asked to move out. You did not get the long-term relationship you desired.

- You go into the supermarket closest to your home, and they are out of the only kind of cereal your sick child will eat. You have to drive across town to another store, and there is lots of traffic. You have less time to care for your sick child.
- Your friend cancels three nights in a row because of a new lover. The result is you miss your friend and end up feeling lonely. Your friend did not treat you the way you think friends should.
- Your business partner leaves the partnership without notice or forwarding address, and you are left holding the business and debts alone. Your economic future has changed for the worse.
- Your mother was self-absorbed and did not give you enough attention. When you were growing up she appeared more interested in her needs than in yours. As an adult, you may be at a disadvantage in establishing satisfactory relationships and likely will have to learn to parent yourself.
- You go to your doctor to help deal with a medical problem, and she is too busy to fully answer your questions. You leave feeling rushed and unheard. You may have to go on the Internet or call the doctor back to get the answers you need.
- On the way home from school a drunken driver seriously injures your daughter. You could not protect the health of your child.
- Your partner does not come home one evening, and you know she or he is with a former lover. You were not able to create a relationship in which your partner was faithful.
- One of your parents regularly came home drunk. You were often afraid and scared and learned not to trust this parent. As an adult you understand that you did not get the nurturing parenting that children deserve, and you are still looking to find emotional support from a source other than your parents.

In each of these situations a grievance is formed when we lack the skills to confront the reality of things not turning out the way we had hoped. These situations range from the trivial, like missing a parking space, to the serious, like having an alcoholic parent. When we deal with our experience well, a grievance can be avoided. When we handle the situation poorly, a grievance is usually the result.

I do forgiveness work with people who have suffered the ultimate horror, the murder of their children. I have seen people cry over the wrongful death of their child twenty years after it happened. I have worked with people who are still trying—and failing—to make sense of that tragedy. No matter how great or small the tragedy, each person faces the challenge of how to make peace with losing something precious.

Most of the people I see struggle to come to terms with the fact that life does not always seem fair. I witness needless suffering because people do not recognize that making peace with this fact is an unavoidable life task. Often people react with depression or fury when a painful life experience happens. They may cling to their initial reactions because they do not understand that the specifics of what happened may be less important than learning how to deal with their reaction to the experience. Abandonment, lying, or injury are difficult enough to address without adding outrage to the mix.

Dana, for example, made not getting a promotion worse by complaining that the company was wrong. To hear her tell it, the previous ten years had been wasted. By focusing on her disappointment, she wiped away the satisfaction she had gained from her job, when she might have focused her energy instead on how best to deal with the situation. Like Dana, many people deal unskillfully with painful life situations by creating and maintaining long-standing grievances. They end up renting too much space in their minds to the hurt.

Grievances are formed when people are unable to deal successfully with not getting what they wanted and then they rent too much space in their minds to the injustice. This is the grievance process we go through even when the disappointment is as severe and horrible as the loss of a loved one. It is the same process when the injustice is waiting an extra moment in a supermarket line or struggling in traffic when we are late for an appointment, or struggling to make sense out of a random act of violence.

RENTING TOO MUCH SPACE IN YOUR MIND

When I first met Charlene she talked incessantly about the horrors of life with her ex-husband. In a sneering and clipped voice she would talk about how he had regularly lied to her. His affairs dominated her conversation. She honed in on any conversation about insensitive or uncaring people and seized the opportunity to chime in with how awful her ex was.

From listening to her you would think that he had walked out on her yesterday, but in fact it was five years earlier. To Charlene, what he had done was wrong and that was the end of the story. To me, what he had done was wrong and that was the beginning of the forgiveness story.

Charlene may not have been married to her ex-husband anymore, but she was still renting out the best part of her mind to him. In that important way they were still living together. In fact, I would be surprised if she thought of him that much when they were married.

Are you like Charlene? Do you talk over and over about what happened to you? Do you let your mind dwell on your grievance many times during the day? Do you have friends or family who do this? Do you get tired of the amount of time that you spend thinking about things from your past? Do you get tired of listening to other people repeat their same story?

If you can view your mind as your house, I can teach you to control how much space you rent to your wounds and grievances. You are the proprietor, and you set the rent. Each of us decides who our tenants are and the conditions of their lease. What kind of accommodations do we want to give our wounds and grievances?

We can rent our grievances the master bedroom and build them a hot tub out back. We can give them a great lease with terrific terms that never expire, or we can grant them only a day-to-day tenancy. We can allow them to put their stuff in all the rooms of the house, or we can restrict them to a small room in the back. In other words, we need to ask: How much time do we spend thinking about our hurts and disappointments? And, When we think about them, how much intensity is there?

The answers to these questions will determine how much of a problem a wound or grievance will cause you. When you have rented too much space in your mind, then you have a grievance. When, like Mike, you have to do work you do not want and then you obsess over it, you create a grievance. Mike did not have to focus on his dislike of the work. He could have focused instead on the real possibility that he was going to make a lot of money when the company went public. Mike did not know how to deal with not getting what he wanted, and so he created out of that inability a grievance.

Just because bad things happen does not mean you have to dwell on them. I regularly ask people why they do not dwell on their good fortune with the same energy that they invest in their bad fortune. This question always catches people by surprise. They rarely consider appreciating their good fortune as an equal option to obsessing over their bad fortune. Are you one of those people who seem to find their problems more compelling than their blessings? Do you, or someone you know, rent out more space to what is wrong than what is right?

What plays on the screen of our mind is like a TV picture that we control with a remote. We can watch horror movie channels, sex channels, soap opera channels, and grievance channels as well as channels that focus on the beauties of nature and the kindness of people. Anyone can tune in to a grievance or choose to switch to the forgiveness channel. Ask yourself, What is playing on my set today? Is your remote tuning in to channels that will help you feel good?

If you remember the air traffic control screen from the introduction, your grievances are the planes that will not land. They fill up your screen, they occupy your mind, and, most important, they make it harder for you to appreciate the things in your life that are wonderful. Missing the beauty in our lives is the unanticipated damage that grievances can create. We just watch one TV channel at a time and what we tune in to often can become a habit.

Just imagine how much of her life Dana is not seeing as she focuses on the fact that she was passed over for a promotion. Do you think she is aware of how lucky she is to have her health or the people in her life who love her?

It saddens me to see countless people who fail to pay attention or be grateful to those they love because they are either thinking of people who have hurt them or feeling sorry for their loss. Let me make one thing clear. I am not saying to ignore problems in your life or deny that people have hurt you. What I am saying is that focusing too much attention on a hurt makes it stronger and forms a habit that can be difficult to break. I am saying that you do not have to dwell endlessly on the painful things in your life. Dwelling on wounds gives them power over you. What you remember, or focus your attention on, can be shifted in the same way that you can change the channel on your TV. If we get used to watching the grievance channel we are likely to see that the world has many grievances, but if we get used to watching the forgiveness channel the world can begin to look very different. (We'll explore this idea further in chapter 9.)

DO YOU HAVE A GRIEVANCE?

Before we delve any further, let's check to see if there is a situation in your life that has become a grievance. I ask you now to revisit an interpersonal wound. In this way we can get a sense of how this is affecting you now. Begin the process by closing your eyes and thinking about the painful situation for a couple of minutes.

When you are clear about what happened, think about or write down a brief summary of the experience. Tell your story about what happened, either on paper or in your mind.

Now examine what happens when you think about this situation today. For example, examine the most common thoughts you have about what happened. Then consider how you feel when you think about the problem. Finally, think about the ways your body reacts when you revisit the hurt.

After you have taken the time to consider your answers, please answer the following questions:

1. Do you think about this painful situation more than you think about the things in your life that are good?
2. When you think about this painful situation, do you become either physically uncomfortable or emotionally upset?
3. When you think about this situation, do you do so with the same old repetitive thoughts?
4. Do you find yourself telling the story about what happened over and over in your mind?

If you answer yes to any of these four questions, you have likely formed a grievance that is renting too much space in your mind. If you answer yes to any of these four questions, you most likely have a grievance that can be healed. You are in the right place and can learn to Forgive for Good. If you answer yes to any of these four questions, then read on and discover how you formed your grievance in the first place.

Remember, the basis of any grievance is that something painful happened to you and at the time you did not have the skills to manage your emotional pain. Then, like Dana, who did not get the job she thought she was entitled to, you rented out some substantial room in your mind, and, voilà, you formed a grievance. This is the way you helped a bad situation become worse. In the next three chapters I will describe in detail exactly how this happens.

In this chapter we learned how a difficult situation becomes a grievance. It all begins with either getting something you did not want or not getting something you wanted. In order for a painful experience to end up renting too much space in your mind, three specific things have to happen. These three elements will be explained fully in the next three chapters of this book.

When we understand the three steps that lead to renting out our mind to a grievance, we will be ready to begin the process of forgiveness. And when we grasp how our grievance was formed and grew, we then learn to forgive those parts of our life that did not work out the way we wanted. Through this process, we can learn to Forgive for Good.

CHAPTER 2

Taking Things Too Personally

A physician is not angry at the intemperance of a mad patient, nor does he take it ill to be railed at by a man in fever. Just so should a wise man treat all mankind, as a physician does his patient, and look upon them only as sick and extravagant.

SENECA

In the first chapter Dana, Charlene, and Mike tried to understand what fueled the long-standing grudges, hurts, and angers that troubled them. They struggled to grasp how they ended up hurt and angry and unable to help themselves. I imagine that many of you, when others hurt you, also wonder why it has to hurt so much. Or perhaps you know people who cannot get over their bitterness and hurt.

We all have seen that some people deal with painful circumstances by developing grievances while others do not. Each of us knows someone who simply does not let things bother them. Some people are able to adapt to difficulty, while others remain stuck for years.

Some of you who hold grudges may surmise that you feel bad because other people simply do not get as upset as you do. Others may think they suffer more because they tend to dwell on the past. People often wonder if the reason they are upset is because what hurt them is worse than what hurt other people. Or they conclude that they feel so hurt because they may be more sensitive than other people.

While each of these hypotheses has some merit, I assert that forming a grievance follows a simple three-step process. The process is clear, easy to understand, and predictable in every case. To form a grievance that interfered with your life, you have done the following three things:

- Took an offense too personally
- Blamed the offender for how you feel
- Created a grievance story

I want to make clear that creating a grievance is not a sign of mental illness. Being hurt is not a sign of weakness, stupidity, or lack of self-esteem. Often, it simply means we lack training in how to do things differently. Feeling hurt is a normal and difficult aspect of all of our lives, and almost everyone creates grievances at some point.

However, just because grievances are common does not mean they are healthy. While reacting to hurt by creating a grievance may be common, reacting differently to painful life events will lead to less suffering. Through forgiveness training, Charlene stopped dwelling on her husband and felt empowered to heal herself. By using this process you too can heal the hurts you already have. You can also recognize the way you create grievances and thereby limit the number you develop in the future.

Learning to handle hurts, wounds, and disappointments more skillfully will not stop things from going wrong in life. People may still be unkind, and random events can still hurt you. The world is filled with suffering and difficulty, and just because you have learned to adapt better does not mean these problems go away. What will change, however, is the space you rent them in your mind and the amount of anger, hopelessness, and despair you feel. I cannot emphasize this point too strongly. Life may not be perfect, but you can learn to suffer less. You can learn to forgive, and you can learn to heal.

ANGER HAS ITS PLACE

Even with all the forgiveness training in the world, there will still be times when it is useful and even necessary to get angry. A personal boundary may have been broken, we may be in danger, or we may have been mistreated. However, the number of situations where acting out the anger is the optimal response is quite limited. Acting out of anger is helpful only in situations where the resulting action resolves a problem.

For example, getting angry with someone who is threatening your child may be the only way to protect the child's well-being. If a family member is abusive, you need to let them know that their behavior is unacceptable. On the other hand, getting angry because three years ago your mother said something unkind neither helps you nor resolves the situation with your mother. Neither does getting angry on the freeway because the traffic jam causes you to be late for work.

There are very few instances where the long-term use of anger will be of help to you. I want to make clear, once a situation has passed, both the long-term naming of angry feelings and the expression of anger rarely lead to good results. Anger can be a wonderful short-term solution to your life's difficulties, yet it is rarely a good long-term solution to painful events. Anger is simply our way of reminding ourselves that we have a problem that needs attention. Yet too often we get angry instead of taking constructive action, or we get angry because we do not know what else to do.

It is my contention that the long-term experience of anger, or what we call a grievance, is almost never helpful. As I will explore in later chapters, grievances lead to frustration, hopelessness, damaged relationships, and health problems.

Now that I have reminded you that anger itself is not bad and distinguished the helpful from harmful expression of anger, let's explore the first step in forming a grievance. This step occurs when you take personally something you did not want to happen. A painful life event, such as an unfaithful friend, cheating business partner, or lying relative, becomes an event you take personally, and you thereby miss an opportunity to transform your hurt or angry feelings into an experience that helps you grow.

PERSONAL VS. IMPERSONAL

All painful life events have both a personal and an impersonal quality. Marilyn's story helps us distinguish the personal from the impersonal and shows how focusing exclusively on the personal creates a grievance.

Marilyn is a woman in her early fifties who struggles with depression and low self-esteem. She traces her emotional problems to her upbringing. She was an only child born to parents who felt trapped in a loveless marriage, and she grew up in the care of a cold and preoccupied mother. She felt loved by her father, but he was rarely home, for he was in the military and they moved often. She remembers the feeling of coming home from school knowing no one would be there to care for her, and forty years later she can easily reexperience that feeling.

Marilyn still complains to her husband and friends that her mother did not love her enough. She did not feel safe growing up. She talks about how difficult it is to make friends and traces this back to her rejection as a child. Marilyn continues to feel genuinely angry and sad about her loss. Her mother is in her eighties now, and Marilyn still hopes that before she dies she can get the love she missed. Marilyn is still mad at her mother, both for the care she did not give her as a child and for the continuing inability to love her in the present. She longs for the loving connection that she says only a parent can give.

Marilyn, at the age of fifty-two, is still taking personally the rejection by her mother and because of that continues to be in pain. Marilyn suffers from a forty-year wound. The neglect she feels is personal because she still wants love from her mother while the love her children and husband offer is often rejected. The neglect is personal because Marilyn feels alone in her lack of love and rents a lot of space in her mind to her loneliness. Moreover, the offense is personal because whenever anyone gets to know Marilyn, the story of her mistreatment is central to how she describes herself.

What Marilyn does to make her poignant experience more difficult is instructive, as she chronically re-creates her sense of injustice. For Marilyn, the wounding process begins again every time she takes what her mother did personally. This is because every painful life event has a personal and an impersonal element and Marilyn has not learned to find the impersonal perspective. The imbalance in her personal-impersonal balance initiates Marilyn's experience of a grievance.

The personal quality refers to the fact that Marilyn's mother did not give Marilyn the love she wanted. In addition, her mother still does not offer the care Marilyn craves. This is happening to Marilyn and to no one else. When something painful, like an uncaring mother, is part of our life, our first response is to cry "ouch" because of the personal nature of the hurt. Having an uncaring parent hurts, and neither Marilyn nor any child deserves to be unloved. In addition, no child is responsible for any emotional neglect they have experienced. Abusive or neglectful parents are a painful and difficult experience to overcome, and I wish that every child were blessed with loving parents. However, Marilyn, like so many others, did not have the attentive parent she hoped to have, and in that way she did not get what she wanted.

As a child Marilyn legitimately took her mother's lack of care personally. Unfortunately, she continues to do so as an adult. When something painful happens to someone else we are able to experience the impersonal quality of the offense, and we rarely feel personal pain. Every day when we read the newspaper or watch TV, we learn of numbers of people who experience tragedy and suffering. Friends tell us stories of the difficulties they or members of their families face. In every city in the country people languish in hospitals and nursing homes without anyone to care for them. Thousands of people are murdered each year in the United States, and drunk drivers kill, maim, and disable thousands more. Rapes, murders, natural disasters, robbery, cheating, lying, and unfaithfulness occur every day in every corner of our country.

We cannot feel the impact of each of these tragedies personally. We have to care more about some than others. The fact that we ignore, or care less about, some tragedies reflects our understanding that we cannot possibly deal with all the suffering in the world. We know that impersonal hurt is everywhere.

The challenge is to locate the impersonal part of the hurt when the rejections, mistreatments, and insults happen to us. Instead of feeling alone in our suffering, we might remember how uncaring or neglectful parents happen to many other people as well, which means that our own mistreatment was not only personal. It is unfortunate that Marilyn does not see the possibility for community with the ranks of other people who did not get the love they craved. She rarely contemplates how other people hurt just as she does. She does not see that it is common both to have neglectful parents and to hurt from it. If she could see some of these things, Marilyn would find the impersonal nature of her hurt.

If Marilyn had been able to shift her attention in this way, she could have shortened the period of her suffering and not formed such a long-standing grievance. Marilyn, because she felt so hurt, acted as if her mother hurt her deliberately. Marilyn's painful and long-standing grievance is a direct result of being unable to understand the impersonal nature of her wound.

FINDING THE IMPERSONAL IN THE HURT

For Marilyn, as for each of us, the impersonal nature of the hurt can be uncovered in two ways. The easiest way is to realize how common each painful experience is. It is a fact of life that nothing that has happened to you is unique. If you remind yourself that you are just one of two hundred people burglarized in your community, it is hard to take it as personally. By looking carefully, we can always find at least ten people hurt in the same way. The large and diverse number of support groups over the country attest to this fact. Remembering how common our suffering is can make it seem like the hurt is being trivialized, but it is worth taking that risk to suffer so much less pain.

Every now and then it is helpful to remember that untold numbers of people are alone because of the neglect of friends and family. Marilyn is not the first, and will not be the last, to crave love from a cold and distant parent. You are not the first and will not be the last to be hurt the way you were.

The second way to uncover the impersonal dimension of hurt is to understand that most offenses are committed without the intention of hurting anyone personally. Marilyn's mother did not want to ruin her child's life. Marilyn's mother was unable to love Marilyn because of a variety of factors. She was in an empty marriage that she entered into at a young age to escape her abusive father. Her husband moved regularly, which made making friends difficult. She also suffered from arthritis, which caused her great pain. In addition, Marilyn's father was crazy about Marilyn, and her mother felt jealous.

Many of the offenses we ache over were not intended to hurt us personally. Some were, but they are rare. Exploring the ways that Marilyn's mother did not deliberately intend to hurt her daughter does not excuse her behavior. To suggest there is an impersonal dimension to many of our offenses is not to deny the pain of loss and neglect. Marilyn needs to recognize what her mother did and did not do. She does well to understand the root of some of her difficulties in life and to trace them to her upbringing.

However, Marilyn would be helped by learning from her mother's cruelty so that she does not repeat those mistakes. When I met Marilyn, she was repeating her mother's coldness with her own children. Her pain and loneliness were such that she was often too consumed with her own loss to offer any love or warmth. Marilyn also did not intend to hurt her children, but my guess is she caused them a great deal of pain.

Each offense carries both the personal and the impersonal within it. Each hurt happens to a specific individual. Marilyn is the one to bear the scars from her mother's neglect, and it is her life that has suffered. If your spouse leaves you, you alone have to create a new life. Even if the offense is toward a group, each person in the group reacts in a personal way to the offense. Simultaneously, each personal hurt can be seen as just one instance of a common experience. More than likely someone has hurt each one of us, whether it is a parent, in-law, business associate, or stranger. If you ask your friends and family, someone has likely hurt every one of them. Being hurt is common. Even the harshest offenses, such as abusive parenting, are common, albeit painful, human experiences.

When we fail to acknowledge the impersonal aspect, we set the stage for creating a grievance. We focus only on the feelings of pain we experience and ignore both the omnipresence of hurt and the frequency with which the event that hurt us occurs. We take an injustice too personally, and for that reason the hurt lingers and a grievance forms.

Marilyn asserts that her parental neglect ruined her life, and for her this is intensely personal. To a sociologist conducting research on parental neglect, Marilyn may be only one subject in a study with three thousand women. The sociologist will see that some women were able to overcome the handicap of their upbringing while others struggled their whole lives. The sociologist will take parental neglect as an interesting object of study—a view far different from Marilyn's. From the sociologist's perspective, Marilyn's experience is typical, not special.

The sociologist sees Marilyn's hurt as impersonal; to Marilyn her hurt is personal. Both perspectives are valid. Each is a different way of seeing the same situation. People deal best with offenses when they can find both perspectives. When you see the impersonal dimension after focusing only on your personal pain, you discover that your specific hurt does not have to cripple you.

I must caution that one can also focus too much on the impersonal aspect of hurts. I see this much less commonly, but it too has its dangers. When we find only the impersonal dimension of a painful event it is often called denial. Saying that something painful was trivial or that the person who did it did not know better, we minimize the legitimate damage done. When responding to other people in pain we want to find the personal aspect of the hurt and be able to offer acknowledgement and support.

When we react to things that happened to us or to others we want to be able to acknowledge the pain but not remain stuck in it. This may be easier to do with the pains that other people suffer, but it is possible with yours as well. I believe we heal best from our offenses when we are able to acknowledge the damage done. At the same time, I want each of us to be able to say that what happened is not a unique catastrophe but the beginning of a new story of forgiveness and healing.

Taking things less personally does not mean that we have to like what was done to us. Marilyn does not explain away her mother's behavior because parental neglect is common. She does not excuse her mother because her mother was also in pain. She does not ignore her own pain by understanding that parental neglect is a difficult but common problem we all face. When she sees the impersonal, she does not deny the impact of the personal. The personal and the impersonal exist side by side.

By focusing on her personal pain, Marilyn feels that her mother wounded her for life and that she was particularly mistreated. Marilyn has created a long standing grievance out of a difficult life experience. Focusing on the personal aspect of a hurt is the first step in creating a grievance. Because Marilyn has ignored the impersonal aspect of the way her cold and neglectful mother treated her, she continues to suffer forty years later.

We know we are focusing too much on the personal when we feel angry long after the specific hurt has occurred. When we take a hurt too personally, our body releases stress chemicals to respond to the perceived danger. These chemicals prompt the fight-or-flight response and lead us to feel discomfort in both body and mind. When we feel this discomfort long after the specific hurt has occurred, it is a sure sign that we have taken something too personally.

In the next chapter, I describe in detail how taking something too personally can hurt us physically as well as emotionally. The link between taking something too personally and endangering our health is the second step in the grievance process. We endanger our health when we blame the offender for how we feel and make a bad situation worse.

CHAPTER 3

The Blame Game

It is circumstances which show what men are. Therefore, when a difficulty falls upon you, remember that God, like a trainer of wrestlers, has matched you with a rough young man. For what purpose? you might ask. So that you may become an Olympic Conqueror; but it is not accomplished without sweat. . . . No man has had a more profitable difficulty than you have had, if you choose to make use of it as an athlete would deal with a young antagonist.

EPICTETUS

In the first two chapters, I showed how the grievance process begins when something happens that we do not like and continues as long as we rent the hurt too much space in our minds. The potential for a grievance occurs when we take something too personally and, like Marilyn from chapter 2, lose sight of the bigger picture. That said, if Marilyn simply took her mother's behavior too personally and then moved on, minimal damage would ensue. But she did much more than that. Marilyn spent her life blaming her mother for all sorts of difficulties she had in her life.

Marilyn had trouble establishing good relationships with men. That was her mother's fault. Marilyn never finished school and so worked at jobs she felt were below her capabilities. That was her mother's fault. When Marilyn got married and started her own family, her husband complained about her parenting skills. That was her mother's fault. Marilyn suffered from a low-level depression much of her life. That was her mother's fault. Marilyn battled her weight for years. That was her mother's fault as well. At the age of fifty-two, Marilyn was still blaming her mother and her childhood for her problems.

I agree that Marilyn has a number of legitimate difficulties. There is also no question that Marilyn's mother contributed to the difficulties she faces. No doubt if Marilyn had had a loving and supportive mother, she would have had a better chance for a successful life and would be less likely to suffer from chronic depression. What I do not agree with is the amount of blame that Marilyn places on her mother. What Marilyn does not know is how harmful blaming can be for both her physical well-being and the health of her relationships.

Marilyn is looking to her childhood and an emotionally crippled mother to explain all current problems. She is looking to the past to help her in the present. She is looking outside herself for solutions to problems that she alone faces. She is unable to see that no matter what happened in the past, in the present she is responsible for the course of her life. Marilyn is knee-deep in the second stage of the grievance process, called the "blame game."

This stage in the grievance process begins after something was taken too personally. Remember Dana, from chapter 1, who took personally not getting her promotion even though she was told that her company was trying to hire people from outside the company? Dana reacted to the lack of promotion as a personal affront even though she was assured her job performance was excellent. Because Dana took the lack of promotion too personally, she felt upset and angry.

To make matters worse, Dana also played the blame game. She blamed her bosses for lying to her. She blamed the company for stringing her along. She blamed her resulting stomach trouble on being humiliated and rejected at her job. She blamed her employer for the stress and struggle in her life.

When we become upset and ask ourselves "Whose fault is this?" and then insist that the reason for our suffering lies with someone else, we have entered the second step in the grievance process. We are playing the blame game, blaming someone else for our troubles. This is a problem because when the cause of the hurt lies outside us, we will look outside ourselves as well for the solution.

Blame is one of the hypotheses we can make about why we feel bad. When people are hurt in the past yet still feel the pain in the present, they look for reasons to explain their pain. They commonly choose the blame hypothesis. A hypothesis is a guess that one offers as an answer to a question when the answer is not clear. When you buy a house and want to know what your monthly house payments will be, you can look up the answer. That answer will be specific in dollars and cents. A real estate agent might offer an educated guess or hypothesis when she does not have her calculator, but the exact answer is easy to find.

In matters of the heart, precise answers are hard to come by. You can never know exactly why another person has acted cruelly. You can never know for sure why you feel angry or upset. You never know any other person's thoughts. You are also not privy to each of the painful things that have happened to a person who hurt you. You cannot know if the actions this person committed were meant to hurt you. You can't know which of the things in your past is actually influencing your experience today.

You can only feel your hurt and offer a hypothesis as to why you're in pain. Some people blame misfortune on the position of the stars in the sky or possibly on a curse. Others blame their suffering on the people who have hurt them. I know people who blame everything on stupid decisions they have made. There is no one right way to explain why things are the way they are.

HOW BLAME WORKS

Alan is a man of thirty-five who found out his wife was having an affair. They had been married for six years, and Alan thought the marriage was solid. When he found out Elaine was cheating on him, Alan was furious and wanted a divorce.

While Alan theorized a lot about what was going on with his wife, it is interesting to realize that Alan had almost no idea of what Elaine was actually thinking. This is because Elaine refused to talk with him. Alan does not know if she felt unappreciated by him or simply wanted better sexual relations. He does not know if Elaine would or could ever tell him the truth. Alan does not know if Elaine hated herself or him or even whether she thought about him at all.

When he talks about her now, he says that she tried to ruin his life. He claims that she was afraid of intimacy and hurt him deliberately. He has chosen the blame hypothesis to explain the pain he continues to feel.

Like Alan, when we are in pain in the present, we often blame our bad feelings on the hurts done in the past. One of the ways we do this is to assume that people meant to hurt us. Another way is to link the cruelty in the past with our current feelings. Both of these hypotheses make it harder for us to heal. This is not to say that understanding some of the causes of our feelings and behavior is not helpful. Remember that feeling hurt does not automatically mean someone meant to hurt you. The crux of the matter is that even when we think we understand where our feelings originated, we still have to develop skills in the present in order to change for the better.

We can learn to make hypotheses that will motivate us to improve our lives and thereby heal our hurts. This is the opposite of blaming. When we blame someone for our troubles, we remain stuck in the past and extend the pain. Unfortunately, we are unaware of how much we limit our chances of healing when we blame someone else.

One of the goals I have for this book is to help you learn to develop hypotheses that help you resolve your pain. Understanding that blame is simply a hypothesis made to try to understand why we hurt is an important step. When we play the blame game we offer the worst kind of hypotheses for why we hurt. Blame hypotheses are usually guaranteed to make us hurt and hurt and hurt until we change them.

The beguiling thing about the blame game is that at first you may feel better. You may feel short-term relief because the hurt you feel is someone else's responsibility. Over the long run, however, the good feelings fade and you are left feeling helpless and vulnerable. Only you can take the steps that will allow you to ultimately feel better.

Alan does not know exactly why he is still in so much pain. His hypothesis is that he suffers because his wife wanted to hurt him and so left him for another man. Alan blames his ex-wife for his pain. The problem Alan faces is that he cannot change something that happened in the past. He cannot go back in time and make his wife love him. He can only change his present circumstances. What is done is done, and for Alan to link his emotional well-being to something in the past is risky. Neither the past nor his wife can be changed.

Yes, Alan's wife behaved poorly. She broke her marriage vows and did so repeatedly. Her behavior hurt her husband, child, and community. She is responsible for her part in the breakup of their marriage and appropriately is asked to pay child support and share parenting rights. I am not claiming that Alan deserved what he got. I am not absolving his wife of responsibility for her behavior. I instead object to Alan's insistence that his ex-wife is causing his suffering in the present. I see how pointless it is for Alan to play the blame game. I object because instead of making Alan feel better, the blame game makes him feel worse. His wife of the past remains in power over his present well-being.

My hypothesis about what ails Alan is that he is renting too much space in his mind to his ex-wife. He is doing something in his daily life that leads to his current suffering. Alan's blaming is causing him pain, and as he reduces his blaming his pain will lessen. Alan is solely responsible for the way he feels in the present. Instead of blaming his suffering on his ex-wife, Alan should ask himself the following question: "What can I learn to help myself suffer less?"

When we blame someone else for our suffering, when we believe that someone else is the cause of our pain, then we need something from that other person in order to feel better. When Alan blames his ex-wife for his current distress, he needs his wife to apologize, admit she was wrong, change, or beg forgiveness before he can feel better. That is a tall order. The likelihood of that is minuscule, and Alan feels helpless as he waits in vain. The sad reality is that Alan's wife has moved on to another long-term relationship and hardly thinks of Alan at all.

As long as Alan blames his wife he makes it harder to get over his rejection. He also makes it harder to develop a good relationship with another woman. Alan thinks he needs his ex-wife to do something for him, and Alan has no power to make her do so. Because he is powerless over her, Alan now adds helplessness and resentment to the rejection and abandonment from which he already suffers. Blaming his wife has made a difficult situation worse.

Alan and Marilyn learned the hard way that we cannot know why other people acted the way they did. Nor do we know for certain the reasons we continue to suffer. In response to painful situations, we offer the best hypotheses we can about what happened. However, it is difficult to know for sure what causes what. Some of the influences on how we feel are from the past, some are from the present, and some are the wishes we have for the future. Some influences result from our behavior, some from the behavior of others, and some due to random factors. We can never know for sure why we hurt. The most practical thing we can do is learn how to hurt less.

FIGHT OR FLIGHT

When we think about a hurt, our body reacts as if it is in danger and activates what is known as the fight-or-flight response. The body releases chemicals whose purpose is to prepare us to respond to danger through fighting back or running away. The chemicals released are known as stress chemicals. They are designed to make us uncomfortable so that we will do something to get ourselves out of danger.

These stress chemicals get our attention by causing physical changes. They cause the heart to speed up and blood vessels to constrict. This raises blood pressure. Our liver dumps cholesterol into our bloodstream so that it can gum up our heart in case we lose too much blood. The stress chemicals alter our digestion and cause our muscles to tighten. Our breathing becomes shallower, and our senses are heightened to cope with the problem at hand. Digestion ceases, and blood flow is diverted to the center of the body. We feel jumpy and uncomfortable.

Most of us blame this unpleasant body response on the person who hurt us. When we do this, we are playing the blame game in a way that can keep us trapped and helpless for a long time.

The physical stress we feel when we mull over an abandonment or deception is the reason many of us struggle so hard to give up our grievances. Every time Marilyn thought about her mother she felt tense. Every time she imagined her unloving parent she felt her stomach tighten and would often get a headache. And each time she felt a physical symptom, she experienced another wave of anger toward her mother for ruining her life. She blamed her mother for her current discomfort, for activating her fight-or-flight response. This normal physical response, and the blame you have for the person who hurt you, cements the grievance that began when you took too personally something you did not like.

When you think about someone who has hurt you deeply, your sympathetic nervous system springs into action. The sympathetic nervous system is the branch of the autonomic nervous system whose goal is to rev up our body to protect us from danger. The autonomic nervous system controls inner organs such as our heart, smooth muscles, and breathing. Our autonomic nervous system has another branch called the parasympathetic system, which calms us down after the danger is past. Both of these systems are operating all the time. When a danger comes into view, our sympathetic system gears up and controls the action in the fight-or-flight response. When the danger has passed or we are relaxed, our parasympathetic system controls the action and we calm down.

The fight-or-flight response of the sympathetic nervous system is quick and predictable. The problem is that it gives us only two choices: fighting back or getting away. We may want to pay back the person who hurt us. We may want that person to suffer the way we have suffered. Alternatively, we may never again want to see the person who hurt us. We may try never to think of them again. While these responses to taking something too personally are common, they are primarily the result of the stress chemicals running through our body. They are primitive responses and usually not the result of careful or productive thinking. Our problem is the choices these stress chemicals offer us are inadequate in helping to regain control of our emotional life.

Simply put, these are poor choices. They do not help us face charged emotional situations with people close to us or come to grips with painful life experiences or deal with the subtleties of intimate relationship.

You may have considered that the ideas of seeking revenge or avoiding harm are carefully thought out responses. Not so. They are the product of a biologically designed system of protection. Your nervous system offers these responses when you perceive danger. What is unfortunate is that your nervous system cannot tell whether the danger you are seeing is occurring now or ten years ago. Your nervous system does not know if your mother is yelling at you today or in 1981. Your nervous system does not know whether your husband had an affair today or in 1993. Your nervous system responds the only way it knows how whether you have thought about a problem once or twelve hundred times.

To make matters worse, the fight-or-flight response alters our ability to think. The stress chemicals do part of their work of protecting us from danger by limiting the amount of electrical activity available to the thinking part of the brain. The stress chemicals also play a part in diverting blood flow from the brain's thinking center toward more primitive parts of the brain. When Marilyn says she is so upset over her mother that she can't even think straight, she is telling the truth. When you get frustrated because you have thought the same thing repeatedly about your grievances, there is a reason.

The body is so exquisitely designed to protect us from danger that it won't allow us to waste our precious resources planning things out or thinking of new ideas. Our biology says survival is most important. Our body is willing to stand guard each of the 100 times we remember the horrible way our boss yelled at us or the 263 times we describe in bitter detail the day our mother walked out on the family.

Think about this. How else could our bodies limit us to only two choices? Our bodies are trying to save our life by diverting some electrical energy from the thinking part of the brain to the more primitive and reactive parts. Your body will try to save your life when you face a saber-toothed tiger. Your body will try to save your life if the car in front of you swerves and you have to jam on your brakes. You will need every ounce of concentration on the task at hand to survive these challenges.

Your body has no need to save your life when you are remembering how unkind your mother was ten years ago. You do not need fight or flight when you tell your spouse that your best friend yelled at you. You do not need sympathetic nervous system arousal to explain for the thirty-fifth time how unfair it was that your father loved your sister more than you. You must learn to distinguish real from imagined danger to function effectively. You cannot learn this critical life lesson when you are busy blaming others for how bad you feel or how poorly your life has unfolded. Playing the blame game, you are trapped in a vicious cycle of hurt and physical discomfort.

GIVING AWAY OUR POWER

The biggest mistake we make while under the influence of the stress chemicals is to blame our distress on the person who hurt us. When we blame another person for how we feel, we grant them the power to regulate our emotions. In all likelihood, this power will not be used wisely, and we will continue to suffer. The number of people who give power over to those who did not care about them is shockingly high.

Feeling bad every time we think of the person who has hurt us becomes a habit and leads us to feel like the victim of someone more powerful. We feel helpless because we are constantly reminded both in mind and body of how bad we feel. When we blame this normal protective response on the offender, we make a mistake. This mistake takes the keys to our release out of our hands and puts them in someone else's hands.

Joanne gave her power away to her friend Nancy. Nancy had advised Joanne on what to do in a love relationship, and the advice had been wrong. Nancy had not given good thought to what Joanne asked, and if the truth were told Nancy was jealous of Joanne's way with men. When the relationship ended, Nancy took up with the man that Joanne had been dating.

Joanne felt like a victim of Nancy's capriciousness and lack of care for her. Joanne wanted Nancy to make things all better to stop her suffering. Nancy did not intend to stop dating Sandy because she thought he was better with her than with Joanne. Nancy wanted to remain friends and told Joanne so. Joanne could not imagine that and was clearly operating from her fight-or-flight experience. Joanne imagined either revenge or never seeing her again.

Clearly, Nancy treated Joanne badly. She gave Joanne bad advice on her relationship, and when the relationship ended, she broke Joanne's heart by taking up with Joanne's ex. But until Joanne was able to take responsibility for her own feelings, Nancy held the power over Joanne's fight-or-flight mechanism. When Joanne gave her power away to someone who did not give her what she wanted, she became and stayed upset. Joanne took the actions of Nancy personally, which triggered anger and the activation of her body's stress chemicals. The resulting stomachaches, muscle tension, and anxiety Joanne blamed on Nancy.

Because of this Joanne was on her way to creating a mighty grievance. She allowed someone who was not going to change continue to hurt her, and the result was that Joanne felt like the helpless victim of an uncaring and unkind friend. There is great danger in giving people without your best interests in mind power over you. There is great danger in giving people who have hurt you power over the way you feel.

If you remember Dana from chapter 1, her bosses meant her no harm at all. In fact, they admired and appreciated her work. They passed her over for a promotion to hire from outside the firm. This did not stop Dana from blaming them for her career, health, and emotional distress.

Stan faced an entirely different situation yet ended up with a grievance like Dana's that was cemented by the blame he placed on other people. Growing up, Stan was treated terribly by his alcoholic mother and absent abusive father. He remembers seeing his mother passed out on the sofa and the embarrassment he felt when friends came to visit. His father came home each day, fought with his mother, and then attacked Stan. Stan was sixteen at the time and ran away from home. Stan had no further parenting from either parent because neither would respond to his calls or letters.

To add insult to injury, Stan's mother blamed Stan for the disruption in the family. Stan would call, and his mother would tell him how he had hurt his father and fractured their family. In their last phone conversation she yelled at him for breaking up their family and then died shortly thereafter.

While I empathize with Stan's terrible childhood and early adulthood experiences, I wonder if there is any value in blaming his mother for his present angry feelings. His mother was an indifferent and often cruel parent. However, his now-dead mother can hardly change things. Stan stays tied to her as long as he blames her for the failures of his life and for his chronic anger. Even more chilling, Stan continues to give up his power to someone who was cruel and to the end of her life unwilling and unable to change.

I see time and again that Stan's experience is common. I see many people who give away their power to people who were cruel to them. I ask you: How many of you give away your power to relatives who did not care for you? How many of you give away your power to business associates who meant you harm or to lovers who cheated on you? How many of you know people who look backward more than they look forward? How many of you spend years renting too much space in your mind to past hurts?

Think of the wasted suffering that emerges from staying tied through blame to people who did not care for you. This suffering is the bottomless pit that awaits those who play the blame game. When Nancy took Joanne's boyfriend, the loss of the relationship should have been bad enough. When Dana did not get her merited promotion, the loss of income and prestige should have been the extent of her suffering. Being raised by and then rejected by an alcoholic mother, Stan clearly had suffered enough. When Alan's wife cheated on him and then left him, his loss alone was painful enough.

Each of these four people kept themselves stuck by blaming their friend, boss, parent, or spouse for their continued pain. Each stayed connected for years to the worst parts of their lives. In trying to solve the problem of an unmerited hurt, each actually made the problem worse. Their problem was how to live their lives so that they heal and move on. The solution they tried, blaming, kept them stuck. It kept them in relationships with someone who hurt them and prolonged their helplessness and pain.

Holding people accountable for their actions is not the same as blaming them for how you feel. It is justified to hold wayward spouses to their commitment to pay child support. It is justified to expect a hit-and-run driver to spend time in jail. What leads to unnecessary suffering is making your spouse responsible for your continued suffering or your inability to enter into another relationship. What does not help you is holding that hit-and-run driver responsible for your ongoing depression or the unwillingness you might feel to take risks ever again.

It is difficult to release hurt when people have been cruel. I have seen repeatedly that forgiveness grants that ability. Forgiveness allows us to reclaim our power from the people who continue to hurt us through our use of blame and personal offense. Staying tied to people who were unkind by taking things too personally is the first step in a process by which we intensify the grievance that began when we did not get what we wanted. Blame is the second step. Forgiveness is the key to unlocking the door to let you out.

In the next chapter I will continue to explore the creation of a grievance. I will discuss the ways that taking an offense too personally and then blaming the other person for how we feel evolve into a grievance story. We will see how mistreatment often ends up as a story of victimization, a story told over and over. Whether we tell it to ourselves or to others, the constant retelling offers scant relief or hope.

CHAPTER 4

The Grievance Story

The attitude of unhappiness is not only painful, it is also mean and ugly.

What can be more base and unworthy than the pining, puling, mumping mood, no matter by what outward ills it may have been engendered? What is more injurious to others? What less helpful to others as a way out of difficulty? It but fastens and perpetuates the trouble, which occasioned it and increases the total evil of the situation.

WILLIAM JAMES

When a friend goes out on a date or takes a vacation, you want them to tell you what happened. You hope to hear an interesting story, and if the vacation or date was a good one your friend will have good tales to tell. While you are interested in the story as a whole, you are not necessarily interested in each moment or detail. We would be bored silly if a friend detailed each second of a taxi ride they took in Manhattan. Only imagine your disinterest if they told you every item on the menu and their deliberation over what to eat for breakfast. We would beg for mercy if a friend told us the minute-to-minute breakdown of every show they saw on television. What we want from them is a good story and not an overly detailed accounting.

When we tell friends about our relationships with our parents, we select particular memories to describe. If we had a mean father, we will give a couple of examples to show his character. If our parents were kind and generous, we will provide some anecdotes that demonstrate their kindness. No one describes each morning of their life or details each situation when they were hurt. It is impossible to describe every moment of a childhood.

What we do instead is craft a story to give our friends a sense of what our childhood was like. We offer a talking snapshot of our life. To tell our story, we pick the events we find most representative of how it was for us growing up. We check our memory banks, and out of the millions of moments of our childhood, we select a few. We create a story that we hope shows the picture of our experience.

In the same way out of the thousands of moments of your friend's vacation, they will select what they think are the interesting ones to tell. While listening you hope they are conveying the most important and interesting aspects. In either instance, whether listening or talking, a story is constructed. How we construct that story has consequences to our well-being. When we are talking about grievances or wounds, the way we create our story will be of the utmost importance.

Our story places what happened to us in sequence and allows us to describe our feelings. We offer commentary on the events and provide interpretation of people's actions. Most important, our story allows us to say what the experience means to us. To do that we must decide which events to highlight and which to minimize or dismiss. Little do any of us know how much is riding on the outcome of what we decide to highlight, interpret, and leave out in our account. Little do we know the potential damage if our story becomes a grievance story.

You may not have considered that the stories you tell emerge from selecting content out of a wide range of possible experiences. You may not have considered that some decision making was involved or that there are many ways to describe any particular situation. You may not have considered that the main purpose of your story is to help you understand what happened. The primary purpose of any story you tell is to help you place what happened in context. The secondary purpose is to describe what happened.

MANY POINTS OF VIEW

Let's look at one simple fact. No matter how clear and obvious the events of any hurtful experience may have been, each person involved will tell a different story. Whether we are the person who committed the hurtful act or the person who suffered from the offense, each person in any given situation notices different aspects. Bystanders, friends, and family all tell their own tale of what happened. Naturally, each of us has his or her personal view, which depends on our role.

There is no story that tells exactly what went on from all points of view. There is no one true story, only many points of view. Your story reflects your point of view and in addition communicates a theme. In choosing your theme, you often have to choose between looking like a hero or a victim or describing other people as heroes or villains. Sometimes the point of your story is how well you acted. Sometimes the point of your story is to promote your accomplishments. At other times the point of your story is to detail how awful things were.

The story can be something you keep to yourself or share with others. Just because you do not tell anyone else does not mean you do not have a particular way of talking to yourself about what happened. For each thing that happens, you create a story. This story, how often you tell it, to whom you tell it, and in what way you tell it dramatically affect your life.

Your story is not simply an objective accounting of reality. There are times when we have to communicate bad news, and to do that we tell a certain kind of story. Tact may be necessary, and we will relay the events in a certain way. Your story provides information as well as communicates ideas and may be intended to influence other people. The kind of story you tell determines how you remember the incident and how it affects your life.

Too often through telling a story we lock in the negative way a hurtful situation has affected us. The danger is that we can get caught telling a story where we take an offense too personally and then blame the other person for something done in the past. We paint the picture of helplessness in the face of someone's cruelty. In so doing, we create a grievance story.

Research has shown the story you tell about hurt changes according to whether you were the offender or the offended. Psychologists in a study asked volunteers to respond to a prompt that described a common situation where one person hurt another, such as a car accident. In this experiment there was clearly an offended party, but the subjects who read the information were given only limited details. The psychologists then asked the research subjects to create a story that filled in the details from either person's point of view. The volunteers could speak as either the offender or the offended.

To make this experiment interesting, the volunteers were given leeway in how they responded. They could describe what happened before the accident, what the participants were thinking, or something else such as the weather or traffic conditions. Their response could be as long as they chose. The reason for the flexibility was to give each person the freedom to answer as they wished.

The results of the study clearly showed one thing. If you are the offender in a difficult situation, you see things quite differently than if you are the offended. The subjects who responded from the point of view of the offended minimized their responsibility for what happened and put blame on the offender. To these subjects, the person who hurt them meant harm, and they themselves were relatively blameless for what happened.

Subjects writing from the point of view of the offender responded differently. These people placed more responsibility for what happened with the offended and minimized the damage done by their actions. In their stories the hurt was more accidental, and the offended party often did something to put themselves at risk. Interestingly, in neither group did people offer an objective reporting of the situation. People on both sides offered the versions that reflected their point of view in the best light. There was no agreed-upon, objective reality.

ARE YOU TELLING A GRIEVANCE STORY?

Depending on whether you are the offended or offender, some of your stories become grievance stories. If you look in your memory bank, I am certain that some of the items stored there are grievance stories. Grievance stories describe the painful things you have endured but not healed from. You will know these stories because telling them makes you mad or hurt all over again. You know it's a grievance story when you feel a flutter in your stomach, a tightening in your chest, or sweat forming in your palms. Grievance stories are the stories you tell when you explain to a friend why your life has not worked out the way you hoped. They are the ones you tell to make sense of why you are unhappy or angry.

Here is a brief test to help you determine whether the story you have been telling to yourself and others is a grievance story.

1. Have you told your story more than twice to the same person?
2. Do you replay the events that happened more than two times in a day in your mind?
3. Do you find yourself speaking to the person who hurt you even when that person is not there?
4. Have you made a commitment to yourself to tell the story without upset and then found yourself unexpectedly agitated?
5. Is the person who hurt you the central character of your story?
6. When you tell this story, does it remind you of other painful things that have happened to you?
7. Does your story focus primarily on your pain and what you have lost?
8. In your story is there a villain?
9. Have you made a commitment to yourself to not tell your story again and then broken your vow?
10. Do you look for other people with similar problems to tell your story to?
11. Has your story stayed the same over time?
12. Have you checked the details of your story for accuracy?

If you answer yes to five or more of the first eleven questions and/or no to question 12, there is a good chance you are telling a grievance story. If so, do not lose hope. You can as easily change a grievance story as create one.

CREATING A GRIEVANCE STORY

The way we create memories is what makes our grievance story so hard to shake. Our mind stores memories in categories. In order to make sense out of things that have happened, we link thoughts by association with other memories. Some memories can be stored in more than one category. When bad things happen to they can be stored in the "griev-ance story" in-box. Or they may be stored in the "people do not love me" in-box. Sometimes we store them in the "life is unfair" in-box. Some of us have large in-boxes for these categories and as a result become easily reminded of hurts and grievances.

After storing memories in various categories, our mind searches to find past events that match our current mood. If we feel sad in the pres-ent, we get instant access to sad memories from the past. If we feel angry in the present, then our tendency is to find memories of other things that made us mad. If we are thinking of a situation where we were mis-treated, other examples of that will fill our head.

The most harmful memory categories are those that remind you of when you were helpless or angry. Grievance stories do this by their nature. Due to the associative nature of memory, things that trigger these categories lead only to more and more painful feelings. We don't realize how many of our moods are determined by the random memories of past hurts. When we focus on painful events in the past, we decrease our self-confidence. In addition, we activate the stress chemicals, which pose risks for physical well-being.

I worked hard to help Victor acknowledge the risk inherent in the way he told his grievance story. Victor is a Presbyterian minister, and when we met he was feeling hurt and angry over the fact that his superi-ors refused to let him relocate. He wanted to move to a warmer climate primarily to help his arthritis. He lived in New England, and winter was brutal.

Victor had an important administrative position. His bosses told him they needed him to remain where he was. To Victor, they were cal-lously indifferent to his health and feelings. Victor complained bitterly about this decision and would often bring up other decisions his superi-ors had made that he did not like. Clearly, Victor was hurting himself by focusing so intently on the unpleasant consequences of his superiors' decision.

As a result, Victor was unable to remember any good decisions his bosses had made. In this way he was taking on a host of poor decisions instead of just his current dispute. It was hard for him to decide the opti-mal course for his future while dealing with all the items he had stored in his "bad bosses" basket. Victor was stuck, feeling like a victim of unfair fate.

Like Victor, when we create a grievance story, we enter the final stage of the grievance process. We suffer if we tell the grievance story repeatedly to others or ourselves. Even though it is the third and final step of the grievance process, the grievance story often signals the onset of future difficulties. The grievance story is our tale of helplessness and frustration based on taking something too personally and blaming someone else for how we feel. The grievance story seems true every time we tell it because familiar stress chemicals course through our body. However, telling a grievance story too often is dangerous to both confidence and mood. It is also a health risk since high blood pressure can become a factor when thinking about a grievance story too often.

When Dana from chapter 1 did not get the promotion she expected, she was devastated. She took the rejection personally, blamed her bosses for the loss of her dream, and told anyone she met how they had ruined her life. Every time Dana told the story she experienced her undeserved loss and triggered anew her anger and frustration. Dana's grievance story placed her squarely at the mercy of unkind fate and capricious bosses. As long as she told this same story, she felt continued anger and helplessness.

Dana's co-workers at first were sympathetic to her plight. They empathized with her loss and frustration. However, as Dana's job performance suffered and she continued to claim, "I have wasted ten years of my life," people at work became less supportive. Soon people avoided her because they no longer wanted to hear her grievance story. Her co-workers began telling a story of their own. In their story Dana was the problem, disrupting the work environment and unable to move on with her life. Dana wondered why her co-workers started to avoid her.

To create his grievance story, Alan from chapter 3 focused on the parts of his abandonment that made his hurt personal. Alan highlighted his ex-wife's infidelity and ignored problems in their marriage. His wife had complained for years about his lack of sexual enthusiasm. Alan focused on his ex-wife's flaws and not on any of the attempts she made to work things out. Alan felt tortured by his own loss and unable to see that a huge number of other people endure similar circumstances. He blamed his ex-wife every time he was lonely, became jealous of other loving couples, or struggled with financial problems. Alan's grievance story solidified his belief that life was empty without his wife's love and support.

Alan did not complete the grievance process until he formed his grievance story. When his ex-wife left he was in a situation that hurt like hell. He could have taken his ex-wife's actions too personally, blamed her for his pain, and still created a story where he had some personal power. It was not until Alan created the grievance story that he lost flexibility in how he could respond. He did not have to describe himself as a victim. There are as many stories of men surviving loss as there are of men who fall apart.

When his wife left, Alan's friends were on his side. They supported him and let him moan and complain. Alan found other men whose wives had left them, and they all agreed that women were unreliable and selfish. This led to a short period in his life when Alan, although in a great deal of pain, felt a good deal of support.

Unfortunately for Alan, the support eroded as his friends developed other interests and went back to their lives. The other recently divorced men moved on and no longer needed or wanted to hear the same complaints. These men got tired of hearing themselves and Alan complain. They began to shun Alan, and this too he blamed on his ex-wife. Grudgingly, Alan began to date but was always disappointed; one was too skinny, one talked too much, one did not listen enough.

When I met Alan he was bitter, alone, and without a clue as to how he had become so unhappy. He did not know the toll his grievance story was taking on him. Each of the mental daggers he was sending to his ex-wife was hitting him instead. The anger he directed at his ex-wife made it difficult for him to attract another woman. The mistrust he felt led him judge people harshly. The pain he was suffering made it nearly impossible for Alan to develop interests with which to engage friends in conversation. Alan blamed it all on the fact that he was dumped, and that is the painful story he told.

I want to make clear the crucial distinction between creating a grievance story and simply telling other people you have been hurt. Alan's story did not become a grievance story because he told other people about his wife's betrayal. Alan was smart to reach out for help when his marriage ended. Alan had a grievance story because he told the same story over and over. He told a story that put the responsibility for his well-being on his ex-wife. His story became a grievance story because at every turn he took his wife's actions too personally. At every turn he blamed his present misfortune on things done in the past. He resisted his friends' and familie's advice to get on with his life and instead remained stuck in a cycle of pain.

FINDING SOCIAL SUPPORT

Researchers have found that people like Alan and Dana who share their life experiences with others tend to deal better with stress. This is called social support, and generally the more of it the better. Research shows that good social support is beneficial for people dealing well stress. People who rely on friends or family are generally happier and report better health.

Scientists have found that people who do not have friends and have to deal with things alone struggle more with difficult life experiences and also die earlier. In fact, one large study showed that people who were socially isolated were at the greatest risk for premature death. Lack of companionship is just as, if not more, dangerous to survival than smoking. In a different study, elderly people who had heart attacks were more likely to die in the hospital if no one visited them. If they had one visitor their odds of leaving the hospital alive increased substantially. With each visitor, their odds for survival increased.

When it comes to dealing with life's difficulties, such as loss of a job, corporate shake-ups, stressful work experiences, or an extended hospital stay, social support is crucial. Research also shows that appropriate help from friends and family can help protect us from getting sick. It can help resolve the stresses we face.

However, in one series of studies, researchers found some interesting things about social support that suggests that there may be both productive and unproductive types of support. We all need the help of people who care. However, we have to use their help wisely.

The people who profited most from social support asked for comfort for a shorter period of time. They requested advice and wished to learn how to cope better with what had happened to them. They wanted their friends and family to be honest with them and then tried to use their assistance to make changes in their lives. These people used the support to help themselves through a difficult period and received health benefits as a result. They saw themselves as faced with a challenge and were up to the task. They could have created a grievance story but instead used gumption and the support of friends to endure a crisis and tell a positive story of their successful coping.

Those who did not profit from social support asked for different things from their family and friends. These folks tended to complain to family and friends about how poorly they were treated. They encouraged their friends and family to support them even if they were wrong. They saw their problems as big and resented the challenges they were faced with. Their self-esteem was so fragile that they resisted advice that would help them change for the better. These people were telling a grievance story and resisted giving up that story. They suffered health consequences as a result.

I want to relate a story of a woman who used the help of her friends and family wisely. Up to this point I have written about people whose grievance stories were more important to them than learning to cope well with their losses. But here is the story of a woman I find remarkable. Her story illustrates that not all offenses must become grievances and that a grievance story is not inevitable just because we are grievously hurt. Reading her story, you see how the help of people close to you can lead you to become a hero instead of a victim.

Renee was hit by a car while riding her bicycle on a quiet side street in a small city. She was an expert cyclist, rode to work regularly, and knew the rules of the road. She was riding on the correct side of the road, signaled properly, and wore a helmet. She was not in a hurry and was careful. None of what she did protected her when a driver in a hurry tried to pass on the inside and hit Renee. Renee was hit flush, the car knocked her flying, and then the driver sped on his way. Renee was badly hurt and spent two weeks in the hospital with a crushed pelvis and a severe concussion. When she was released from the hospital she recuperated for six months at home.

Her pelvis never fully healed, she suffered from chronic headaches, and Renee needed a cane for five years after the accident. She never found the driver who hit her. She had to quit her job, and her husband had to change his to earn more income. Renee, however, survived the accident, survived the loss of her job, survived the random act of violence, and continues to tolerate her chronic pain. She did this by becoming a person whose suffering developed into her compassion for the pain of others. Besides a new full-time job, she volunteers regularly in a pain clinic helping others deal with their injuries.

Instead of complaining, Renee talks with gratitude about the help given to her by her husband and family. She reminds visitors that she could not have survived without their help. She is thankful they showed her love but not pity. Renee commends her husband for pushing her to go back to school when she was still hurting. She has kind words for her father, who told her to talk with other people who overcame similar problems. She remembers her father saying, "While you can't change the past, you are the only one who can make your future." Renee, while frustrated about her pain, admits she is a much better person today because of what she has gone through.

Each of us can learn to deal with our wounds and hurts like Renee. We do not have to tell endless stories of victimization. We can forgive those who have hurt us and move on with our lives. We can forgive ourselves for being stuck and getting hurt. We can forgive our parents if they have hurt us and our friends and family if they have not been supportive. We can help our friends to forgive and move on if they are stuck. We can create a story that shows us as hero instead of victim.

CHOOSING A STORY

We begin the process of creating a new story by taking care every time we talk about the unresolved painful things that have happened to us. When you hear yourself talking about a past hurt, stop for a moment to see if you are telling a grievance story. If so, pause and take a deep breath. Your grievance story, which seems so comforting and familiar, is your enemy. That grievance story, more than what hurt you, has imprisoned you. It keeps you in the past. It alienates your friends and family and reminds you and others that you are a victim. Once we change our grievance story, we are on the road to healing.

Remember the grievance plane metaphor I used in the introduction? I would like you now to think about these planes in a different way. I am going to use this metaphor to illustrate the variety of ways we can use to describe any difficult situation.

The planes are in the air and have been circling for hours and hours, but now each of us is a passenger stuck waiting to land. Finally the plane lands, the door opens, and we have arrived at last at our destination. I am interested in the different ways we react when we see our friends and family who are waiting for us.

Some of us will have grievance stories already developed to spring on our friends. We will complain about the delay, talk about the lousy food, describe in minute detail the airline's incompetence, and discuss all the ways we can be compensated for our pain and suffering. Others will see their loved ones and exclaim how glad they are to see them. These people will talk about how they missed their family and friends and how thankful they are that they finally landed safely. These folks will want to catch up with their friends and when asked may say they found it a challenge to stay hopeful when they were stuck in the air so long.

It seems reasonable to assume that the passengers who already have a grievance story will suffer longer than the people who don't. For the people who are simply happy to land and delighted to see their family again, the plane ride is over. For those with a grievance, while the ride is over, the grievance may keep them tied to the plane for months. Each of us chooses which kind of story we want to tell. Remember, we can either forgive and move on with our lives or be tied to things over which we have no control.

Now that you know the three steps in forming a grievance, I will teach you to how to forgive. I will teach through the experience of forgiveness to tell a different story. You will see that you have the choice to amend your story so you no longer highlight the wrong done or the hurt you have suffered. You will learn to tell your story so your problems become challenges to overcome, not simply grievances on which to dwell. By the end of this book, your story will show you as the conquering hero capable of overcoming difficult obstacles. Your story will be that of a hero who succeeded on a journey of forgiveness.

CHAPTER 5

Rules, Rules, Rules

What has passed and cannot be prevented should not be grieved for.
BIG ELK, MAHA CHIEF, FROM *Commonplace Book of Prose*, 1830

In each of the previous chapters, I asserted that a grievance begins when something unwanted happens and too much space is rented to that event. The three-step grievance process lays the foundation for understanding what is happening when past hurts cause us to feel a painful mix of emotions and thoughts. I described the three steps needed to form a grievance: taking something too personally, playing the blame game, and creating a grievance story. However, the question remains: What causes some situations and not others to become grievances? Every time we do not get what we want, we do not form a grievance. Is there a factor that determines why in one situation more than others we are likely to create a grievance? The answer is a resounding yes. Before a grievance is formed, we reacted to a painful situation in a certain way. Why we reacted in this way is the subject of this chapter.

The underpinning of the grievance process is something I call "unenforceable rules." In this chapter I show how making a simple and common mistake can cause us to react poorly to disappointment and setbacks and begin the vicious cycle of the grievance process. Making this simple mistake is at the root of all grievances. Before we can move forward into forgiveness, we must go back to examine the hurtful moment when we still had a choice about how we would respond.

Let us return to Sarah's experience as an example. Sarah, whom we met in the introduction, did not want her husband, Jim, to stay out late.

But staying out late, along with poor work habits, was just one of the many signs that Jim had substance abuse problems. His addictions soon became a nightmare of late-night phone calls, huge debts, and abandonment. He left her with an infant son and a host of unpaid bills. Sarah, of course, did not want any of this to happen and in response felt overwhelmed and angry.

Sarah's picture of how her life should unfold likely had no place for the ravage of unrestrained substance abuse. Sarah dreamed of a loving family nurtured by an industrious and caring father. She reacted to not getting what she wanted with outrage, hurt, and anger. She took Jim's substance abuse personally, blamed her husband for all her distress, and created a grievance story that she told for years. Sarah thought her husband caused her problems, both in her life and in the way she felt. She was unaware of the role she played in becoming upset. She did not know that her reaction to the situation made it more painful and long-lasting.

Think about this obvious fact. Every person married to a substance abuser does not end up like Sarah. Each person who deals with an alcoholic partner does not create a grievance. Some people are able to recognize the signs of trouble and take a stand quickly and firmly. While they may suffer pain and embarrassment, they survive. They may even grow because of what they have overcome. Other people make heroic efforts to help their partners and stay centered in their positive efforts. Others join with those who struggle with similar problems and gain support through the group connection. Still others do their best to manage the problem and after exhausting their resources move on. There is nothing etched in stone that says you have to create a grievance because you married a substance abuser.

UNENFORCEABLE RULES

There is a specific way of thinking that gets us from point A when something happens to point B where a grievance takes hold. The particular way Sarah thought about her experiences led to her increased distress. Certain mental habits made some of her problems big and others small. The thinking process that leads to grievances is the process of trying to enforce unenforceable rules. The rest of this chapter explains unenforceable rules and how you create them.

To better understand unenforceable rules, imagine an industrious police officer whose job it is to patrol a busy stretch of interstate highway. Sitting in his car, the officer notes a late-model BMW speeding by at eighty-five miles per hour. He begins to write out the ticket and tries to start his car. His engine, however, will not turn over. It sputters but does not catch. Stuck and unable to move, the officer soon notices another car speeding by. Then another. Wondering what to do, he gets mad at first and then feels helpless.

Questions go through his mind: "Do I write out a ticket for each car, or do I let them go by? If I write out tickets, what do I do with them since I can't issue them? What do I do about the cars that continue to speed by?" Stopping speeders is the police officer's job, and because of a damaged engine he cannot do his job. He is faced with the predicament of having rules to enforce but no ability to do so. What does he do with his unenforceable rules?

The officer is faced with a worse predicament if a car whizzes by at ninety miles an hour and the driver appears drunk. The officer sees the driver not just speeding but putting other drivers at risk. The officer faces a crisis if he sees a drunk driver speeding by who causes a hit-and-run accident. The officer is still stuck and helpless to intervene. The squad car still does not work, and he cannot do his job. The officer is faced with the predicament of trying to enforce rules that at that moment are unenforceable.

The question the officer ponders is the one you deal with every time one of your unenforceable rules is broken. The question you confront is, "Do I continue to write tickets that I cannot serve?" Like the police officer, you are often faced with situations where you have to figure out what to do when you have no control over the situation.

Let's imagine the police officer is stuck for two hours before another police car can pick him up. During that time he sees fifty cars whizzing by at eighty miles per hour. Let's say he writes a ticket out for each of them. What does he do with the tickets? He may put them in the back of his squad car, or he may put them in his date book. Wherever he puts them, they will clutter up some part of his life. In the same way, when you write mental tickets that you cannot enforce to your friends, spouse, neighbors, and business associates, you clutter up your mind.

Often when trying to enforce unenforceable rules we write mental tickets to "punish" the one who has acted wrongly. Unfortunately, if our rule is unenforceable, the only person we end up hurting with our ticket is ourselves. We clog up our minds with these tickets. We become frustrated because things do not go the way we want. We become angry because something wrong is happening. We feel helpless because we cannot make things right.

I am convinced that when you try to enforce something over which you have no control, you create a problem for yourself. That problem gets in your way as you try to figure out what is the best thing to do. It is much harder to know what to do when you are angry, frustrated, and helpless. Making a good decision is tough when you are constantly writing tickets and there is no one to give them to.

Being upset got in Sarah's way as she tried to figure out what to do with her crumbling marriage. Sarah's vain attempt to enforce her unenforceable rules, not just her husband's substance abuse, contributed to her near breakdown. Sarah's constant writing of tickets was as big a problem as her husband's behavior.

We have as much chance of enforcing our unenforceable rules as of getting blood out of a stone. Think for a minute about why trying to do so makes our lives so hard. Have you ever tried to force someone to do something they did not want to do? How successful were you? Have you ever tried to get what you needed from a person who did not want to help? How successful was that? Have you ever demanded your spouse or partner be nicer to you? Were you successful? Have you ever gotten mad at yourself for making a mistake? Did getting mad help? Ever demanded your boss treat you better? Did this change your boss's behavior? Each of these normal desires is an example of trying to enforce an unenforceable rule. Trying to change what cannot be changed or influence those who do not want to be influenced will meet with failure and cause us emotional distress.

OUR RULES DETERMINE OUR FEELINGS

The rules we have for other people's behavior and for our own behavior will to a large degree determine how we feel. Why? Because some rules are enforceable and others not. When you have too many unenforceable rules or try too hard to enforce the ones you have, you create a problem. Trying to enforce only those things you can control will help your life go more smoothly.

When I tell my two-year-old son to stay out of my bedroom, I can put up a gate to keep him out. If somehow he crawls over the gate, I can bring him back to the living room or I can put up a bigger gate. If I have the will and energy, I can keep my child away from my bedroom. Generally, I can make my two-year-old stay where I want. I am able to enforce my rule to keep my child out of our bedroom.

When you make a house rule that your eighteen-year-old son bring your car home by 10:30 every evening, you are setting yourself up for frustration. You can insist until you are blue in the face he have the car home by 10:30. However, your son makes the ultimate decision about when he returns home. Unless you have an unusual relationship with your child, you are not sitting in the car with him as he is driving.

Your son could be late for a number of reasons. He may be late because there is a lot of traffic. He may decide to follow his friends and not you. He may forget the time he was supposed to be home. He may not care what you think. To demand he return at a specific time is an unenforceable rule. You can physically control your two-year-old, but you cannot control your eighteen-year-old in the same way. The difference is the eighteen-year-old has a choice whether or not to obey you.

We are trying to enforce an unenforceable rule when we blame someone else for how we feel. We are certainly trying to enforce an unenforceable rule when we take someone else's behavior too personally. When we have created a grievance, rest assured there was at least one unenforceable rule. Whenever we are very upset about anything, at the root of it is our attempt to enforce an unenforceable rule. In fact, feeling angry or helpless or depressed is an indication that we are trying to enforce an unenforceable rule.

We know we are trying to enforce an unenforceable rule if anything, except a very recent grievous loss or illness, causes us a good deal of emotional distress. When facing the recent death of someone we love or the loss of one's home or the news of a major illness, it is natural to feel overwhelmed and not be able to think clearly. However, after a short period of time we must confront the problem of enforcing a rule we cannot enforce.

None of us has ultimate control over our health or the life and death of the people we love. Put bluntly, when something unpleasant happens, we have the choice of accepting it or not. The reason we do not accept what happens to us is we cling instead to our unenforceable rules. This is analogous to a drowning person, who just fell off a ship, clinging to the anchor of that ship. The drowning person is gasping the last breath and still complaining that the anchor was supposed to keep the boat from moving in the storm.

WHAT IS A RULE?

A rule is any expectation you have for how something should turn out or how someone should think or behave. I deliberately make this definition broad. We all make rules for how we should act and think, how other people should act and think, and how life should turn out. We have rules for just about everything, including what is appropriate dress, appropriate language, proper amount of traffic on the expressway, correct numbers of items in the supermarket checkout line; how other people should talk, how our kids should treat us, and even what kind of weather we should have.

An unenforceable rule is an expectation you have that you do not have the power to make happen. This can be an expectation for your parents to treat you as well as they treat your brother or an expectation that you win the lottery. It can be an expectation that you win first prize in a race or that you get a raise. It can be an expectation for sunny weather or a short line at the supermarket. There is no end to what we can expect that we do not have the power to make happen.

An unenforceable rule is one where you do not have control over whether your rule is enforced or not. An unenforceable rule is one where you do not have the power to make things come out the way you want. When you try to enforce one of your unenforceable rules you become angry, bitter, despondent, and helpless. Trying to force something you cannot control is an exercise in frustration. Trying to force a spouse to love you or a business partner to be fair or a parent to treat each sibling fairly is unenforceable.

Anyone would feel frustrated if they stared at a rock waiting for blood to emerge. Most parents get frustrated and angry watching the clock tick by when their teenager is late. Children of harsh parents get upset when they want their past to be closer to *The Cosby Show* than *Married with Children*. You get frustrated when you want someone to treat you better than they choose to. Each time we try to enforce an unenforceable rule, frustration and helplessness ensue. Try to imagine how frustrated and angry Sarah got each time Jim stayed out late. Imagine how many tickets she must have written and stored in her mind.

The more unenforceable rules you have, the greater likelihood that you will feel agitated and disappointed. The stronger you try to enforce something you cannot control, the worse you will feel. If you cling to even one unenforceable rule, you leave yourself open to suffer every single time the rule is broken. Each and every time Jim was late, Sarah got upset. She was upset because he was out drinking. She was upset because she was alone. In addition, she was upset because Jim was not obeying her. Jim was not doing what she felt he was supposed to do. Sarah was helplessly trying to enforce an unenforceable rule.

In response, Sarah wrote out a huge number of tickets. Jim was breaking rules left and right. He broke so many rules Sarah lost track. The problem was Jim did not take her tickets seriously. He did not care if Sarah wrote out tickets all day long. Sarah's tickets started to fill up her mind, crowding out other thoughts.

Part of Sarah's frustration was a legitimate response to Jim's carelessness and destructive behavior. As we will learn in the next chapter, in order to forgive it is important that we know what behaviors are not okay with us and what boundaries must not be crossed. However, another aspect of the suffering was Sarah's insisting Jim be a certain way when she did not have the power to make him be that way. She couldn't make him stop abusing drugs. She didn't have the power to make him come home at night. She couldn't force him to show up on time for work, and she couldn't make him love her. Yet instead of accepting his lack of reliability, Sarah tried to maintain her illusion of control. Therefore, every time Jim violated her unenforceable rules, she became angry. Sarah never thought to examine the rules she had for Jim to see if they were realistic.

Sarah thought about Jim's behavior in the specific way that is required for a grievance to take hold. She thought about him in the way that caused her to take his behavior too personally and blamed him for her host of troubles. Sarah thought that her husband was wrong to abuse drugs. Sarah thought Jim should come home at night. Sarah thought Jim should show up on time for work. She thought he should love her. Sarah created a host of rules that Jim brazenly broke time and time again, and she wrote out tickets by the dozens. The unenforceable rules Sarah tried to enforce led her to suffer even more.

I do not claim that Jim's behavior is acceptable. I do not suggest that it is easy to live with a substance abuser. He is acting irresponsibly, mistreating his wife, and neglecting his marriage. I do not suggest that Sarah could live with a substance abuser or face the shambles of her marriage without pain. What I claim is that trying to enforce unenforceable rules leads to feeling helpless and angry instead of empowered. Writing tickets is not the same as taking constructive action. Writing tickets is what you do when you cannot figure out what constructive action to take.

Lorraine is now a single mom with two kids. She was married to Larry for seventeen years. When they were together Larry worked all the time, and she in effect has been a single parent for years. They spent virtually no time together, and Larry went to none of his children's school functions. Their relationship was withering from neglect, and Lorraine felt more and more bitter.

One day Lorraine got fed up and confronted Larry with her feelings. They made a date to spend the next Saturday together. Saturday came, and when Lorraine woke up she found a note from Larry saying he was going to the office for a few minutes. Four hours passed, and there was no sign of Larry. Lorraine was furious, and when Larry did come home she screamed at him and threw some kitchen utensils at him. She screamed that she was sick and tired of his lying to her. Larry broke Lorraine's unenforceable rule for the last time, and she wrote him a major ticket. Larry could not understand why his wife got so upset. After all, he was just getting some work done.

"My husband must not lie to me" is a common example of an unenforceable rule. Lorraine and Larry would have had a better marriage if Larry had been more honest. Maybe Larry did not want to be home with Lorraine and did not know how to say that. Maybe he had his own grievances with her behavior. Lorraine's fury at his actions made meaningful discussion difficult. Lorraine was too busy throwing tickets at Larry to engage in mutual dialogue. She was convinced Larry was wrong for breaking her rule, and she did not feel the need to listen to his side of the story.

Each of us would love it if our significant others were honest with us. Our partnerships would be the better for it, since we could trust our partners more easily and would feel safer. Unfortunately, the reality is we cannot make a partner be more truthful than she or he chooses to be. We cannot force a spouse to do anything that person does not choose to do. If Larry wants to go to work and lie about it, Lorraine can do nothing to prevent this. I imagine that many if not all of us with lying spouses had unenforceable rules buried under the mound of tickets we wrote.

Before exploring this further, I want to make one pertinent distinction. Many of us confuse unexpected events with unwanted ones. Often, what you do not want, you also do not expect to happen, but these are not the same. For example, if there is a knock on your door at 3:45 in the morning, you will likely be anxious. You may either angrily or haltingly ask who it is. If the voice says there is a cashier's check made out to you for a hundred thousand dollars, this announcement would be unexpected but clearly wanted. You likely would not get upset at being given a huge check.

However, if the knock at your door is from someone repossessing your car, then the event may be both unexpected and unwanted. If your payments are delinquent, the knock may be clearly expected and just as clearly unwanted. If you are upset, you may have an unenforceable rule saying that even though you did not fulfill your financial obligation there should be no consequences.

For Sarah, her husband Jim's substance abuse problems were both unexpected and unwanted. When Sarah married Jim, she did not have any contingency plans for his latent substance abuse. In a way, she was not realistic. While Sarah did not want an alcoholic husband, it was certainly possible; many people have alcoholic spouses. At first Jim's drinking was both unexpected and unwanted. As time went on and Jim was rarely sober, his substance abuse became expected but unwanted. However, Sarah's unenforceable rules clouded her judgment and made it hard for her to react to what had become expected but unwanted behavior.

In Lorraine's case, Larry's withdrawal was unexpected and unwanted. They had a loving courtship and a good couple of years of marriage. But later Larry's absences became the norm; his not being home became expected but unwanted. Lorraine too was unrealistic. While she did not want a neglectful husband, she had one, and so do millions of other women. She responded by getting angry and looking for ways to pay Larry back.

For both women, much of their suffering arose because they could not accept the truth of their lives. They lived with husbands who were more likely to disappoint than satisfy them. Rather than taking constructive action, each woman kept on trying to enforce her unenforceable rule. Each woman wrote out tons of tickets and suffered because she did not understand the deadly power of her unenforceable rules. Each woman claimed that her rule was correct and her husband wrong. Neither realized there is no way to win when you are trying to enforce an unenforceable rule.

The pain both women felt was related to how strongly she tried to enforce her rule. Each woman got angry as her unenforceable rule was broken. Neither woman had the power to make her husband do what she wanted, which led to feelings of helplessness. Sarah had an unenforceable rule in her mind that her husband was not supposed to drink. If Jim was not supposed to drink, why did he? He must have had a different rule. His rule was that it was OK to drink. He may have had a rule where wives are supposed to mind their own business. Sarah did not follow his unenforceable rules and that may have frustrated him.

She did not know that her nondrinking rule was unenforceable. To her, sobriety was a normal expectation for a wife to have for her husband. To me this is an unenforceable rule that destroyed Sarah's chances for recovery from a painful and difficult experience. In Sarah's case, her unenforceable rule made living with a drunk more difficult. Jim was an alcoholic and did exactly what alcoholics do: he drank. Sarah wrote out many tickets for behavior that was expected but unwanted. She did not adapt well to expected behavior because she kept on insisting that Jim stop. For Sarah, having an unenforceable rule that was regularly broken began the cycle that led her to form a grievance.

Unenforceable rules are everywhere and are at the root of almost all our suffering. Often, husbands and wives have different rules governing the same situation. This can lead to all types of problems. A rule I often hear from women is, "I've had a hard day at work, and I need my husband to be understanding tonight and not pester me to have sex." But husbands often have a very different rule. They may think, "I've had a hard day at work, and I need a loving and sexually available wife." When this occurs, both partners have unenforceable rules.

Linda and George were such a couple. When George wanted sex and Linda was too tired, her response was to get mad at George for breaking her rule—although she did not put it that way—and view him as an inconsiderate oaf. Unfortunately, George had a different rule. He perceived Linda's lack of sexual desire as unkindness on her part. As a result, Linda was often angry with George while George felt shunned by Linda. Both were trying to enforce unenforceable rules instead of facing the reality of their own and their partner's limitations. Their marriage improved when they stopped trying to enforce their rules and instead started forgiving each other.

Underlying every grievance is the reality that the offended party had an unenforceable rule that was not followed. The rule can be as generic as "I should not suffer," "People should be nice to me," or "I have to be loved." Or it can take the form of specific rules of conduct such as "My lover should have cleaned the bathroom exactly as I told him to." In either case, demanding adherence to rules that cannot be enforced lies at the base of the grievance process.

When you say that someone you love must love you back, you are creating an unenforceable rule. Just because you love them why do they have to love you? When you say that your husband should not drink but instead come home to you at night, you are creating an unenforceable rule. Just because you want your husband to be sober does not mean he wants the same thing. When you say your friends must not lie to you, you are creating an unenforceable rule. Just because your relationships would be easier with truth telling does not mean your friends have to make the relationship easier on you.

When you say your family should be sensitive when you are in pain, you are creating an unenforceable rule. Just because you want care does not mean your family has to offer it when you want it. On your vacation when you want the weather to be perfect, you are creating an unenforceable rule. Just because you want good weather does not mean it will happen. When you say your boss should be patient with you, you are creating an unenforceable rule. Just because you want a sensitive boss does not mean that becomes a priority for him.

WHAT YOU HOPE FOR IS NOT THE SAME AS WHAT YOU GET

In each of the above examples you are clearly stating what you hope will happen. Each example consists of a good and positive wish. The world would be a better place if everyone were loved and treated fairly. Each of these desires is a good one, and it is helpful for you to know what you want. The problem comes when you forget that what you hope for is not the same as what you get. Just because Alan from chapter 3 really wanted his ex-wife to come crawling back to him did not make it likely. He forgot that he could live without her. When Lorraine confused wanting Larry to work less with thinking Larry had to work less, she forgot she survived for years with him gone.

Unenforceable rules warp our judgment. We try so hard to get our rules met that we do not see the damage that our rules are causing. We blame people for breaking our rules. We write out tickets to punish them. We withhold our love. We do all sorts of things arising from upset and hurt instead of doing the one that might help: we do not look at whether our rules are enforceable.

The grievance process begins when we want something and make an unenforceable rule about getting it. Remember Dana who felt she must get the promotion she wanted. Dana made the critical mistake that turned her wish into an unenforceable rule. Dana wanted the promotion, but made believe she was owed the promotion. She confused ten years of service to her company with a guarantee that the promotion was hers. Dana could not control the decision about who was promoted so she created an unenforceable rule. Not knowing she even had a rule and certainly not knowing her rule was unenforceable, Dana acted as if wanting the promotion meant that she was owed the promotion. This caused her no end of grief and led her to take everything too personally, blame her failure and depression on her employers, and create a grievance story.

Each of the people I talked about in this chapter suffered because of their unenforceable rules. For Dana or Alan not getting what they wanted followed by years of writing tickets led them to tremendous emotional suffering. Their hurt, anger, and hopelessness led to an exaggerated attention on the person who hurt them. This clouded their judgment and made it almost impossible for them to lead full lives. Their decision making suffered and they felt stuck for years.

The first step in unraveling your unenforceable rules is to recognize them. When you realize you make unenforceable rules, you have taken the first step toward helping yourself. Simply by doing this you have taken back some of the power you gave other people to hurt you. As a next step you can construct rules that will lead to more peace and greater control over your emotions. With that peace and control come improved judgment and decision making.

Sometimes we have to resolve a difficult situation. As an example, living with an alcoholic spouse is often a troubling experience. Simply making better rules will not resolve the problem. We may have to figure out what to do to protect ourselves and maybe our children. To do this we need our wits about us. When our minds are filled with helpless anger because our rules are not being followed we have less energy available to think through our options. It is difficult enough to leave a spouse or obtain a restraining order. We make the challenge greater when we insist our spouse do something they are not able to do: drink responsibly.

In the rest of the book you will learn how to stop making unenforceable rules and how to make alternative rules that are enforceable. You will learn the research-proven method of writing fewer tickets. With an enforceable rule, you are more able to stay on top of things when your spouse does something different from what you wanted. With an enforceable rule, you retain the flexibility to make good decisions even when faced with an alcoholic spouse. With enforceable rules, you can forgive and make decisions that work toward your good instead of simply reacting to your wayward spouse. The peace and control you feel will lead to improved judgment and decision making.

Remember that in almost every circumstance in which you feel significant emotional pain, you are trying to enforce an unenforceable rule. There is hope. Each of us can learn to change our rules. We can reclaim our power. We can learn to forgive.

PART TWO

Forgiveness

CHAPTER 6

To Forgive or Not to Forgive:
That Is the Question

Good-nature and good sense must ever join;
To err is human, to forgive, divine.
ALEXANDER POPE

Thus far we have discussed creating grievances at length but have paid little attention to forgiveness. This is a book that teaches the importance of forgiveness for both health and happiness. With that in mind, let us now shift our focus to this book's purpose: to help us learn to forgive ourselves and others who may have hurt us.

I begin where I always begin discussions of forgiveness: with my assertion that forgiveness is a choice. Neither you nor I have to forgive anyone who has hurt us. On the other hand, we can forgive all who have done us harm. The decision is ours to make. Forgiveness does not happen by accident. We have to make a decision to forgive. We will not forgive just because we think we should. Forgiveness cannot be forced. I have no intention to demand that you forgive, but I will show you how and then the choice is yours. To help you choose, let me show you why I believe forgiveness is in your best interest. This choice exists whether or not someone asks for forgiveness. Each of us can learn to land the planes endlessly circling on our radar screen. When we choose forgiveness we release our past to heal our present.

What I want is for forgiveness to be on your menu of choices when you are mistreated. I see over and over that many people forget there are a variety of ways to react when hurt. Sometimes we get angry and stay angry. Sometimes we get hurt and stay hurt. Other times we simply let the problem slide off our backs. Sometimes the wounds of the past fester and contaminate our present. Sometimes we have no patience for coping at all. There is no single way to react.

In another situation we may feel compassion for the person that hurt us. Or we become furious with ourselves. Other times we don't understand exactly what happened and don't know how to react at all.

Each of us reacts to hurt in different ways at different times. I want to teach you to put forgiveness on your response menu so that you can choose it when needed.

In the initial chapters of this book, we learned the process by which a grievance is formed. Renting too much space in our mind to a problem comes from taking something too personally. Blaming someone else for our feelings then takes away our power, and we progress to forming our grievance story. Behind the process lies our tendency to make unenforceable rules that the world or other people are supposed to follow.

Throughout, I have used examples of actual people, with real life problems, to show how grievances unfold. I have done this for one reason. I want to make clear beyond the shadow of a doubt that a grievance does not occur by chance. Just because we were mistreated does not mean we have to create a grievance. A grievance isn't inevitable just because of a deep wound. A grievance forms when you react to painful situations in a specific way.

The first chapters detailed that what we think and feel after a hurt plays a major role in whether or not we form a grievance. When we realize our role in the grievance process, we can then decide to play the central role in our healing. The most powerful way to heal is through forgiveness. When we forgive, we take something less personally, blame the person who hurt us less, and change our grievance story. Through learning the process of forgiveness, we can forgive anyone who has hurt us in any way.

In this and the following chapters, I explore the reasons you are better off when you choose to forgive. I describe the differences among forgiveness, condoning, reconciliation, and justice. I have conducted research studies that conclusively prove that what I am teaching you works, and I describe these studies in detail. Other scientific studies have shown that forgiveness can improve your health, relationships, and emotional stability, and I distill the essential data from this ground-breaking research as well.

GETTING READY TO FORGIVE

Forgiveness is only one response of many you can choose from when you are hurt. Unfortunately, forgiveness is rarely discussed and less often practiced. This is so even though forgiveness is a major tenet of religious teaching and world politics. Research suggests that most people do not consider forgiveness when deciding how to deal with the cruelties of life. The omission of forgiveness from our menu of responses is hurting us in mind, body, and spirit.

Forgiveness is not something esoteric or otherworldly. Forgiveness is a skill that you can learn. Forgiveness takes place by undoing each of the steps of the grievance process. We learn to balance the impersonal aspect of hurt with the personal, which most of the time means taking something painful less personally. We take responsibility for how we feel when someone hurts us. Finally, we change our grievance story to a forgiveness story, where we become the hero instead of the victim.

Before moving forward, we need to make clear the three preconditions needed before we are ready to forgive. These three preconditions are simple, and most people reading this book will have already satisfied them:

- Know what your feelings are about what happened.
- Be clear about the action that wronged you.
- Share your experience with at least one or two trusted people.

If you have not completed these preconditions, forgiveness needs to wait. You do not have to rush to forgive, and when you are ready forgiveness will be easier and deeper. I often see people like Darlene, who put themselves at risk by repeatedly satisfying these three preconditions. Darlene was jilted at the altar by her fiancé, Jack, and three years later she still rented Jack a lot of space in her mind. Darlene complained about how bad she felt and how wrong her boyfriend was for ending their relationship, and she told her tale of woe to anyone within earshot. She took all three preconditions to the extreme. I see more people like Darlene, stuck in rehashing their wounds, than those not ready to begin.

The first precondition is to be able to describe how you feel. This does not mean the feelings will be simple or always clear. Your feelings may alternate from day to day or come and go. Sarah was angry with her ex-husband for his substance abuse for a couple of days and then mad at herself for getting into such a desperate situation. This was also accompanied by feeling like a failure for her part in creating such a poor relationship. In addition, she was ashamed that she was a single mom on welfare. At other times she was defiant, saying that no stinking ex-husband was going to ruin her life.

When mistreated, we can expect a variety of painful feelings. There is nothing unusual about feeling upset, confused, furious, abandoned, alone, or scared. It is common when hurt to feel numb and overwhelmed. It is common to feel one thing one day and another the next.

Sarah benefited from naming her feelings. Naming fights the tendency to deny or minimize how we feel. It is both easy and common to deny the intensity of our feelings as a way to save pain. Sometimes we have a hard time admitting bad things really happened and that they hurt. We may deny the intensity of our feelings to remain in problematic relationships. Acknowledging how you feel is one step in the fight against the tendency to stay in abusive and painful relationships. In any case, you are not ready to forgive until you are clear about how you feel.

It is just as important to know exactly what was done that was unacceptable. This means trying to remember details as best we can. It does not mean we have to exhaustively examine every minute of what happened. The purpose is to free us of the tendency to deny and minimize what occurred. We want to know that what we experienced was unacceptable behavior and to be able to state in clear language what was not okay. How can we know what to avoid in the future if we are unclear about the lines crossed? Coming to clarity about what causes us pain makes us less likely to repeat a hurtful situation.

Darlene at first said simply that her boyfriend sucked, that he was a lying son of a bitch and she hated him. She said that he cheated on her and she hated him. At least every twenty words she said she hated him. I asked her if there were any other feelings she had. After a few moments Darlene, looking sad and vulnerable, responded by saying that she felt lonely and was afraid to trust again.

Darlene's feelings were complex and often felt contradictory. She was confused about which of her feelings were real. Was she scared and therefore mad, or was she mad and therefore scared? I reminded her she did not have to sort everything out; she just had to know what she felt. Darlene was scared of being alone, angry with her ex, angry with herself, confused, and deeply hurt. She also felt self-doubt wondering if Jack's behavior reflected upon her desirability. Would other men dump her as well? Would she ever find someone to love her faithfully?

Darlene's fiancé left her by taking up with another woman. I asked her what was wrong with this behavior. She looked at me like I was from Pluto and said he ruined her life. Darlene said she hated him and that he was a son of a bitch. After some prompting and tears, she said, "He lied to me, he dishonored our family, and he broke my heart." Darlene had such a difficult time calming down it was hard for her to be clear about what Jack had done wrong. Her negative feelings overwhelmed her. When she was able to articulate what was not okay, Darlene satisfied the first two preconditions.

The third precondition to forgiveness is to tell a handful of trusted people what happened. This means talking about how you feel and what about the hurtful situation was not okay. Sharing your pain with a few trusted people helps you cope; it helps you put feelings into words and makes them clearer. Sharing pain allows other people to care for us and provide us with guidance and support. Sharing our pain helps us to connect with the universality of hurt and allows us to feel less alone.

To talk openly with one to five people does not mean it is better to tell twenty people. When we share our story with a couple of people we do so for support and guidance. When we share our story with a larger number of people, we often do so to denounce the offender, offer a cry of pain, or let people know how we have been victimized. These reasons are different from looking for support and guidance and are too often simply the retelling of our grievance story.

If you cannot find trusted friends or family, I suggest a therapist or support group. If no one is available, you can write down your experience on paper and then review it. You can share what you have written anonymously in chats on the Internet. I must mention one caution: please do not share your pain with people who can hurt you or take advantage of your confidence. You also do not have to share your pain with the person who has hurt you, for that person is not necessarily an appropriate one.

When you have shared your pain with a few trusted people, you can take the next step and learn to forgive. You know how you feel, you know what is wrong, and you have shared your pain.

Darlene had long ago told a number of people all there was to know about being left standing at the altar. She found out that telling her story over and over again become less and less helpful, only further confirming her distress and victimization. For her, as perhaps for you, the harder part may be naming the wrong that was done. In any case, when each of these steps has been completed—knowing what your feelings are, being clear about the wrong, and sharing your experience with one or two trusted people—you are ready to forgive.

WHAT IS FORGIVENESS?

The major obstacle to forgiving is a lack of understanding just what forgiveness is. Some of us confuse forgiveness with condoning unkind actions. There are those who think that we forgive in order to repair the relationship with the offender. Some of us are afraid to forgive because we think we will not be able to seek justice. Some think that forgiveness has to be a precursor to reconciliation. Some of us think that forgiveness means we forget what happened. Others of us think that because our religion says we should forgive we have to be able to. Each of these conceptions is wrong.

Forgiveness is the feeling of peace that emerges as you take your hurt less personally, take responsibility for how you feel, and become a hero instead of a victim in the story you tell. Forgiveness is the experience of peacefulness in the present moment. Forgiveness does not change the past, but it changes the present. Forgiveness means that even though you are wounded you choose to hurt and suffer less. Forgiveness means you become a part of the solution. Forgiveness is the understanding that hurt is a normal part of life. Forgiveness is for you and no one else. You can forgive and rejoin a relationship or forgive and never speak to the person again.

I am often asked if there is a timetable for forgiveness. The answer is no. No single pace is right for all of us. Sometimes just deciding to forgive can be all we need. Ruth had been angry for years at her aunt for not attending her wedding. Her aunt and her mother had bickered all their adult lives, and when Ruth's wedding date came the sisters were at odds. Ruth had been close to her aunt and took her snub personally. Years later she had a baby, and this brought to the surface how much she missed her aunt.

Ruth could not bring herself to call her aunt because she could not get past the snub of her wedding. When she learned from me that forgiveness was not only possible but could be learned, she called her aunt and told her she missed her. Luckily for Ruth her aunt was receptive and apologized for her immature behavior. All it took for Ruth to make the call was the suggestion that she forgive her aunt. She was poised to heal; she only needed the encouragement. She just needed to learn that forgiveness was a reasonable alternative to hurt and anger. Ruth put forgiveness on her menu and then at the first opportunity used it.

At the opposite end of the spectrum is Will. Will was devastated by his wife's affair. They had been married for ten years when she told him that she was in love with another man. She moved out of the house and within a week had begun proceedings for custody of the children. Will did not see it coming and felt furious, hurt, and deeply rejected. The affair hurt his self-confidence in many ways.

Will became depressed and started to drink. His performance at work suffered, and he lost friends. He was a bitter man four years later when I met him. Will's friend gave him one of my forgiveness training sessions as a birthday present. Will took the gift but was often a pill in class. He would argue and say that some things are just not fair. He spoke more in class than the other twenty people combined. At the end of the series he told me that my material was interesting, but he insisted that his hurt and the mendacity of his wife were beyond the range of forgiveness.

I did not see Will for six months until he showed up at another one of my classes. This time he paid for the training himself. To put it mildly, I had mixed feelings about seeing him. He went through the class series and asked the same probing and just-short-of-hostile questions he had asked the first time around. However, at the end of the six weeks, he told me that even though forgiveness would never work with his wife, he had tried it with other people in his life with success. I told Will that there might come a day when even his wife could be forgiven.

Again a few months passed, and this time I got an e-mail from Will. He was letting me know he had started to date a nice woman. He said that as he started to date Julie he acted in the same bitter and caustic manner I knew all too well. Julie told him that she would listen to his pain and provide emotional support, but she was unwilling to be mistreated. Will realized he had to make a choice about whether or not to trust her.

Will wrote that he was wrestling with my metaphor of the air traffic controllers. He suddenly understood that his long-standing grudge about his ex-wife was taking up precious space in his mind. He was with a woman who would not accept that because of his past mistreatment he had a right to be unkind to her. Will decided that Julie was more important than his ex-wife and began to practice some of the things I had taught. He opened his heart to Julie and by doing so gave their relationship a chance. He wrote to thank me and ask me if he was my toughest nut to crack. Will forgave his ex-wife. He had to wait until he was ready, but forgive he did.

We choose forgiveness because it is good for us and good for our community. When we forgive we help ourselves and serve as an example for others. When we forgive we allow our airplanes that have been circling for years to land. As I will discuss in the next chapter, I have conducted scientific research that demonstrates that clearing up our air traffic control screen is good for mental, emotional, and physical health. The remainder of this chapter will be devoted to the three broad reasons why forgiveness is beneficial.

WHY FORGIVENESS IS BENEFICIAL

The most important benefit of forgiveness is our assertion that we are not victims of the past. Clearly, our past influences our present. Marilyn from chapter 2 will see the influence for the rest of her life of growing up with her cold and distant mother. She cannot change the past. She cannot turn back the hands of time. However, she can more readily learn new ways of living in the present when she forgives her mother.

Some people grow up in families that teach them things as children they find difficult to unlearn as adults. Unfortunately, some of the things parents teach their children are harmful.

Tim grew up in a home where conflict resolution meant screaming at the top of one's lungs, and someone was always yelling in his home. Linda grew up in a home where when she was wrong her father humiliated her. She remembers going to her room at least once a week in tears. Unfortunately, no one can change the past. However, they can forgive their parents and learn new ways to live.

Those who had an abusive parent learned that the world is not always safe. We can forgive that parent and to the best of our ability create a new and safer environment. When we forgive we become calm enough to say confidently that what our parents taught was dead wrong. With that calmness, we can chart the best course for our lives. Forgiveness is the beginning of a new chapter, not the end of the story. Too many people make acknowledging a wrong an end in itself and miss the chance to forgive and grow.

No one's past has to be a prison sentence. We cannot change the past so we must find a way to resolve painful memories. Forgiveness provides the key to acknowledge the past and move on. When we can forgive we have less to be afraid of. For example, Sarah was terrified to start another relationship after the disastrous experience with her alcoholic husband. On dates she was often timid and guarded, for she carried Jim with her and he lurked in the back of the car. When she finally forgave Jim, she knew by that act she became a more powerful woman. She began to date in earnest but not in desperation.

After forgiving Jim, Sarah knew she would never let another man treat her the way he did. She knew that if she were hurt again, she could recover. She had learned the skill of forgiveness and knew that she could use it whenever she needed. When we prove to ourselves that we can survive one painful situation, we also realize that we can survive another. In this way, as we forgive our self-esteem develops. We become stronger and learn what is and is not okay for us.

After forgiving Jim, Sarah did not forget how he treated her. She remembered not as a victim but as a survivor. She did not condone his unkindness and substance abuse problems. She knew his treatment of her and their child had been wrong. She no longer allowed him much space in her mind, and she had proven to herself he was not responsible for her emotional experience.

Sarah learned she could live without a man. She learned to be more assertive. She learned to trust herself. In addition, Sarah carried no fantasies of reconciling with Jim. As far as she was concerned, that movie was over and she was glad to be out of the theater.

The second benefit of learning to forgive is how much help we can offer to others. You may not know the power an example of forgiveness can provide. If you look around you will see friends, family, and acquaintances filled with hurt, sadness, and anger. You can help many others with your example of how you overcame adversity and pain. So many people confront the same types of painful situations that have affected us. We forget how many people may be helped through our example of forgiveness.

When Dana finally forgave her bosses for not promoting her, she took it upon herself to help others. She was so tired and worn out she decided that her suffering had to be for something. She began to caution her friends not to have unrealistic expectations at work. She advised others to not react with the same ferocity when they did not get what they wanted. She laughed at how crazed she had been. Dana tried to help other people avoid the pain she felt. In that way, she knew her suffering had not been in vain.

Forgiveness is an act that shows strength. We can forgive from strength only when we know, have named, and shared those feelings. We can forgive from strength only when we have made clear we are hurt and that we are not ashamed of being hurt. Our strength can be an example to others.

The third benefit from forgiveness emerges as we give more love and care to the important people in our lives. I know from my own experience and those of many others that hurts from the past often cause us to draw away and mistrust the very people who are trying to love us. Too often the people who suffer from our grievances are not the people who hurt us but those who care for us today.

If we rent too much space to what went wrong, where is the space to appreciate the good in our lives? If we focus our attention on past defeats, how can we give our full loving attention to our significant other, friends, or co-workers? If we remain bitter over past parenting cruelties, who suffers—our parents or our current friends and loved ones?

Tim grew up in a tumultuous home with lots of anger and bitterness. When Tim carries that legacy into his friendships and love relationships, who reaps the consequences? If Tim is mad at his parents for their out-of-control home and develops a short fuse, do his parents or his current partner bear the brunt?

As Tim learned to forgive he saw that the people he had been pushing away were those who really cared for him. As he began to forgive his parents for their out-of-control home, he was able to see more clearly the damage his anger had done to his present relationships. Through forgiveness he created more time and energy to embrace and appreciate his friends and loved ones.

WHAT FORGIVENESS IS NOT

Forgiveness does not mean that you have to think that what happened was okay. Forgiveness does not mean condoning the unkind, inconsiderate, or selfish behavior of someone who hurt you. Will was correct when he condemned his wife's adultery. She acted with cruelty and violated their wedding vows. She lied and embarrassed him. For Will to acknowledge his feelings was necessary and healthy. The problem for Will was he acknowledged his pain repeatedly. Listening to Will was like hearing an old-fashioned record with a scratch that played the same notes over and over. The music that Will repeatedly played was not particularly pretty.

Anger and hurt are appropriate responses to painful events. We must know how to say no when our boundary is crossed. We do not have to be a doormat in order to forgive; neither does forgiving mean that it is okay for people to treat us unkindly. Forgiveness is the decision to free ourselves from the personal offense and blame that have us stuck in a cycle of suffering. While anger and hurt are appropriate, they, unlike wine, do not improve with age.

Forgiving is not the same as forgetting. You do not want to forget what happened. In fact, you want to remember it. First you remember to ensure that something bad does not happen again. Sarah made a vow to herself that if her date drank too much or admitted to previous drinking problems she was not going to go out with him again. Sarah was cautious with her dates as she remembered how she had ignored the early signs of Jim's drinking.

Also, you remember what happened so that you can pat yourself on the back for forgiving. You deserve praise for forgiveness, for letting something go and moving on. You have succeeded on a difficult journey, and that is cause for celebration. You remember your hurts from the point of view of healing, not from that of helpless victimization. You do not need to dwell on what happened or get a swelled head because you have forgiven. You do want to acknowledge the courage and perseverance that led to overcoming the wounds of the past.

Finally, you have the opportunity to use your healed memories to offer compassion and support to those in need. When you forgive you become a model for those still struggling. They benefit from seeing people who have healed. You can serve as an example of what is possible. You show people through your example that forgiveness is possible.

Darlene ultimately forgave her boyfriend, Jack. This took both time and effort. She stopped blaming him for how she felt. She realized that people change their minds and often do not know how to talk about it. Darlene was able to change her story to reflect her newfound sense of mastery. She stopped complaining to other people and took responsibility for her life. She knew she had forgiven. However, even though Jack was now calling and wished to see her, Darlene did not want to see him ever again. She mentioned this to me in hushed, timid tones. I commended her for her growth and told her that forgiveness and reconciliation are not the same.

Reconciliation means you reestablish a relationship with the person who hurt you. Forgiveness means you make peace with a bitter part of your past and no longer blame your experiences on the offender. You can forgive and decide there is no reason to have any further relationship with the person who hurt you. In fact, every time we forgive someone who is dead you do this. Every time we forgive someone we only knew for a short painful moment (like the victim of a hit-and-run car accident), we do this. With forgiveness we have a choice. We can forgive and give the offender another chance, or we can forgive and move on to new relationships. The choice is ours.

In the same way, to forgive does not mean that we give up claims to justice or compensation. I once worked with a man who was the victim of a hit-and-run accident. I met Russell only nine months after the accident, and he was bitter and in chronic pain. He insisted that he could not forgive because it meant that he could not pursue his lawsuit. I told him to pursue legal action if that was his choice. I told him forgiveness was for his emotional and physical well-being: his head would be clearer and his decisions more sound. I told him to forgive so that he was a victim of the driver for as little time as possible.

I also knew that the criminal justice system and monetary compensation would not fill the need Russell had for his emotional healing. Russell needed to both win in court and win in his life—to both win a lawsuit and reclaim his heart. I told Russell to set up a two-pronged plan. The first prong was for his emotional healing and involved learning to forgive. The second prong was to try to ensure that the offender was punished. Russell's two approaches were complementary but not the same. Forgiveness would not ensure a speedy trial, and justice would not necessarily heal Russell's emotional pain.

Russell, Dana, Darlene, Marilyn, Tim, and Sarah all learned to forgive. Each had different issues to resolve, but what joined them was their sense that something wrong and unfair had happened. Their lives improved as they forgave the person who hurt them. However, there is more proof of the power of forgiveness than just these anecdotes. Other scientists and I have conducted studies on forgiveness that show how beneficial this is. In the next chapter, I will review the research. Then I will teach you my proven forgiveness method, one that has helped thousands of people recover from painful life events.

CHAPTER 7

The Science of Forgiveness

Of the seven deadly sins, anger is possibly the most fun.

To lick your wounds, to smack your lips over grievances long past, to roll over your tongue the prospect of bitter confrontations still to come, to savor to the last toothsome morsel both the pain you are given and the pain you are giving back—in many ways it is a feast fit for a king.

The chief drawback is what you are wolfing down is yourself.

The skeleton at the feast is you.

FREDERICK BUECHNER

Scientific research clearly shows that learning to forgive is good for one's health and well-being—good for mental health and according to recent data good for physical health as well. A number of conclusive scientific studies attest to the healing power of forgiveness. In this chapter, I distill the key research from these scientific studies to demonstrate clearly the power of forgiveness to heal both body and mind. At the end of this chapter and in the following one, I detail the groundbreaking research I have conducted on my forgiveness training methods and the resulting health benefits.

A handful of specific forgiveness studies show that becoming more forgiving enhances one's health. Preliminary studies from research in allied fields such as psychology, medicine, and religion show that feeling more positive emotions such as gratitude, faith, and care have a positive impact on cardiovascular functioning.[1] Both kinds of studies suggest positive results in one's life as one learns to forgive.

Studies from a variety of disciplines demonstrate that people with higher degrees of spirituality live healthier and longer lives.[2] Practicing forgiveness is a form of spiritual practice that likely is beneficial to health in a similar way. Forgiveness is offered as a balm for hurt and angry feelings by many of the world's religious traditions.

Other studies show that people who evidence higher degrees of blame suffer more from a variety of illnesses.[3] You will remember that blame is at the core of holding a grudge. Blaming others emerges as the result of an inability to manage anger and hurt. Medical and psychological studies have shown for years that anger and hostility are harmful to cardiovascular health.[4] These studies show that people who have difficulty managing anger have higher rates of heart disease and suffer more heart attacks.

The research from these diverse fields suggests that learning to forgive benefits us in a variety of ways. As you Forgive for Good you may experience an increase in positive emotions. You may have easier access to the feelings of hope, care, affection, trust, and happiness. You may benefit from experiencing less anger. You may see a reduction in depression and hopelessness. You may also develop an enhanced spiritual point of view. You may see the world as a more benign place and feel more connected to people and nature. In whatever way forgiveness helps you, the science to date is clear: relinquishing your grudges will be good for you.

I have conducted four of the studies that prove the positive effects of learning to forgive. My studies fit into a larger picture of successful forgiveness studies. Almost uniformly, the forgiveness studies show positive results in psychological and emotional well-being. People who are taught to forgive become less angry, more hopeful, less depressed, less anxious, less stressed, more confident, and they learn to like themselves more.

Well-conducted research shows that it is helpful to teach forgiveness to adolescent children of neglectful parents,[5] elderly people who felt uncared for,[6] women abused as children,[7] men whose partners had abortions,[8] and partners of unfaithful lovers.[9] In each study as the people in the particular group are taught to forgive they experience improvement in psychological, emotional, and/or physical functioning.

Currently, three studies have examined the effect of forgiveness on physical health. Each of the studies shows positive results. In addition, in the largest forgiveness study I conducted, we asked participants to rate the number of times they felt symptoms of stress such as racing heart, upset stomach, and dizziness. The people who completed my forgiveness training reported a significant decrease in the symptoms of stress and thus as a result showed improved health at the end of the training. Even more important, the forgiveness group maintained this improvement in a follow-up assessment four months after their forgiveness training ended. Those participants in the study who did not receive forgiveness training showed no improvements in their reported health.

The first study to look specifically at how forgiveness improves physical health disclosed that when people think about forgiving an offender it leads to improved functioning in their cardiovascular and nervous systems.[10] In this study, college students were asked to imagine that they had forgiven their offender. They were instructed to actively give up vengeance against the offender and adopt an attitude of goodwill. The periods of imagining forgiveness were interspersed with periods of rehearsing their grudge. When rehearsing the grudge, the subjects' blood pressure, heart rate, and arterial wall pressure all rose. These are negative experiences for one's cardiovascular system. If these responses occur for too long they can damage the heart and blood vessels.

In addition, during the period of unforgiving imagery participants' muscle tension increased and the students reported feeling uncomfortable and less in control. During the forgiveness condition, there were no physiological disturbances and the students reported greater feelings of positive emotion and relaxation. This study exposed that both forgiveness and holding a grudge generate immediate physical and emotional reactions. The reactions were experienced as positive in the forgiveness condition and negative in the grudge condition.

This study showed that holding a grudge in the short run could stress participants' nervous system. Holding a grudge caused these students to feel more stressed and increased their sense of discomfort over a short period. No study as of yet has proven that holding grudges causes long-term health damage, but many studies hint at it.

A study at the University of Wisconsin, Madison,[11] showed that the amount of forgiveness people felt was related to their reporting a variety of disease conditions. The more forgiving people were, the less they suffered from a wide range of illnesses. The less forgiving people reported a greater number of health problems. This relationship held constant for both short-term physical complaints and longer-term general well-being.

In this study, the relationship between forgiveness and health held true for the frequency of symptoms reported. People who had a higher capacity for forgiveness reported fewer symptoms than those with a less developed ability to forgive. People with higher capacities for forgiveness also reported fewer medically diagnosed chronic conditions. This study established a fundamental relationship between learning to forgive and reported incidences of health complaints.

The third study that looked directly at forgiveness and health was completed at the University of Tennessee. The study's researcher interviewed 107 college students who had been deeply hurt either by a parent, friend, or romantic partner. In a series of interviews, they were asked to recall the event, and then their blood pressure, heart rate, forehead muscle tension, and sweatiness were measured. The study found that the people who forgave the betrayal had decreased blood pressure, muscle tension, and heart rates when compared to those who had not. The forgivers also reported less stress in their lives and fewer physical symptoms of illness.

The results of these studies suggest there are health benefits from learning to forgive. Short-term forgiveness appears to reduce the stress on the body. We can all benefit from reduced stress, and there is no downside to learning to forgive. Even with these positive results, remember forgiveness research is a budding science. Only a limited number of studies have been completed. In the physical health field the studies are small and do not conclusively demonstrate the long-term effects of forgiveness.

The study I completed comes the closest to illustrating that people who learned forgiveness reported improved health over a six-month period. I imagine that over the next couple of years research will emerge that shows forgiveness to be one of the things we can learn that heals us physically, emotionally, and spiritually.

In order to learn more about my work and the science of my forgiveness studies, I will detail each of my experiments. I have conducted my forgiveness research with college-age adults, younger to middle-aged adults, cardiology patients, and Catholics and Protestants from Northern Ireland who have lost family members to political violence. My first study shows that people who were taught to forgive become less angry, feel less hurt, are more optimistic, become more forgiving in a variety of situations, and are more spiritually inclined, compassionate, and self-confident.[12] My other studies show a reduction in experience of stress, physical manifestations of stress, and an increase in vitality.

I was cofounder and director of the largest study to date that taught people to forgive someone who had hurt them. I also completed two successful studies that taught forgiveness to people from Northern Ireland who had had one of their family members murdered.

My forgiveness methodology is now being tested in two other research projects. A group of hospital-based cardiologists is using my forgiveness training with patients who have high blood pressure. The doctors are recruiting three groups of patients to test whether an eight-week class in forgiveness can lower blood pressure. Preliminary results from the first group suggest that forgiveness leads to a small reduction in blood pressure. This reduction in blood pressure is accompanied by a diminution of anger and an improvement in day-to-day quality of life. In the other study, researchers adapting my forgiveness methodology are looking to see whether forgiveness training can help premenopausal women reduce the levels of stress chemicals in their bodies. This project is currently in the recruiting stage.

BEGINNING FORGIVENESS RESEARCH

My first forgiveness study served as the dissertation for my Ph.D. degree in counseling and health psychology at Stanford University. I was interested in forgiveness for many reasons, including the struggle I had with forgiving my longtime friend Sam. I figured that if I had such a difficult time with learning to forgive, others must as well. For my experiment I wanted to test if the methods I had developed and used in the past might be proven to work for others.

When I dove into the scientific literature I saw that only four forgiveness training studies that taught people to forgive had been reported up to that time. It seemed clear that forgiveness was an area ripe for new methods. Most important, forgiveness was an area that needed methods that were proven effective.

Prior to undertaking my first project I held a number of assumptions about forgiveness that at that time were untested. First, I thought that forgiveness was the same process no matter what the offense. I had read books that taught that forgiving one's parents was a different process than forgiving one's neighbor. These books also suggested that forgiving oneself was a different process as well. That idea did not make sense to me. To me, forgiveness is forgiveness. Learning to forgive is difficult enough without having to sort offenses into different categories, and I wondered if this was one reason that people had such a difficult time forgiving.

This is not to say that many offenses do not hurt more when committed by your parents than by a friend or another adult. Certainly, being beaten when a child is a grievous wound and can cause significant harm. I do not claim that all offenses will be forgiven at the same pace or that murder is an equal offense to a parking ticket. What I am saying is that the process of forgiveness is the same regardless of the offense committed. Therefore, for my study I recruited volunteers who were hurt by a wide range of offenders, unlike earlier researchers, who had recruited people suffering from a specific offense.

The second assumption I had was that forgiveness was more about one's present life than one's past. The goal of forgiveness training was to reduce pain and suffering so people could move on in their lives. I understood that it is only in the present that anyone can feel better. For good or bad, the past is the past. We only have the present with which to work. And with present happiness as the goal, I created my first forgiveness training.

My third assumption was that the power of forgiveness was wasted when applied to only the worst aspects of our lives. Why just forgive an abusive parent or an alcoholic spouse and find peace? Why not learn to forgive the daily hassles and problems we all face? Why not forgive everything that does not go our way? I saw that forgiving smaller offenses would be good practice in forgiving life's higher hurdles. I decided to teach people to forgive all sorts of things to bring more peace into their lives.

Since I was a graduate student at the time I decided to conduct my research on other students. I recruited student volunteers between the ages of eighteen and thirty who still carried a grudge toward someone close to them. I worked with students who had to forgive their parents for hurting them, forgive their teachers for unfair grading, forgive their close friends for sleeping with their lovers, forgive their lovers for cheating on them, forgive their bosses for lying to them, and forgive their sisters or brothers for being the family favorite.

The only offenses I excluded were instances of physical or sexual violence that occurred in the previous five years. I recruited fifty-five volunteers and randomly assigned them to two groups: one that received my forgiveness training immediately, and one that received the forgiveness training when the first group was finished. Each person had an equal chance of getting the forgiveness training early or late.

The people in the late group served as a comparison group for those in the early group. A comparison group allowed me to know that any positive changes were due to my forgiveness training and not to other factors. Assigning subjects randomly meant that I put all of the volunteer's names in a pile and then had a research assistant sort them into two groups using a numerical formula. Randomizing the subjects gave me the best chance to have two equal groups to compare.

The results of my first study were very positive and validated my hypotheses. When I say my research was successful, I mean that almost all the positive results were statistically significant. Success in research does not just mean that at the end the forgiveness group's scores were better than the comparison group's scores. Often one group will have better scores than the other at the end of an experiment. That is not enough to be sure that the numbers mean that the experiment worked. Statistical calculations tell whether the difference is significant; that is, due not to luck or to one or two people who made huge improvements. Statistically significant means there is 95 percent certainty that the positive results are not a result of chance.

For this experiment I was interested in working with students who had something to forgive but were not overly hostile, vengeful, or depressed. I was interested in seeing if the average person who held a grudge could benefit from learning to forgive. I wanted a training that could be given to anyone whether they were dealing with a slight or a serious grievance.

In order to participate, each student had to volunteer to be in the study. Then each had to fill out standard paper-and-pencil psychological tests three times. The first time was at the beginning of the study, the second at the end of the forgiveness training, and the third ten weeks after the training ended. On the psychological tests the students' initial scores fell in the average or normal range. These were psychologically and emotionally normal young people who had trouble forgiving someone but who were not depressed or hostile. In fact, on some measures the students were less angry and wanted less revenge than the average person their age.

It is quite difficult in scientific research to get significantly positive results with people who begin the study in the average range. The goal of almost all psychological research is to get people who start depressed, anxious, or angry to end the experiment close to the average range. My students started average and still improved significantly. In addition to learning to forgive, the students improved their psychological and emotional functioning in a variety of ways. I am proud to say the positive results remained unchanged two and a half months after the training ended. These results showed that almost everyone can benefit from learning to forgive.

When the students signed up for the experiment they did not know whether or not they would be in the forgiveness group. After they filled out the first set of questionnaires they were told to either stay and begin the first class or return home. The people in the forgiveness class met weekly with about twelve to fifteen other people. Each class lasted an hour and was held for six consecutive weeks.

I had five basic goals for this experiment. I will discuss each specific goal and describe how that goal was met. I highlight my most important goal, which was to reduce the level of anger the forgiveness group participants experienced. I save this discussion for last because unmanaged anger is a significant risk factor for heart disease and deserves elucidation.

The first goal was to help forgiveness group participants feel less hurt about the situation that brought them into the study. This was successfully accomplished with a significant reduction in pain from the beginning of the study to the end. The subjects were asked to draw a line that would indicate on a scale from 1 to 10 how hurt they felt at that time. The forgiveness group as an average initially rated their hurt as above 8 on that scale. At the end of the experiment, ten weeks after the forgiveness training ended, the forgiveness group rated their hurt as just a little over 3 on the same scale.

The second goal of this study was to help participants learn to forgive as a general problem-solving strategy. I wanted people not to only forgive the person who hurt them but also to put forgiveness on their menu of choices in many situations. We measured this by two different methods.

First, another forgiveness researcher developed brief descriptions of the different situations that could elicit forgiveness, reconciliation, revenge, or a host of other responses. Examples were similar to a close friend lies to you, someone steals from your home, your lover leaves without notice, or you are the victim of unfair treatment at work. Participants were asked to select from a range of choices and only the number of forgiveness responses were scored by the research team.

For the second assessment, we created a vignette that described a hurtful interpersonal situation. For instance, a lover calls and says she or he slept with their ex and now wants to talk. Study participants had to describe their strategies for working through the possible hurt and relationship difficulty generated by this situation. On both of these measures the students in the forgiveness group showed they had learned to forgive. The students in the forgiveness group possessed better strategies for dealing with their pain and showed a significantly greater confidence that they could forgive their lover.

The third goal of my training was to help participants forgive the specific person who hurt them. First the entire group of study participants indicated they were more likely to forgive their offender. And second, we saw that the women participants, who comprised 75 percent of the study, forgave the offender more quickly than did the women in the comparison group.

The results showed us something interesting and full of common sense: the passage of time was an important factor in letting go of hurts.

All of the participants hurt less over time. Even though the forgiveness group made significantly more progress than the comparison group, both felt less pain over time. The old saying, "Time heals all wounds," has merit. The big difference is that when people learn to forgive they also become psychologically and physically healthier and learn strategies that make them more confident so they can better handle future hurts and difficulties.

The fourth goal of the training was to improve the psychological, emotional, and spiritual functioning of the forgiveness group members. I was interested in seeing how the forgiveness training improved participants' hope, self-confidence, compassion, personal growth, and quality of life. On each and every test the forgiveness group improved significantly relative to the comparison group. This means that the forgiveness group members became emotionally healthier through learning to forgive. It may be an important by-product of learning to forgive that we become emotionally stronger. We feel more confident and optimistic. For the people in the comparison group, time lessened their hurt, but it did not improve their psychological or emotional functioning.

FORGIVENESS IMPROVES HEALTH

The positive emotional changes I found have implications for health. Higher levels of hope have been shown to help people deal successfully with pain and some forms of illness.[13] Optimistic people live longer and have fewer illnesses.[14] Spiritually minded people cope better with loss and illness.[15] Depression is a risk factor for heart disease and may predict who will leave the hospital alive after a heart attack.[16] A recent study showed that depressed people are at significantly greater risk of a stroke.[17]

The primary goal of my forgiveness training was to reduce the amount of anger the forgiveness group participants held. Specifically, I was interested in reducing the students' angry reactions to interpersonal hurt. I accomplished these goals. The forgiveness group reduced their levels of anger by about 15 percent from the beginning to the last measurement period ten weeks after the forgiveness training ended. The students showed less anger both in how they felt on the particular days they were tested and in how they responded to situations over the long term.

I was concerned with anger because of the research that shows anger to be a significant risk factor for heart disease.[18] Heart disease is the leading cause of death for both men and women. Autopsies of young adults who have died show that coronary artery disease, with narrowing of arteries and the beginning of cholesterol plaque, starts in many people by their early twenties. Even young adults are not immune to cardiovascular disease and the harmful effects of unmanaged negative emotions.[19]

A recent study looked at adults who all had normal blood pressure. The subjects were given a psychological test to measure their levels of anger. Those with high levels of anger were found to be three times more likely to develop heart disease than those with low levels of anger. This is because anger causes the release of stress chemicals, which alter the functioning of your heart and cause the narrowing of your coronary and peripheral arteries.

In the past, the major psychological risk factor for heart disease was thought to be Type A behavior. Early studies had shown that people who were Type A had a greater risk of suffering a heart attack. The thinking at the time was that the Type A person was always in a hurry, overly competitive, excessively hardworking, and easily angered. The mix of these traits was thought to be the cause of the enhanced cardiovascular risk. However, a variety of research studies showed that hostility is the dangerous component of Type A personality. Being a workaholic or always in a hurry, when not accompanied by anger, does not pose a risk to your health.[20]

The University of Wisconsin forgiveness study[21] showed that learning to forgive might help prevent heart disease in middle-aged participants. In this study the more the subjects showed a high level of forgiveness, the fewer heart-related health problems they reported. At the same time, the more these participants reported a lack of forgiveness, the higher was their reported incidence of heart disease.

The same study revealed that the more hostility a subject had, the larger the number and the greater the frequency of health problems reported. The relationship between forgiveness and the absence of health problems was stronger than the relationship between hostility and the incidence of health problems. The author concludes that the "failure to forgive in this study is a greater predictor of physical health problems than hostility alone."

A fascinating study showed that simply thinking of something that makes you angry for five minutes could depress heart rate variability (HRV).[22] HRV is a crucial measure of nervous system health and shows the flexibility of the cardiovascular system. Our hearts require flexible functioning to respond to stress and danger. In addition, depressed HRV is a significant predictor of who will not survive heart disease.[23] In this study the five minutes of anger were also shown to depress subjects' immune response. The researchers tested for salivary IgA, which is a common measure of immune competence. For the angry subjects in this study, their IgA was diminished for between four and six hours after their angry episode.

In that same study the researchers showed that when participants thought about someone they cared for, their body responded with positive physical changes. They found improvement in both HRV and immune function. In addition, the researchers found that reflecting on positive feelings caused participants' brain waves to harmonize. Harmonized brain function leads to an increased ability to think clearly and creatively. I have seen that when people forgive they end up making better decisions. It is exciting to note that forgiveness may help harmonize our brain functioning as well.

My first study showed that learning to forgive helped people in a variety of ways. Forgiveness is a complex experience that changes an offended person's spiritual feelings, emotions, thoughts, actions, and self-confidence level. I believe learning to forgive the hurts and grudges of our life may be an important step for us to feel more hopeful and spiritually connected and less depressed. These changes improve our health and give us more energy to create a better life for ourselves. They allow our bodies to function in an optimal way. These scientific results demonstrate to me the importance of continued research into the effects of forgiveness.

THE STANFORD FORGIVENESS PROJECT

Because of the success of this first study, my dissertation adviser, Dr. Carl Thoresen, and I obtained a grant to redo and expand the study. We called this experiment the Stanford Forgiveness Project, and it was significantly larger than any attempted at the time. We were overwhelmed with the response to our recruitment. The grant we received was for 110 people, but because of the interest in forgiveness, more than 260 people participated.

Two years had passed since the first forgiveness groups, and had I learned a lot in that time. I had done a clinical psychology internship and had a full year of patient contact. I therefore was able to improve, strengthen, and expand the forgiveness training. The result was the subjects in the Stanford Forgiveness Project attended six weekly ninety-minute sessions. Again we measured participants at the beginning of the experiment, at end of the training, and eighteen weeks following the training.

In the Stanford Forgiveness Project I worked with hurt adults between the ages of twenty-five and fifty. Again, I did not limit the participants according to offender, excluding only people who were victims of abuse or assault within the last five years. We recruited people unable to forgive their spouses for cheating on them or for having alcohol or drug problems, their best friends for abandoning them, their parents for mistreating them, business partners for lying to them, or siblings for not caring about them. Again we randomized people into forgiveness and comparison groups, and we measured participants' spiritual well-being, hurt, anger, physical health, stress, optimism, and forgiveness.

One interesting thing we learned from the Forgiveness Project was that more women than men sign up for forgiveness experiments. This gender difference has been corroborated by other forgiveness studies and by my experience in teaching public classes. Of the calls we received, about 80 percent were from women. We wanted to recruit an equal number of men and women to determine if forgiveness is different according to gender. As an interesting aside, we recruited more men when we changed our ads to ask for "people who held a grudge."

As I write this, results from the Forgiveness Project are still coming in. So far the data have been extremely positive. We know that the forgiveness group felt less stressed because of the training, and this change held steady sixteen to eighteen weeks after the training ended. We know that participants became more forgiving of the person who hurt them and more forgiving in general. Both of these results held steady for four months after the training ended. Forgiveness group participants also became more confident in their ability to forgive and their ability to feel less upset and more in control of their emotions.

The people who went through the Stanford Forgiveness Project became significantly less angry, both in how angry they felt at the moment and in their more general experience of anger. They also reported they felt less hurt than the people in the comparison group at the end of the training and also sixteen to eighteen weeks later. In addition, the subjects became significantly more optimistic from the beginning of the experiment to the end.

In addition to monitoring changes in stress, optimism, and anger, we asked people to rate how healthy they felt. Participants were asked to simply state on a scale of 1 to 5 how healthy they felt with 1 signifying great and 5 poor. The forgiveness group participants reported a small improvement in rated health, while the comparison group showed no improvement. Compared with the general population, the average health of the participants in the study was very good, and so the showing of any improvement is noteworthy.

Finally, we asked the participants to indicate which common body responses to stress they regularly felt. Examples were headaches, stomachaches, dizziness, tiredness, and muscle aches. I am delighted to report that learning to forgive significantly reduced the number of physical symptoms the forgiveness group experienced. That is, forgiveness training helped people report not only less stress but also fewer symptoms of stress affecting their body.

These first two forgiveness projects showed that people experienced definitive positive changes through forgiveness. One interesting feature of these studies is that we did not recruit people suffering from extreme examples of grievances. We recruited people in all walks of life who had a grudge against someone close to them. It is noteworthy that we did not solicit victims of death or abuse. In my next two projects I completely shifted my focus. In these projects I worked with people who had suffered the greatest of tragedies, the loss of a close family member to murder. In that way I could show that my forgiveness process would work with the whole gamut of interpersonal injury.

The next two forgiveness studies my research partner and I called the Northern Ireland HOPE Projects. We used the word *HOPE* to stand for Healing Our Past Experience. In the first project, a Presbyterian minister named Byron Bland and I brought to Stanford five women who desperately needed to learn to forgive. These were Catholic and Protestant women from Northern Ireland. Four of the women had their sons killed in the political violence that has racked Northern Ireland for the past thirty years. The fifth woman suffered a grievous loss and also needed to forgive.

We completed the forgiveness training for the second HOPE Project in the winter of 2001. In this project we brought seventeen men and women from Northern Ireland who had a loved one murdered. Again we worked with Catholics and Protestants who came from all over Northern Ireland. Some of the participants had lost their parents, others had lost siblings, while still others had their children murdered. These two projects are, to say the least, a significant test of my forgiveness training.

I imagine there is nothing harder to forgive than the murder of a family member. In the next chapter I will describe the HOPE Projects in detail and give you a sense of what it was like to work with people who have experienced such great loss.

In this chapter I reviewed scientific research that shows forgiveness helps heal people in physical, mental, and emotional ways. Some of the studies attest to the value of learning to forgive, while others point to the positive effects of becoming more spiritual or experiencing more positive emotions. Each and every forgiveness study shows benefit to its participants. The forgiveness studies have been conducted with a wide range of offenses and subjects. Forgiveness simply works; it heals people's lives. It leads to greater peace and hope. I have seen it work many times and I have data to prove it. I have presented case studies of people who have forgiven and I am teaching you how to forgive. I am convinced that forgiveness will work in your life as well.

I highlighted my first two studies because they are relatively large, well designed, and worked with a variety of people with a multitude of hurts. In this book you are learning the same process that helped college students, middle-aged adults, and people from Northern Ireland to suffer less pain. My confidence is such that if I showed people who have lost their children how to heal their wounds I can certainly help you and those you love.

1. W. Tiller, R. McCraty, and M. Atkinson, "Toward Cardiac Coherence: A New Non-Invasive Measure of Autonomic System Order," Alternative Therapies 2 (1996): 52–65.

2. L. K. George et al., "Spirituality and Health: What We Know, What We Need to Know," *Journal of Social and Clinical Psychology* 19, no. 1 (2000): 102–16.

3. H. Tennen and G. Affleck. "Blaming Others for Threatening Events." *Psychological Bulletin* 119 (2000): p 322–48.

4. T. Q. Miller et al., "A Meta-Analytic Review of Research on Hostility and Physical Health," *Psychological Bulletin* 119, no. 2 (1996): 322–48.

5. R. H. Al-Mabuk, R. D. Enright, and P. A. Cardis, "Forgiveness Education with Parentally Love-Deprived Late Adolescents," *Journal of Moral Education* 24, no. 4 (1995): 427–44.

6. J. H. Hebl and R. D. Enright, "Forgiveness as a Psychotherapeutic Goal with Elderly Females," *Psychotherapy* 30 (1993): 658–67.

7. S. R. Freedman and R. D. Enright, "Forgiveness as an Intervention Goal with Incest Survivors," *Journal of Consulting and Clinical Psychology* 64 (1996): 983–92.

8. C. T. Coyle and R. D. Enright, "Forgiveness Intervention with Post Abortion Men," *Journal of Consulting and Clinical Psychology* 65 (1997): 1042–46.

9. M. S. Rye, "Evaluation of a Secular and a Religiously Integrated Forgiveness Group Therapy Program for College Students Who Have Been Wronged by a Romantic Partner" (Bowling Green, Ohio: Bowling Green State University, 1998).

10. Van Oyen, C. Witvilet, T.E. Ludwig, and K. L. Vander Laan, "Granting Forgiveness or Harboring Grudges: Implications for Emotions, Physiology, and Health," *Psychological Science*, no. 12 (2001): 117–23.

11. S. Sarinopoulos, "Forgiveness and Physical Health: A Doctoral Dissertation Summary," *World of Forgiveness* 3, no. 2 (2000): 16–18.

12. F. M. Luskin, "The Effect of Forgiveness Training on Psychosocial Factors in College Age Adults," unpublished dissertations (Stanford University, 1999).

13.   C. R. Snyder, "The Past and Possible Futures of Hope," *Journal of Social and Clinical Psychology* 19, no. 1 (2000): 11–28.

14.   B. Q. Hafen et al., "Mind/Body Health: The Effect of Attitudes, Emotions and Relationships," (Needham Heights, Mass.: Allynand Bacon, 1996).

15.   F. M. Luskin, "A Review of the Effect of Spiritual and Religious Factors on Mortality and Morbidity with a Focus on Cardiovascular and Pulmonary Disease," *Journal of Cardiopulmonary Rehabilitation* 20, no. 1 (2000): 8–15.

16.   A. Ferketich et al., "Depression as an Antecedent to Heart Disease Among Women and Men in the NHANES I Study," *Archives of Internal Medicine* 160, no. 9 (2000).

17.   B. S. Jonas, "Symptoms of Depression as a Prospective Risk Factor for Stroke," *Psychosomatic Medicine* 62, no.4 (2000): 463–71.

18.   R. Williams and V. Williams, *Anger Kills: Seventeen Strategies for Controlling the Hostility That Can Harm Your Health* (New York: Random House, 1993).

19.   C. Iribarren et al., "Association of Hostility with Coronary Artery Calcification in Young Adults," *Journal of the American Medical Association* 283, no. 19 (2000).

20.   Williams and Williams, *Anger Kills*.

21.   Sarinopoulos, "Forgiveness and Physical Health."

22.   Tiller, McCraty, and Atkinson, "Toward Cardiac Coherence."

23.   R. C. Carney, "Depression Affects Heart Rhythm" (Yahoo News, 1997).

CHAPTER 8

Northern Ireland:
The Ultimate Test

If you do not wish to be prone to anger, do not feed the habit; give it nothing which may tend to its increase. At first, keep quiet and count the days when you were not angry: "I used to be angry every day, then every other day: next, every two, then every three days!" and if you succeed in passing thirty days, sacrifice to the gods in thanksgiving.

EPICTETUS

I briefly mentioned in the last chapter that I have completed one Northern Ireland HOPE Project and am in the middle of the second. In both of these projects, my research partner and I worked with the families of murder victims from Northern Ireland to help them heal from their loss. In the first project we worked with women who had lost sons to murder, and in the second we worked with seventeen men and women, each of whom had lost a family member to murder. We worked with these families as a way of trying to help people in strife-torn countries make peace and begin a dialogue with each other. For this reason we brought both Catholic and Protestant people from Northern Ireland to both workshops.

The first Northern Ireland project began its planning in the summer of 1999. My HOPE partner, Reverend Byron Bland, is a minister who does peacekeeping work in Northern Ireland. He had made extensive contacts with people in that country. One such person he befriended was Norma McConville. Ms. McConville has been a peace activist in Northern Ireland for the past thirty years. She knew the country and its people, and Byron trusted her to find political-violence victims willing to join us for forgiveness training. Norma was our link to Northern Ireland, and through her we gained the trust necessary for mothers to fly ten thousand miles away from home and open up old yet still-festering wounds to people they had never met.

Reverend Bland initially contacted me because he heard of the work I was doing in the Stanford Forgiveness Project. He knew I was teaching people to forgive. He had read newspaper accounts of my research but did not know if what we were doing would work in Northern Ireland. He knew firsthand of the deep need of the victims there to recover from their personal tragedies. He knew these tragedies were the result of years of religious and politically motivated violence. He saw with his own eyes the damage the hurts and grievances were doing to individuals, families, and communities.

Byron asked me if I was willing to try my forgiveness training with deeply hurt people in Northern Ireland. Each of the women we recruited for the first HOPE project had lost a son to murder; for some, the murder had taken place as long as twenty years ago. We found out that no matter how much time passed since the murder, the women still suffered tremendous pain. To make matters worse, these women felt that their need to heal had been ignored.

Byron and I realized we had a number of difficulties to overcome if we were to pull off a project like this. First, we did not have the money, nor did we know whether my forgiveness training would work with such extreme loss. Arranging lodging, transportation, food, and forgiveness training and providing sightseeing and entertainment for a week are also arduous tasks. We agreed to try because we wanted to help and to the best of our knowledge this kind of forgiveness project had never been done.

None of the women could afford the transatlantic journey, nor did they have the resources to house themselves in the United States. These people were from working-class families and simply did not have the funds for a weeklong trip to America. We were able to obtain donations for the plane fare and food, and each of the women was housed in a volunteer's home. Stanford University provided us with space to conduct the workshops, and in January of 2000 the women arrived at San Francisco International Airport.

I taught my forgiveness methods to these women, and we measured the results. As with the other experiments, I asked the women to fill out questionnaires at our first meeting for a baseline evaluation. At the end, when they were about to leave for home, they filled out the questionnaires again; this is called the post-test. Finally, six months after they had returned to Northern Ireland, we mailed them a set of questionnaires for the follow-up evaluation.

When these women first arrived the stories they told about their losses were heartbreaking. One woman described how her son had been kidnapped on his way to work one day. He was ushered to a shallow grave with his hands tied behind his back and then shot hot in the head. His body was then hidden for twenty-one years. I can only imagine the horror a mother must feel knowing how her child's life was taken.

Another mother told how her son worked in a restaurant fixing platters of fish and chips. One day a gunman walked up to the takeout window and started shooting. Her son was shot seven times and died on the spot. A third woman said that her son was fatally shot while with his childhood best friend. The woman and her son were Protestants while the friend was a Roman Catholic. The two friends were sitting in a pub when a Protestant Loyalist rushed in and shot both young men dead. The fourth woman's son was a policeman and was killed in the line of duty.

Each of the women's stories was gruesome and sickening. Listening to them, one could only wonder how people could be so cruel. I sat with these mothers and saw firsthand how devastating is the loss of a child.

The upshot is that these women came to Palo Alto in January 2000 and participated for a week of my forgiveness training. When they arrived eighteen months had passed since we began the Stanford Forgiveness Project. In that time I had taught literally hundreds of people to forgive and had refined my teaching methods.

The results from the HOPE Project back up my assertion that I had strengthened my forgiveness training approach. The proof is seen in the positive results we got from the scientific measurements and in the changed stories the women told about their loss and their lives. The women learned how to tell a different story, one that allowed them a degree of peace and a renewed sense of hope.

Unlike the first two studies, this time we did not use a comparison group to evaluate changes. We did not want these people to feel their suffering was being used primarily for the advancement of science. There was no way we could bring a dozen women who had suffered grievous losses to the United States and then offer only half of them forgiveness training. Therefore because there is no comparison group, by scientific standards my results are considered less robust. However, even with that caveat the results we achieved are remarkable.

On the measure of how hurt the Irish women felt by their loss, on a scale of 1 to 10, they began the week with a score near 8.5. Again, this is a simple, standard psychological test where each woman draws a line across a page to represent her current level of pain. When they left at the end of the week, they registered their hurt a bit over 3.5. When the questionnaires were returned at the six-month follow-up, their hurt score still stood below 4. The change in hurt scores is a similar result to those obtained in my two previous studies. The change was gratifying because these women's wounds were much more grievous.

On a separate measure, that of stress, the women reduced their stress by almost half from the beginning of the training to the follow-up six months later. The stress questionnaire asks people how they are coping with the difficulties in their lives.

These Irish women showed an increase in forgiveness toward the person who committed the murder, of about 40 percent over the week of the training. This positive result remained constant at the follow-up evaluation. Their depression scores also improved. Given a list of 30 items indicating depression, the women checked an average of 17 at the beginning, an average of 7 at the end of the training, and 10 at the six-month follow-up. The women also showed that by the follow-up assessment they had become significantly more optimistic.

I knew to succeed I had to offer these women the strongest forgiveness training I could develop. I worked hard to clarify my thinking and broaden my understanding to include such heartbreaking loss as the death of a son. The result turned out to be a process strong enough to help these women. The forgiveness process I used with the women from Northern Ireland is the same one you are reading in this book.

The positive effects of the Northern Ireland HOPE project exceeded our expectations. We started with women who understandably felt extremely hurt and very angry in their grief. We ended with women who mourned the loss of their children but through forgiveness gained a measure of strength with which to cope. As one participant reminded herself, "Life is for the living." Another participant said, "We must move on with the memory of our sons in our hearts."

I still marvel that on each and every variable, the women showed improvement. I marvel that the forgiveness training worked and the positive effects lasted, even after the women returned to Northern Ireland, with a political climate pitting culture against culture.

I do not want to make any claims that these women are completely over their loss. I make no claim that I can heal every person who has suffered tragedy. A child is irreplaceable. After a grievous loss one's life will never be the same. But each of us has the choice on how we react to the tragedies of our lives. For these Irish women, we were able to calm their emotional distress so that they could find life choices that they may have missed. Each, in her own way, chose to focus on the living and to honor the memory of her dead sons by being more hopeful and less angry.

THE SECOND HOPE PROJECT

About six months after our first Northern Ireland Project ended, the Reverend Bland and I decided to set up another round of the HOPE Project. We contacted Norma McConville and asked how we could expand the training to work with up to eighteen wounded people. We knew we could be effective with five, but would our approach work with three or four times that many? Could it work with other family members, not just mothers?

We have just finished the forgiveness training of our second Northern Ireland HOPE Project. In this project the original five women returned to Stanford for another week of forgiveness training. Each woman also brought with her two or three friends, family, or community members who had also suffered the loss of a family member to murder. The original five women served as both participants and guides in their companions' forgiveness process. Arriving from Northern Ireland were sons whose fathers were killed, women whose husbands were killed, men and women whose brothers were killed, and women and men whose sons were killed.

In HOPE2, as in HOPE1, the stories were painful to hear. One man told of the loss of his father. He was a young boy when his father was shot, and he grew up with only his mother and his brother. He knows the only reason his father was killed was because he was a Protestant. As a result, this man developed an intense hatred for Catholics, a hatred that to a large degree dissolved during the HOPE Project. This man learned that Catholics who lost a family member grieved as much as he did. The pain of loss transcended religious and political boundaries.

Another participant reported the loss of her husband. He was kidnapped from his home and forced to drive a van loaded with explosives to a military checkpoint. The bomb was detonated as he sat in the driver's seat. A different woman told how her husband was murdered while baby-sitting his grandchildren. A third woman's husband was murdered almost thirty years ago, and subsequently his house was bombed. The stories were numbing in their cruelty and senselessness.

In this second HOPE Project, we again provided a week of forgiveness training. We met twice a day as a group throughout the week. We measured the effectiveness of the training at the post-test completed at the end of the week. In addition, after six months we will send follow-up questionnaires to measure the long-term success of the Project. It is one thing to help people while they are sage and visiting the United States. It is another to provide guidance strong enough to withstand a return to the communities that bred the mistrust and the pain.

We have just begun to examine the HOPE2 post-test data and do not have any follow-up results. In common with each of the other forgiveness experiments, the HOPE2 group showed statistically significant improvement. Their level of hurt went down almost 40 percent over the course of the week, to the same level at which the first group ended its week. In addition, the HOPE2 group showed a 15 percent decrease in their level of anger and a similar decrease in their levels of stress.

In the psychological domain, the HOPE2 participants arrived suffering from a high degree of depression and left with a much-improved disposition. The members of the group demonstrated a statistically significant decline in their experience of depression. The reduction in sadness was in the range of 20 percent from the beginning of the week to the end.

One new area we explored with the HOPE2 group was physical well-being. We asked each to fill out two health-related questionnaires. The first checklist asked participants to report how often they experienced physical symptoms of stress or emotional distress, such as headaches, nausea, sore muscles, or trouble falling asleep. At the end of the week the HOPE2 group reported an almost 35 percent reduction in these symptoms of distress.

The second questionnaire looked at the level of energy and vitality experienced by the participants. On a scale from 1 to 5 participants were asked to indicate how well they slept, what kind of appetite they had, how much energy they felt, whether or not they had aches and pains, and if they were stiff and sore. At the end of their forgiveness week the HOPE2 group showed a statistically significant increase in their experience of physical vitality and well-being.

To put it mildly, I am gratified by these results. Over the course of a week we helped people who had suffered a grievous loss to feel better both emotionally and physically. We gave people encouragement to let go of a grievance and move on in their lives with love. They did so and benefited in both mind and body.

To round out our assessment, we asked the Northern Irish participants to fill out a questionnaire that showed how much they had forgiven the person who murdered their son, brother, or father. This yielded both interesting and provocative results. Two of the seventeen participants showed a marked decrease in forgiveness from the beginning of the week to the end. Something in the attention paid to the death by murder made them feel less forgiving toward the murderer. When we evaluated the forgiveness outcome from the questionnaires the other fifteen HOPE2 participants filled out, we saw a statistically significant positive change in forgiveness.

This somewhat mixed result makes a lot of sense. Not everyone will feel better after spending seven days revisiting a horrible part of his or her life. I am delighted that a large majority of the HOPE2 participants used the week to become more forgiving and at the end were less depressed, hurt, and angry and felt better physically. I marvel at the implications of these results. They demonstrate the incredible power of human beings to heal from even the most blatant of horrors. They reinforce my belief that people can learn to forgive.

During each of the HOPE Projects, I was privileged to be a part of healing and emotional growth. I am in awe at the courage these victims of senseless tragedy showed. I reflect upon what it must take to fly to a foreign country and allow your deepest pain to be opened to people you do not know. Each of these people is a hero. They trusted and listened and learned, and they forgave and healed.

The Reverend Bland and I will continue to offer our forgiveness training with people from Northern Ireland and other places in the world. We are already planning our next workshop, where we will have some of the HOPE2 participants work as trainers to help a new contingent of hurt people. Our goal is to empower people in strife-torn areas to teach forgiveness approaches directly.

My hope is that these forgiveness weeks can launch a process that helps heal divided and embittered societies. It is my sincere hope that each of us will do the same in our families and with our friends. Forgiveness is needed not just in the harshest of political environments but in the safest as well. That people who have seen family killed in a bitterly divided society and learned to forgive should give us all hope.

The rest of the book describes in detail the forgiveness process offered to the HOPE2 participants. Starting in the next chapter I relate step-by-step instruction in how to forgive. You have little to lose and so much to gain when you put forgiveness on your menu.

PART THREE

Forgive for Good

Forgiveness Techniques for Healing:
Changing the Channel, Breath of Thanks, Heart Focus, and PERT

A wise man will make haste to forgive, because he knows the true value of time, and will not suffer it to pass away in unnecessary pain.
SAMUEL JOHNSON

In the first eight chapters I explored how and why we form grievances. I defined forgiveness and gave reasons to add forgiveness to your menu of choices. I described research that affirms the power of forgiveness to heal the body and mind and highlighted my own research. Now I will show you how to take the concepts presented and forgive anybody, including yourself.

It is now time to heal your grievances. In chapter 6 I highlighted the three preconditions for forgiveness. They are to know how you feel, to know what was wrong, and to tell a couple of trusted people what happened. If you have completed these steps you are ready to learn to forgive.

I do not claim that you will always find forgiveness easy or that you will choose to forgive all those who have hurt you. I assert that when these preconditions are satisfied, forgiveness becomes an extremely beneficial option.

OBSTACLES TO FORGIVENESS

But first, let's clear up a few common obstacles to forgiveness. The first is our tendency to confuse an unforgivable offense with an inability to forgive. I have found this misconception makes it harder for people to forgive, and I know that clearing this up will be of help to those reading this book. I often meet people who confuse their lack of motivation to forgive with a feeling that a specific offense is unforgivable. These people, even when they have met the preconditions dozens of times, have a hard time giving up their grievances. They resist the idea of forgiveness and argue about whether their offense is forgivable.

Mike, whom we met in chapter 1, is a good example. During a workshop I wrote the three preconditions on the chalkboard and said that we were now ready to begin. Mike raised his hand and said he did not think those conditions would allow him to forgive. What had happened to him was so unfair, since he had been promised a job as a Web designer and now was doing technical writing. Didn't I see that he was lied to? How could anyone forgive such liars? Wasn't it wrong to forgive people who lied like that? Wouldn't that mean he was letting them off the hook?

I asked Mike to imagine that twenty million dollars was deposited in a Swiss bank account in his name. The money was his, on one condition: that he agree not to think harshly again about his grievance. He was to imagine that the bankers had a thought detector that would know if he still held negative thoughts about his bosses. If they caught him in vengeful or angry thoughts, he would lose the money. I asked him if, in this scenario, he could let go of his grievance.

Mike replied, "Of course I could. My mama did not raise a fool, and only a fool would give up twenty million dollars." So I said to Mike, "We are really talking about your motivation to forgive, not whether your bosses should or could be forgiven. It is obvious that it is okay to forgive your bosses; you just won't do it until you have a good enough reason." I then said, "It seems to me you would forgive your bosses if the reward were good enough. Is that true?" He looked sheepish and said, "Yeah, I guess so." Mike learned that it was not the dishonesty that stopped him but whether or not he had sufficient reason to forgive.

In response to the offer of twenty million dollars, some people have told me that on principle they would not forgive the person who hurt them for money. I find this logic unconvincing, in particular because if someone hurt me I would love to get paid not to suffer anymore. In addition, I wonder why anyone would want any more suffering to come from an injustice. Giving up twenty million dollars seems like a lot of suffering. I picture a nice beach house, unlimited funds, and being able to do only work I love. For people who find money insufficient, I pose an alternative question. Dana, the woman who was passed over for a job promotion, was one such person. And before I continue I want to warn you, this second image can be difficult for some people.

I asked Dana to imagine a loaded gun pressed to her right temple— to picture the trigger is cocked and there is an itchy finger holding the gun. To picture that the person holding the gun is ready in a moment's notice to kill you, only waiting for the go-ahead. Dana's only way out is to agree to let go of her grievance. Her only condition is to eliminate negative thoughts about the offender from her thinking, and she will be released safe and sound.

After imagining this, Dana looked shaken and said of course she would not get killed for her grievance. Her tone said it was obvious, and I agree. However, to me it is equally obvious that grievances hurt us in many ways and do not require a loaded gun to provoke the need for change. Interestingly, I have yet to find anyone willing to hold on to his or her grievance in this scenario. No one wants to die for the privilege of remaining hurt and angry.

Unfortunately, many of us suffer for years from grievances we have not released. I showed in chapter 7 the proven positive effects of forgiveness and the harmful effects of grievances, anger, and depression. I am certain you are hurting your psychological well-being, your relationships, and likely your physical health by holding on to your grievances. Besides the anger and hurt, the loss of joy, love, and intimacy mar the lives of those who do not forgive. Please choose not to be one of these people. Please choose to Forgive for Good.

The good news is that we are more ready to forgive then we think. Our major obstacles are not the offenses themselves but the lack of tools with which to work. We only imagine it is the nature of the offense that is unforgivable. However, if any of us look around we will find people who have forgiven the very same offense. Remember, I have worked with people who made significant progress to forgive unprovoked violence. No offense is unforgivable to everyone. If you look you can always find someone who has forgiven in a similar situation.

When you put yourself into one or both of the scenarios above you will see that the hesitancy to forgive is principally a question of motivation. We feel unmotivated because lacking such compelling reasons as wealth or death we do not know how good we will feel when we have forgiven. We wonder if it will be worth the effort. Because we lack the tools to forgive, the effort can feel overwhelming. This book gives you the tools to forgive. You still have to make the effort.

The motivation to use the techniques is primarily to regain the power you give the past to ruin your present. Often we forget that forgiveness is for us and not the offender. Forgiveness in no way condones cruelty or unkind treatment. Forgiveness gives us back peace of mind.

WHAT DOES NOT WORK

In addition to lack of motivation and inadequate training, we face one other obstacle to forgiveness, and that is our tendency to continue reacting to hurt in ways that do not work. When we are hurt we do not know how to suffer less and find peace. Each of us tries a variety of solutions to this problem, and some solutions work better than others. If we would only stop doing what does not work, we would hurt less and be open to new approaches to problem solving. Let me give you an example.

Alice never got along with her in-laws. She and Hugh were married young and had a child right away. They had their second child a year later. The early years of their marriage were difficult and made worse by harsh feedback Hugh's parents. They were always telling Alice and Hugh what they were doing wrong and how their generation was better. The in-laws were intrusive and critical, and neither Hugh nor Alice welcomed their visits.

Alice tried everything she could think of to solve this problem. She tried confronting her in-laws. She tried saying nothing when they visited. She tried being overly friendly and hospitable when she spoke to them on the phone. She tried complaining to Hugh. She tried threatening Hugh if the parents showed up again. She tried whining to Hugh, and she tried accusing Hugh of not caring about her. Nothing Alice tried changed her in-laws or made her relationship with Hugh better. The in-laws continued on their nasty, merry way no matter what she did.

I asked Alice to write a list of all of the strategies she could think of to deal with the problem of her in-laws. Then I asked her to put a star next to those she had tried that failed. A failed strategy was one that neither helped her feel better nor changed the behavior of her in-laws.

I told Alice that at the least she could acknowledge her strategies "that did not work" and then stop doing them. Alice could improve her life if she never again tried one of her failed strategies. She suffered from both strategies that did not work and not having strategies that did work. She could solve some of her difficulty by at least not doing again "what does not work."

When Alice did this exercise she saw that nothing she tried had worked. She still had the problem of her in-laws. She also saw that she continued to use failed strategies. Alice got upset with her in-laws or her husband every time she tried what does not work. When she looked at her list of failed strategies with the conviction that she would not do them again, new ideas actually came to her mind. These strategies contained words such as *let it go*, *forgive them*, and *relax*. Alice then recognized what did not work and was free to see if the practices of forgiveness and letting go might work. She found that they did.

FORGIVENESS IS PRACTICAL

The three obstacles I have reviewed are common impediments to trying forgiveness. I bring those up because acknowledging these is part of my practical approach to forgiveness. I have structured this book so that throughout I provide hints that teach forgiveness. From the first to the last page, my goal is to make forgiveness practical. Throughout this book I provide practical hints for learning forgiveness. I want each of you to learn to forgive. My definition of forgiveness centers on the benefits of feeling peaceful, and I unravel the steps of how we formed our grievances. Finding peace does not need to be complicated.

Remember, all grievances begin when something in a person's life happens that they do not want to happen. From that initial unpleasantness they take things too personally, blame the offender for how they feel, and tell a grievance story. The grievance means that too much space is rented in their minds to hurt and anger. In chapter six I defined forgiveness as the feeling of peace that emerges as you

- take a hurt less personally
- take responsibility for how you feel
- become a hero instead of a victim in the story you tell.

I urge you to remember this definition of forgiveness. It is first and foremost a practical definition. Your goal is to feel peaceful. The feeling of peace comes as you heal your grievances—blaming less, taking responsibility for how you feel, and changing the story you tell. I call this peace forgiveness. As you feel more and more peace, you are progressing in your goal to heal from your grievances. You are learning to forgive.

In my definition of forgiveness there are three components. The most critical component is the story we tell. When we tell a story of victimization we have already taken something too personally and are blaming the offender for how we feel. When you tell the story of your heroic overcoming of an injustice, you will naturally blame less and take things less personally. However, it is very difficult to move directly to changing a well-rehearsed grievance story.

To avoid that problem, I suggest you begin by taking responsibility for how you feel. We have to remember that we are responsible for our emotional experience. Our past is not responsible for our present feelings. Just because something unpleasant occurred in our past or may occur in our future does not mean that day after day should be ruined. Difficulties, mistreatments, and unkindness do not have an extended warranty. We become helpless when we give the person who hurt us excessive power over how we feel. Our painful feelings will diminish only when we take that power back and show we are responsible for how we feel.

I teach two complementary techniques to help us reclaim responsibility for how we feel. The first technique is easy to practice and available to everyone. It is to not lose sight of the good things in our life. This sounds simple but takes some effort. What this means is we spend time and energy finding the beauty and love in our life to balance the time we spend on grudges, grievances, and wounds. The second technique is to practice PERT, the Positive Emotion Refocusing Technique, to immediately reduce our distress when we feel upset, hurt, or angry. PERT is a simple technique and will work whenever you feel upset. I will discuss it toward the end of this chapter. Right now, I want to walk you through the first technique: finding the positive in your life.

Both components to take responsibility for how you feel are important. Both make you feel better and reduce the power of your wounds to ruin your days, weeks, and months. Remember, taking responsibility for how you feel does not mean you have to like what happened. Responsibility only means we are the one in control of our emotional and behavioral reactions. Forgiveness is not a focus on what happened in the past and neither is remaining upset or holding on to grudges. You may have been hurt in the past, but you are upset today. Both forgiveness and grievances are experiences you have in the present.

Our parents may have been rotten in 1978. That does not mean on July 7, 2002, at 4:15 PM we have to feel upset. Or, our lover may have cheated on us in 1996. That does not mean that on August 4, 2001, at 9:00 we have to feel angry. Alternatively, we may be in a difficult ongoing relationship with a sibling. That does not mean that at odd times during the second week of October we have to feel disgust and resentment.

I want to make clear that taking responsibility for how you feel does not mean that what happened is your fault. You did not cause your parents to hurt you or your lover to cheat on you. You did not cause the car to hit you or the illness to strike you. You did not cause your boss to be grouchy nor did you cause the weather to stink on your vacation. While you did not cause these things to happen, you are responsible for how you think, behave, and feel since those experiences occurred. It is your life, and they are your reactions and emotions to manage.

CHANGING THE CHANNEL ON YOUR REMOTE CONTROL

Taking responsibility means first and foremost that even though we are hurt, we continue to make the effort to appreciate the good in our life. When we understand that pain is a normal part of life, we make the effort to keep our hurts in perspective. I challenge the common tendency to feel that our experience of hurt is more real than our ability to feel good. I challenge the tendency to assert that painful experiences are somehow deeper than rapture over the beauty of a sunset or the love we feel for our children.

Many of us are renting more space to rehashing our grievances than focusing on gratitude, love, or appreciation of nature. My central message here is when you bring more positive experiences into your life, your hurts will diminish in importance. In fact, this is the first step to taking responsibility for how you feel and beginning to forgive. If I rent out more and more space in my mind to appreciating my children or the loveliness of a rainy day, there is as a result less space and time for dwelling on the hurts.

To help you understand this idea I want to share with you a helpful metaphor. Imagine that what you see in your mind is instead being viewed on a TV screen. Picture that what you see and hear comes as a TV program. On your TV screen at home you change the channels with your remote control. You choose what programs you want to see. When you want to watch a horror movie you may have to tune in channel 6. To watch a love story you have to watch channel 14. To watch a nature channel you have to select channel 51. By your control of the remote you determine what shows on your TV.

Imagine now that each of us has a remote control that changes the channel we are viewing in our mind. Imagine if the pictures in our mind could be changed in the same way you change the channel of your TV. From this point of view, a grievance can be seen as the remote control stuck on the grievance channel. For some of us, like Denise, that means endless reruns of the show *I Had Rotten Parents*. For others, like Mike, there are endless episodes of the show *Lousy Rotten Lying Bosses*. There are so many programs running on people's grievance channel that they do not wait for the summer to show reruns. Many of us who have a grievance have probably worn down the remote buttons that access the grievance channel. *My Life Was Unfair* often plays to standing-room-only audiences. *My Parents Mistreated Me* is an all-too-familiar tearjerker.

My challenge is to teach you to reprogram your remote control. I want you to program your remote to regularly tune in to the gratitude, beauty, love, and forgiveness channels. Programs on these channels are always listed in *TV Guide* and are always playing on someone's TV set. Just because Sarah's husband used drugs, cheated on her, and then left her does not mean her gratitude and beauty channels must go unused. There is always a beautiful sunset to find or a story in the newspaper about a heroic act of kindness to read. The truth is Sarah needed access to those channels desperately at that bad time in her life. She increased her suffering by locking her remote in to the grievance channel.

Often people find that tuning in to the forgiveness, gratitude, beauty, and love channels is more easily said than done. Their remote may be stuck. If you can't find anything to view on your beauty or love channel, you can watch other people who have TVs with good reception. If you have been hurt in love, don't miss the joy as other people connect with each other. If you do not have a lover but do have a cat, put the cat on your love channel. There is always a way for the voices of little children to bring a smile. There is never a moment we cannot give thanks for the gifts of our life. Each breath we take is a precious gift.

Because I work in California I regularly suggest people dust off their Big Sur channel. Big Sur is an area on the California coast where nature is stupendous and the views are gorgeous. Big Sur is, like Yosemite National Park or the Grand Canyon, a place of magnificent beauty. It is so beautiful it is hard to be there and stay in a bad mood. I ask each of you to occasionally tune in to the Big Sur channel as a reminder that the exquisite beauty of nature is always nearby. Watching Big Sur is as real as any hurt from the past. It is just a button away on the remote. We do not have to get up off our recliner. What we watch on our mental TV is a choice.

The world is full of things to appreciate and find beautiful. The challenge is to teach ourselves how to look. The forgiveness and gratitude channels remind us that even though we have been hurt, we do not have to focus our attention on that hurt. The love and beauty channels remind us that in each and every moment we have the choice to determine what we see, hear, and experience.

The one thing no one can take from us is where we place our attention. In other words, we alone control our remotes. If we have made a habit of tuning in to the grievance channel, remember that any habit can be broken. The world is full of heroes who have overcome difficulty by tuning in to channels of courage or bravery. Each of us can become a hero, and then other people will benefit from watching our lives on their TV.

When you tune in to the gratitude, love, beauty, or forgiveness channels you give your body a rest. When you are focused on your problems and grievances your body is under stress. Your stress chemicals are active and you feel tired and beaten down. You blame the offender for your distress and feel disempowered. In this way you can actually restore some of the damage done by your stress response.

For those of us whose remotes may have a little rust I offer some suggestions for how to improve reception on the gratitude, love, beauty, and forgiveness channels. Each of these suggestions has been practiced and found useful.

Gratitude Channel

- Walk into your nearest supermarket and give thanks for the abundance of food available.
- Go to a nursing home or hospital and give thanks for your good health.
- When driving, mentally thank each of the drivers who follow the rules of the road.
- If you have a significant other, thank this person for caring for you. Make it a point to do this every day.
- Remind yourself of any kind act done by your parents.
- Notice a salesperson or clerk at a store, and thank this person for waiting on you.
- In your home, give thanks for all of the labor that went into making your furniture, appliances, and food.
- As you wake up each morning, give thanks for your breath and the gift of your life.

Beauty Channel

- When stuck in traffic, notice the beauty of the sky or the remarkable movement of birds or clouds.
- Stop at a schoolyard and observe the delightful play of little children.

- Find a favorite spot in nature that you can go to easily. Remember what that spot looks and feels like.
- Watch nature shows on television.
- Deeply appreciate your favorite piece of music.
- Walk slowly, and absorb the smells and sights of nature.
- Notice how beautiful well-prepared food looks and tastes.
- Observe the beauty and wonder of flowers, in particular the array of colors.
- Notice how attractive the people you love look.
- Go to a zoo, and marvel at the variety of animals.
- Envision the beauty of Big Sur.

Forgiveness Channel

- Look for people who have forgiven others, and ask them to tell you their stories.
- Remember when you have forgiven, and remind yourself you can do it.
- Read books about people who have forgiven hurtful situations.
- See if there are any forgiveness stories in your family.
- Practice forgiving the littlest offenses against you.
- Practice forgiving for just a minute at a time.
- Forgive a driver who cuts you off in the road.
- Think of times that you have hurt others and needed forgiveness.
- Notice whenever someone is kind to you after you have hurt him or her.
- Notice how often you naturally forgive those you love.

Love Channel

- Look for people who are in love, and smile at their happiness.
- Go to a hospital, and observe the love of family who care for those who are ill.
- Remember the times in your life when you were loved.
- Remember the times in your life when you were loving.
- Call up a friend, and tell them you care about them.
- Look for memories of kindness done for you by your parents.

- Ask yourself what you can do to become a more loving person.
- Ask someone about a time when she or he felt really loved.

In addition to the above ways to tune in to positive emotions, the following two exercises will help keep the rust off your remote. These exercises give best results when practiced often. You will need to remind yourself to practice until you develop the habit of finding beauty and gratitude naturally.

BREATH OF THANKS

1. Two or three times every day when you are not fully occupied, slow down and bring your attention to your breathing.
2. Notice that your breath flows in and out without your having to do anything. Put your attention on your stomach, and as you inhale, allow the air to gently push your belly out. As you exhale, consciously relax your belly so that it feels soft.
3. Continue breathing this way for about three to five slow, deep breaths.
4. Then for each of the next five to eight inhalations, say the words *thank you* silently to remind yourself of the gift of your breath and how lucky you are to be alive. Often people have a stronger response when they imagine their experience of gratitude centered in their hearts.
5. After those five to eight breaths of thanks, return to the soft belly breathing for another one to two breaths.
6. Then gently resume your regular activity.

HEART FOCUS

1. Assume a comfortable position you can maintain for ten to fifteen minutes.
2. Gently bring your attention to your breathing as it flows in and out. As you inhale, allow the air to gently push your belly out. As you exhale, consciously relax your belly so that it feels soft. Prac-

tice this focusing of your attention for about five minutes.

3. Then bring to your mind either a memory of an experience with another person when you had a powerful feeling of love or a scene in nature that fills you with beauty and tranquillity. Do not choose someone for this exercise that you are trying to forgive.

4. When the image of that experience is clear in your mind, try to reexperience in the present moment the associated peaceful and loving feelings. Many people like to imagine the good feelings are centered in their hearts.

5. Hold those peaceful feelings for as long as you can. If you find that your attention wanders, return to step one and the unforced rise and fall of your stomach.

6. After ten to fifteen minutes, slowly open your eyes and resume your regular activities.

Practice the Heart Focus exercise at least three times per week.

FORGIVENESS: THE PRACTICE

Helen was an attractive woman in her midthirties who lived alone. In my workshop she mostly sat quietly and listened, yet I often saw tears forming in the corners of her eyes. When she talked the tone of her voice revealed a chip on her shoulder. She always resisted the possibility of forgiveness, arguing that her hurt could not be repaired. She said she could never forgive her sister for breaking her heart.

Helen and her sister had always been competitive. Joan was two years older, and Helen remembers getting the short end of the stick. Helen reported that while they were growing up, Joan was her parents' favorite. Recently, Helen and Joan both liked the same man. Helen started dating Rick and introduced him to Joan. Within a few weeks Rick and Joan were living together. Helen was crushed. She felt betrayed and unattractive. Her parents told her to let it go, as Joan and Rick were in love. They asked her why she didn't want her sister to be happy.

Helen was miserable, as almost anything could trigger the memory of her loss. She was also angry and let anyone within earshot know that her sister was a disreputable louse. One day I asked Helen why she was upset when her sister was not to be seen. She looked at me like I was crazy. I said, "Helen, I do not see anyone or anything in this room to be upset with. Nevertheless, I see you upset. Where does that come from?" I wondered aloud if Helen had formed the habit of being upset. I told her it is possible that she has become accustomed to feeling these negative emotions.

I asserted that this is common when we get hurt. We often get stuck in a habit of repeatedly remembering the betrayal and mistreatment. I reminded her that she was the landlord who rented out the space in her mind. I went to the chalkboard and showed Helen that her sister was a plane she was keeping in the air long after it needed to land.

I then led the class through a guided visualization on appreciating a safe and beautiful scene in nature, an example of tuning our TV to the beauty channel. At the end of the visualization, I asked Helen how she felt. She responded that she felt good but was confused about what that had to do with forgiveness. I asked her whether bringing up those peaceful feelings when she got upset would make a difference. She said that she thought it would make a difference. I reminded her that the peaceful feelings she had just experienced are her goal.

Forgiveness is the practice of extending your moments of peacefulness. Forgiveness is deciding what plays on your TV screen. Forgiveness is the power that comes from knowing a past injustice does not have to hurt today. When we have good experiences, such as moments of beauty or love, then for those moments we have forgiven those who have hurt us. Forgiveness is the choice to extend those moments to the rest of our life. Forgiveness is available anytime. It is completely under your control. It does not rely on the actions of others; it is a choice you alone can make.

I reminded Helen that her goal was to learn how to feel good more often during her day. During those few minutes when Helen visualized a scene of beauty, her sister could not hurt her. As the painful action took place in the past, the only way her sister could hurt her again was for Helen to focus on the betrayal. For Helen, the critical thing was to control her mind and as a result her emotions.

Helen learned that how she feels is directly related to what plays on her TV. Since Helen paid relentless attention to her sister, she felt overwhelmed with pain. The times when she feels good or peaceful are when she has forgiven her sister. I asked her to imagine that her goal was to extend those peaceful times. I told Helen that she alone holds the power to determine how many peaceful moments she experiences.

PERT

The first step when we take responsibility for how we feel is to remind ourselves to look for the good and beautiful in life. We have learned three parts to this process. First is to dust off our remote control so we can find what is playing on our beauty, gratitude, love, and forgiveness channels. Second is to practice the Breath of Thanks a couple of times every day. This breathing will help you relax and remind you that the most important gift you may not be fully appreciating is life itself. Third is to set aside about an hour each week to practice the Heart Focus. The Heart Focus helps you develop slow and deep breathing. It helps you to relax and teaches you to take your good feelings and bring them into the present.

These three steps help us refocus on the positive and prevent times of prolonged pain or upset. They are not designed for use when a painful memory or seeing someone again causes us to feel significantly upset. That is when we need a different technique. PERT can help us at the moment a painful experience comes onto our TV screen.

PERT: POSITIVE EMOTION REFOCUSING TECHNIQUE

We need to learn how to maintain our peace in any situation, no matter how upsetting. We gain tremendous confidence when we are suddenly faced with a painful situation or memory and are able to sustain our positive focus. Practicing PERT helps us stay calm so we can make good decisions.

Practicing PERT when faced with a raging boss prevents anger and hurt from overwhelming you. On a crowded freeway it prevents distress from making the situation worse. Practicing it while anticipating visiting a relative you do not like enables you to decide whether the visit is in your best interest. Practicing it while remembering an alcoholic parent prevents falling into despair.

Helen practiced PERT and slowly her sister became less of a threat to her. PERT is helpful in any situation where you feel anger, hurt, depression, or bitterness. Students of mine practice PERT when they remember how an ex-spouse or parent mistreated them. Students of mine practice PERT when they find themselves getting upset in an ongoing marital struggle. When you practice PERT and remain calm you will notice your grievance starts to weaken its hold over you.

PERT takes about forty-five seconds to practice and can be done anytime and anywhere. No one has to know you are practicing. You can practice in an argument to stay cool or while your lover is telling you good-bye. You can practice when you need to be assertive and are worried about the offender's reaction. PERT is the most powerful technique I know to help you remain in control of your emotions. As you practice PERT the people who hurt you become less threatening. You take away their power to hurt you and replace it with increased self-confidence and calm.

PRACTICING PERT

When you are feeling the effects of an unresolved grievance or ongoing relationship problem:

1. Bring your attention fully to your stomach as you slowly draw in and out two deep breaths. As you inhale, allow the air to gently push your belly out. As you exhale, consciously relax your belly so that it feels soft.

2. On the third full and deep inhalation, bring to your mind's eye an image of someone you love or of a beautiful scene in nature that fills you with awe and wonder. Often people have a stronger response when they imagine their positive feelings are centered in the area around their heart.

3. While practicing, continue with *soft* belly breathing.

4. Ask the relaxed and peaceful part of you what you can do to resolve your difficulty.

When I met Helen she felt okay only when plotting revenge on her sister or while distracting herself. She was a nervous wreck who watched a number of movies each evening and tried to keep busy. She never considered she had any control over how she felt. Her boyfriend dumped her for her sister so she was upset, and in her mind this conclusion followed like the sun rising in the morning. Helen never realized that by spending over two hours a day lamenting her loss, she would continually feel bad. When she couples that with the fact that she spent almost no time every day filled with gratitude, it was inevitable that she would stay unhappy.

I told Helen PERT was cheaper than a daily pint of ice cream. In her desperation, she practiced the technique faithfully every day. At first she felt nothing except her familiar pain. I told her that the crucial task was to keep her attention on her belly and not on her distress. With time the positive feeling would come.

Helen practiced each day for two weeks. At the end of that time, she could think of her sister without reacting like a puppet on a string. Through the practice of PERT Helen gained control over her feelings and became more confident. As this happened Helen started to think about what she wanted out of life. She started to wonder why she was spending so much time on Joan's life. She understood she was renting Joan too much space in her mind. She also realized that it never would have worked with Rick if he could so easily leave her.

Helen understood none of this during the months she was upset each and every time Joan came to her mind. PERT, Heart Focus, Breath of Life, and tuning in to the beauty channel gave Helen a second chance. Until learning to forgive, Helen had been listening only to the hurt and angry parts of herself. After practicing these techniques, she tuned in to the loving and peaceful parts of herself as well. Finding those parts of herself, which had never gone away but were only tuned out, gave Helen back her life. I have full confidence they will give you back yours as well.

Many people find relief through the practice of PERT alone. Some people who take my training forgive and move on from what I have already showed you. They see that a focus on their grievances hurts them more than the offender. Through practice of PERT, Heart Focus, and the Breath of Life they retain power over their emotions. PERT combined with Heart Focus and dusting off the beauty and love channels are powerful tools.

I did not intend PERT to be a stand-alone practice, but often it is sufficient. However, my forgiveness methods work like peeling an onion. Peeling an onion takes time, and there are a lot of layers. The first in this process is to look for beauty and love with the same determination that grievances and hurts come to mind. The second is to practice Heart Focus and Breath of Life. The third is PERT practice.

In the next chapter I will teach you to create more enforceable rules. In a future chapter I will show you the best way to amend your grievance story. Over a number of chapters I will show you the HEAL method, a powerful tool that will help you forgive even long-standing grievances. The HEAL method is a step-by-step approach for resolving specific hurts you may have had for years.

What I ask from you is to begin daily practice of the techniques offered you in this chapter. Become a scientist. Use your life as an experiment, and see how much better you can feel.

CHAPTER 10

From Unenforceable Rules to Wishes and Hopes

If you are distressed by anything external, the pain is not due to the thing itself, but to your estimate of it; and this you have the power to revoke at any moment.

MARCUS ANTONIUS

The four techniques from chapter 9 will help a great deal in reclaiming your power from someone or something that hurt you. Each technique requires practice, but results appear almost immediately. Practice the PERT technique a few times in situations where you feel angry and upset and you will notice remarkable changes. Practice the Heart Focus and Breath of Thanks and you will create good habits that help the PERT technique to work. Practice finding your gratitude channel and you will see that you have less to forgive. You will soon see the world in a different and better way. People report feeling more assertive and comfortable with others. As you learn to naturally tune in to the gratitude, beauty, and love channels, a world of things to appreciate appears.

With practice many people have healed and forgiven using just these methods. Some people have healed from their grievances through one practice of PERT while others try for weeks to tune in their fuzzy gratitude channels. In this chapter and the following I will teach you other forgiveness techniques that augment and complement what you have learned.

Bill was a middle-aged man who came to one of my daylong forgiveness training classes. He sat in the back and did not say anything during the class. His face showed little expression, and he neither smiled at my jokes nor frowned at my exhortations to forgive. At the end of the class, he came up to the front of the room and started to talk. He said that he had been angry for about eight months at his business partner, Tom. His partner had made a decision to buy some stock in an Internet start-up company. Bill and Tom had argued about the stock purchase. Bill thought it was risky, and the two men agreed to wait before taking any action. Unknown to Bill, Tom purchased the stock immediately after their meeting.

Bill found out about the purchase about a week later and was furious. He was furious about the betrayal, the loss of money, and the deceit. He felt that he could not trust his partner. After all, they had a deal to wait and see. When Bill found out what his partner did he checked the stock price. He was even more furious when he discovered the stock had lost almost 30 percent of its value.

When Bill confronted Tom, he soon found that Tom did not know what Bill was so upset about. Tom said that the deal was too good to pass up. He thought Bill would be happy when the deal showed a profit. When Bill asked him about the broken trust, Tom said that occasionally he had to do what he knew was best. Tom also said that they should wait to sell because the stock price would certainly go back up. When Bill came to my class the value of the stock had not recovered, and Bill and his partner held thousands of shares of a company whose value was 40 percent less than when they had bought it.

Understandably, Bill was still angry. Bill was extremely uncomfortable in situations he could not control. He hated the way his partner had acted; he hated the fact that he was losing money; and he hated that there was nothing he could do about it. When he came up to talk to me it was to let me know how the class had helped him.

He told me that from the moment he started breathing into and out of his belly slowly he felt calmer. From the lunch break on he had practiced the PERT technique literally a hundred times, and it worked. He still did not approve of what his partner did, but it was not going to steal his peacefulness or ruin a twenty-year business friendship. What Bill learned was that he could control the way he felt. He learned that he might not be able to control what his partner did, but he could control how he reacted.

The purpose of PERT, Heart Focus, and the Breath of Thanks is to change the way you feel. The practice of these techniques will increase feelings of peace and help us recover control of our emotions. One of the unintended consequences of feeling more peaceful and less hurt is to be able to think more clearly.

For example, at the start of class Bill was contemplating ending a twenty-year business partnership. After practicing PERT a number of times he calmed down and he was able to put the actions of his partner into perspective. Bill was not thinking clearly because he was trying to enforce one of his unenforceable rules. In Bill's mind his partner had to be trustworthy all the time. As Bill cooled off, his expectations for his partner fell in line with his long-term business goals. He also understood that sometimes even good friends and business associates do things we do not like.

Bill's experience is not unique. We all suffer from cloudy thinking when we are upset. Too often, we think our frazzled minds are thinking clearly. To me, thinking clearly is being able to focus on whether we have a chance to get what we want. When we are thinking clearly we can ask the question, "Is there a good probability that what I want will occur?" If the answer is no, then a clear-thinking person relaxes, works hard at discovering alternatives, and hopes for the best. A person who is not thinking clearly gets mad, hurt, and frustrated. Usually that person becomes filled with blame, which if not checked leads to bitterness and loss of hope.

Usually when we are not thinking clearly, we are trying to enforce an unenforceable rule. The problem we face is that the probability of getting unenforceable rules to work is close to zero. For example, Marilyn from chapter 2 may demand with all her might that her uncaring mother acknowledge her needs. However, if her parent chooses otherwise, there is nothing Marilyn can do to change her. Lorraine, from chapter 5, may demand with all of her might that her husband, Larry, not stay out late working and then lie to her about it. However, if her husband chooses otherwise, there is nothing Lorraine can do to change him.

In each frustrating scenario, there are things we can do to change how we think and feel. In this chapter, I show you how to challenge your unenforceable rules. Before I continue, let me remind you that in addition to changing how you think and feel, you can take action to change your situation. For example, Bill could have left the partnership to make sure his partner never bought stock again or Dana could look for another job.

The problem faced by people when they are angry, hurt, or frustrated is these emotions make it hard to make good decisions. When we add blame to feelings of anger and hurt, then good decision making becomes more difficult. When a wrong is personalized by insisting that your unenforceable rules be followed, good decision making becomes almost impossible.

CHALLENGING OUR UNENFORCEABLE RULES

In chapter 9 we learned PERT, Heart Focus, Breath of Thanks, and channel changing and I recommend them as baseline practices for forgiveness. The next step is to challenge our unenforceable rules so we can develop realistic hopes and wishes. I will teach us how to think more clearly and take our offenses less personally. Why? Because having unenforceable rules is the primary reason we take things too personally.

In chapter 2, I reviewed the dangers of taking an offense too personally. Now I will illustrate that by challenging these unenforceable rules we can help release the grip of the grievance process. When we challenge our unenforceable rules we take the next step in learning to forgive.

As an example, let us revisit the beleaguered police officer from chapter 5. This officer is sitting by the side of a highway with a car that does not work. He is frustrated as car after car speeds by and he is helpless to intervene. So he is now feeling tense, frustrated, and helpless. He is not doing his job, and neither he nor the cars speeding by are following his unenforceable rules. I posed the question in chapter 5, "What do you do when you have rules that you cannot enforce?" Here's the answer.

The officer had a rule that cars should not speed. The community pays him to issue tickets to cars that did speed. However, neither the law nor his authority stops the host of speeding drivers. His rule is unenforceable. A life lesson to remember is, no matter how good the rule, there are always people to break it.

Our officer also had a rule about how his car should work. This rule says that police car engines should always start. His expectation was that each and every time he turned the key his car would work. No matter how hard the officer turned the key his car did not start, so this rule too was unenforceable. Auto repair shops attest to the number of times this rule is broken.

The officer also had unenforceable rules for his own behavior. In his mind a good officer always gives out tickets to speeders. A good officer can always anticipate car trouble and does not make mistakes. Our police officer had rigid and high standards for himself, which made normal human and automotive frailty dangerous. They were chock-full of unenforceable rules. When his car did not work the unenforceable rules made our officer feel angry, helpless, and frustrated.

His rules are unenforceable because the officer did not have the ability to make what he wanted happen. Each of the officer's unenforceable rules was a personal statement of right and wrong. His rules were blueprints for how he wanted certain things to be. Unfortunately, the speeding drivers operated under different rules. Perhaps they had a rule that it was more important to be on time for work than to follow the speed limit or that they follow the speed limit only when everyone else does.

The people who manufacture police cars had different standards for car performance than did our officer. They did not listen to our police officer when they were designing his car. The car manufacturer's rule might be that it was more important to make a profit than build a car that would never break down.

Our police officer did not consider that other people operated under different rules. He thought his rules were the correct ones. He took the breaking of his rules as a personal offense and so suffered hurt and anger. These feelings did not make him a better officer. Helplessly writing tickets that he could not give out actually made him a less effective police officer. We are all in this same position. Helplessly writing tickets we cannot give out does not help us be better parents, spouses, friends, or workers.

Each of us, like our officer, experiences distress when the breaking of an unenforceable rule becomes a personal affront. Holding unenforceable rules makes life more difficult. Unenforceable rules we take personally may be dangerous. I have shown you in chapter 2 the problem with taking the actions of other people too personally. One of the ways this occurs is when breaking an unenforceable rule becomes a personal offense. Too often, when people break our unenforceable rules they break something dear to us. Then, even though we are in pain we tend to cling to our rules rather than examine whether the rules make sense or not.

The good news is that challenging unenforceable rules is a simple process. Unenforceable rules make their presence known. You do not have to look far to find them. They do not hide under the rug. *Every* time you are more than mildly upset with the actions of someone else it is because you are trying to enforce an unenforceable rule. EVERY time you are more than mildly upset with your life it is because you are trying to enforce an unenforceable rule.

You will not stay angry or hurt unless an unenforceable rule of yours has been broken. You can be sure an unenforceable rule is operating when you feel angry, bitter, depressed, alienated, or hopeless. I am not saying there will be no sadness or frustration without unenforceable rules. I am not suggesting having feelings is wrong. What I am saying is that underneath your most painful feelings are rules you are helplessly trying to enforce. If you worked on challenging your rules when you start feeling upset, then your bad feelings won't last and won't be as severe.

SIX STEPS TO CHALLENGING UNENFORCEABLE RULES

There are six simple steps to challenging unenforceable rules. The first step is simple: recognize when you are upset, and acknowledge that the upset is taking place in the present. Taking this step is as easy as getting mad when someone cuts you off on the freeway. You are mad because you had a rule that drivers should not cut you off. Did you have the power to stop them from doing that? No. Was your rule enforceable? No. The result: anger and frustration. Does it do you any good to write out a ticket for the offense? No. Will that make the roads safer? No. Does it help your health or mental well-being to write out tickets for the next three days when you tell your friends and family about the terrible drivers on the highways? No, it destroys your peace of mind.

Alternatively, taking this first step is as simple as recognizing you are upset when you remember how poorly you were parented. Joanne remembers her mother yelling at her to get better grades. She did poorly in school, and her mother had no patience for her difficulty. Each of her siblings did well in school, but Joanne had struggled since the first grade. Every time she remembered being yelled at, she felt tense and sad. Each memory renewed feelings of stupidity and incompetence.

In the seventh grade, Joanne was discovered to have learning disabilities. Her mother refused to admit there was anything wrong with her. Mom thought Joanne was just lazy and stupid. Luckily for Joanne, her special education teacher was able to convince her that she had a problem that could be corrected. However, from that time on Joanne remembers hating her mother. She remembers thinking that her mother could not be forgiven for being so cruel and insensitive.

Joanne still thought this way when we met thirty years later. She regularly got upset remembering her mother's insensitivity. Joanne at this time was forty-six years old. She was thirty-three years removed from the seventh grade. However, she often felt upset remembering her mother's cruelty. Joanne was still trying to enforce an unenforceable rule. She still demanded a caring parent. She still had an insensitive one even if that was only in a memory.

Joanne had a rule that a mother must be understanding and sensitive. This is generally a good desire, but a lousy rule. Joanne's problem was she was as unable to make her mother be sensitive in 1999 as she had been in 1966. I told Joanne that she could try until she died to change the past. Every time she tried to change the past she would get more upset. Every time she got upset she would blame her mother. Moreover, every time she got upset she reinforced her feelings of helplessness.

I led Joanne through the steps of challenging her unenforceable rule. The first step is to acknowledge that she is upset and that upset is occurring in the present. She was able to acknowledge in class that her upset was occurring in the present. When Joanne recognized this, she became able to take action to help herself. Until then, her past was determining her present and she felt helpless, like a victim.

Remember, the first step in challenging rules is to acknowledge that you are upset today, not yesterday. If the upset is current, therefore, the unenforceable rules you hold must also be current. The second step is to realize that your upset is due not only to the situation but also to an inability to enforce an unenforceable rule. I reminded Joanne that her unenforceable rule is more of a problem to her than is her mother. Anyone would feel hopeless at the thought of changing something in the past. Anyone would be upset demanding that his or her mother develop sensitivity she does not possess. I reminded Joanne that many people had bad parenting experiences and therefore good parenting is a rule commonly broken.

I then gave Joanne the key to challenging her unenforceable rules. I explained to her that her suffering is the result of turning her desire for a sensitive mother into a rule that her mother must follow. Wanting a good parent is a legitimate wish. Unfortunately, insisting on a good parent is a recipe for disaster.

When Joanne insists on obtaining something she cannot have she becomes upset. Joanne turned her wish for a good parent into a rule that her mother must behave a certain way. Since her mother exercised her free will and was not sensitive, Joanne was left with a lifetime of pain and suffering.

Let me review once more the first two steps in challenging unenforceable rules. They are first to acknowledge our upset and know we are upset in the present. Step two is to remind ourselves that our urge to write a ticket comes from unenforceable rules. Then, step three is to assert our willingness to challenge the unenforceable rules that are causing us so much pain. That means we focus on changing the way we think and not the person with whom we are upset. Joanne was desperate when she saw how much pain her unenforceable rules were causing her. She was at that point willing to try almost anything. The fourth step in this process is to uncover the unenforceable rule. What is exciting is this is much easier than one may think.

The unenforceable rule is simply the desire or hope you have for something good that has been turned into an expectation or demand.

The desire could be for love, safety, good health, friendship, loyalty, money, sex, and/or good grades. Joanne wished for a caring parent, but she turned that wish into a demand for a good parent. Rita desired a less lustful husband, but she turned that wish into a demand for less sex. None of us has the power to expect other people to always do what we want and therefore people often break our rules. Our mistake comes when instead of challenging the unenforceable rules we try harder to enforce them. That mistake costs us dearly.

Some people spend their whole lives trying to get their unenforceable rules to be obeyed. These people complain about something they cannot change. Instead of realizing that they should think more clearly, they remain angry and unfulfilled. Once you learn how to challenge your unenforceable rules, you will understand it is easier to change your thinking than to get unenforceable rules to be obeyed.

Joanne was always trying to make her mother different. She was trying to make her sensitive. Joanne was also trying to make her past different. She wanted a *Leave It to Beaver* home and did not have one. Trying to change her past made her upset at least once a day.

To look for your unenforceable rules, ask yourself, Am I demanding that other people treat me better than they do? Am I demanding my past be better than it was? Am I demanding my life be easier than it is or turn out more fair than it has? When you find yourself thinking in any of these ways, you have an unenforceable rule. When we do not have the power to make what we want happen, we suffer. As we try harder to enforce the rule, we feel more and more helpless. The bottom line is when we feel helpless, angry, or upset, we know we are trying to enforce an unenforceable rule. And we know we can stop and suffer less.

When you find an unenforceable rule, the goal is to return to the desire and get rid of the demand. I urge each of you to fervently hope things go the way you want. At the same time, remind yourself that it is foolish to demand things go a certain way when you do not have the power to make it happen.

The fifth step follows easily from the fourth. After you have identified your unenforceable rule, you can ask yourself to deliberately change the way you think about what you want or need by substituting the words *hope* or *wish* for the unenforceable expectation or demand.

I suggested to Joanne that she say to herself that she hoped for a mother who was sensitive to children with learning problems. I also suggested she say to herself that she cannot change the past but can hope and work for a better future. I asked Joanne to practice thinking in this way. Joanne reported to me a week later saying that she felt better but was struggling to get used to such a different way of thinking.

The sixth and final step of challenging your unenforceable rules is to realize that you are thinking more clearly and feeling better when you stop demanding and start wishing. I reminded Joanne that the goal of forgiveness is the feeling of peace that comes from taking things less personally and assuming responsibility for how she feels. In time, I assured her, she would get used to this way of thinking, which leads to forgiveness and greater peace.

SIX STEPS TO CHALLENGE YOUR UNENFORCEABLE RULES

1. Recognize that you feel hurt, angry, alienated, depressed, or hopeless. Acknowledge that your feelings may be from memories of the past but that you experience the feelings in the present.
2. Remind yourself that you feel bad because you are trying to enforce an unenforceable rule.
3. Assert your willingness to challenge your unenforceable rule.
4. Find your unenforceable rule by asking yourself the following question: "What experiences in my life am I thinking of right now that I am demanding to be different?"
5. In your mind change from *demanding* you get what you want to *hoping* you get what you want.
6. Notice that when you wish or hope things be the way you want, then you think more clearly and feel more peaceful.

A major advantage when you desire or hope for a loving parent as opposed to demanding a loving parent is you remain open to the possibility that you may not get what you want. When you hope for a good outcome you try hard to make it happen. Joanne wanted a sensitive mother. Joanne wanted an upbringing that was full of care and support. She did not have that upbringing and can do nothing about the past. In the present, she has choices. When Joanne confused her desire for a sensitive mother with the unenforceable rule of demanding a sensitive mother she felt angry and stuck in the past. Joanne's unenforceable rule left no room for handling the parent she actually had.

It is not the desires, wishes, and hopes that get us in trouble. The desire to find loving friends, family, and lovers is critical to our happiness. The problem arises when we demand that our friends, family, and lovers be the way we want them to be. I am suggesting that we be realistic and accept the fact that people can be hurtful. I want us to hurt and suffer less and forgive more.

To heal, forgiveness is important. I am convinced that the frustration you feel enforcing unenforceable rules is the biggest threat to your motivation to succeed. Most of us give up more readily when we demand something we cannot have then when we make plans to optimize our chances to get what we want. When we hope for a caring parent, we leave room for having to make other plans. When we demand a caring parent, there is little room to maneuver.

I want to use our frustrated police officer again to illustrate how to challenge unenforceable rules. First, our officer must acknowledge he is upset in the present even though some of the cars passed by an hour ago. Second, he acknowledges that his upset is caused by his rules about speeding drivers and broken cars and is not caused just by the circumstances. Third, he asks himself the following question: "What am I experiencing right now that I am expecting to be different?"

The officer sees that he is expecting cars to stop speeding as well as demanding that his car start. Since he is clearly agitated and upset, he knows his rules must be unenforceable. He takes a few moments to practice PERT and calms down. Following this he challenges his unenforceable rules directly by saying, "I was expecting cars to follow the speed limit. I made myself upset when I could not enforce what I wanted. I spent wasted time and energy trying to make these rules hold. While I would like drivers to follow the rules of the road, clearly it is beyond my control."

The officer then challenges the rules he had for police cars because the same process is true for his car. He acknowledges that he demanded his car start and made himself upset when it did not. Our officer understands it is healthier to hope his car works and then do what is necessary when it does not. He thinks to himself, "While I wait for a backup, maybe I could catch up on my paperwork." The officer reminds himself how much better he feels when he can think clearly.

COMMON UNENFORCEABLE RULES AND HOW TO CHALLENGE THEM

I want to end this chapter with a short list of some common unenforceable rules. I also provide some simple strategies to challenge the rules and show how people have learned healthier ways of thinking. This is not an exhaustive list, and these are not the only ways to challenge them. This list is a guide to show you some common rules and some realistic ways of looking at life. I hope this list and alternative responses will show you how to take disappointment and frustration less personally.

My Partner Has to Be Faithful

Alan, from chapter 3, discovered his wife, Elaine, was having an affair, and blamed his wife for ruining his life. Through forgiveness training he learned to challenge his rule that a partner has to be faithful. He found it was more realistic to say he hoped his wife would be faithful, since he had learned the hard way he could not force her to. Alan learned through a subsequent relationship how precious that choice of faithfulness is, and he committed himself to appreciate the gift. Alan had the best chance, but no guarantee, of his wife's faithfulness by treating her with kindness and respect. He learned there is a risk in love and offering trust. He found the rewards are great, but there are no guarantees.

People Must Not Lie to Me

Lorraine, whose husband, Larry, was staying out late and then lying about it, found it more realistic to say she hoped Larry would be truthful. However, she saw numerous examples of his deceit and learned to ask herself why her husband should be immune from a common human problem. She learned that husbands and wives and marriage are complex, and when under stress people do all sorts of selfish and destructive things. As long as Lorraine demanded otherwise she was foolhardy and suffered accordingly. As Lorraine became less hysterical she made some significant demands on Larry. When he did not change she moved out, which forced him into counseling if he wanted to keep his marriage.

Life Should Be Fair

Dana, from chapter 1, felt she was owed the promotion at work. When it was given to someone else her lament was, "It's not fair." She learned the hard way it is more realistic to hope than to expect that life is fair. Dana would have been a happy camper if she got the final say at work. Unfortunately, she did not get that privilege, and as the twelve-step programs proclaim, she had to learn to "deal with life on life's terms."

People Have to Treat Me with Kindness or Care in the Way I Want

Nathan is married to a woman who often speaks bluntly and has a gruff exterior. Nathan demands that his wife treat him with more kindness. He forgets that he cannot force her to. Nathan had to learn that expecting kindness in a specific way from a spouse who cannot give it that way is foolhardy. Nathan's wife is also a loyal, hardworking partner and parent, and he believes the marriage is worth saving, so he asked his wife to enter marital counseling to work on their relationship.

My Life Has to Be Easy

Many of us forget that is it great to hope for wealth and pleasant experiences but dangerous to expect them. Jerry had always lamented how hard he had to work, laboring at two jobs to make ends meet. Jerry started to look around and saw that almost everyone was confronted with challenges. He saw that few people had it easy. So he changed his thinking to "I would love an easy life, but until I get one I will appreciate the one I have."

My Past Should Have Been Different Than It Was

This is the most common unenforceable rule I see. Yet it is the simplest to challenge. Remember, the past is done. John was a thirty-year-old who still felt his little brother had been treated better than he. The siblings had little contact in the present, but John blamed his current experience on the past being wrong. He was able to challenge his unenforceable rule and say, "I would have liked my parents to treat us equally, but I can learn to deal with it."

My Parents Should Have Treated Me Better

Joanne had many years of grief because she demanded to have been properly loved by her parents. However, too many adults, including Joanne, were not treated well as children. Joanne's parents were likely troubled, immature, lazy, or selfish. While Joanne had a legitimate desire to be cared for, neither as a child nor as an adult did she have the power to make it happen. As she learned to hope for rather than demand a loving mother, she was able to find elder adults willing to mentor and guide her.

As we learn to challenge our unenforceable rules, we take responsibility for how we feel. When we challenge unenforceable rules we take things less personally. We become aware that much of what we took too personally was simply our set of rules that we could not enforce. As we do this, we come to understand that our thought process played a significant role in experiencing anger and hurt. As we challenge our rules, we see in day-to-day life how clear thinking leads to peaceful experience. In addition, like the police officer, we will have more energy available to make good decisions when things do not go our way. Finally, just like our police officer, we discover that we certainly will not miss the excessive hurt and anger. We can throw away the host of tickets we have written and could not serve. We can and will forgive.

CHAPTER 11

Your Positive Intention

Forgiveness is the key to action and freedom.
HANNAH ARENDT

As we practice the techniques in chapters 9 and 10, we gain control over the way we think and feel. We reflect upon the beauty in nature and our good fortune, and we find that hurts and grievances have less power to disturb us. When we calm down in situations where we used to become upset and angry, we notice increased self-confidence. Practicing PERT in difficult moments helps us feel better and think more clearly. When we understand that our desires and hopes are sometimes manifested as unenforceable rules, we realize that we have the ability to change the present. Through the practice of these techniques the first two steps of forgiveness emerge. We assume greater responsibility for how we feel, and we take the hurtful actions of others less personally.

A HERO'S STORY

As you work with these techniques the third component of the grievance, the story, also begins to change. Your story gradually shifts from attention on the hurt to your emerging power and self-confidence. Through the practice of channel changing, PERT, and the challenge of your unenforceable rules, you gain control over your thoughts, feelings, and actions. As this occurs your story changes from the tale of a victim to the story of a hero. Amending the grievance story is a powerful experience and is the true signal that forgiveness has taken hold.

A victim is one who often feels helpless to respond to painful circumstances or to control thoughts and feelings. A hero has worked hard to overcome adversity and refuses to be beaten by difficult life events. Forgiveness is the journey of moving from telling the story as a victim to telling the story as a hero. Forgiveness means that your story changes so that you and not the grievance are in control.

It is unfortunate but true that no one can alter all the distressing things that have happened. You may not be able to get better parents or undo the damage done by a hit-and-run driver. You may not be able to make your spouse love you again or your children care for you. You may not be able to succeed in school or get the job promotion you wanted. You may never regain perfect health or write the great American novel. However, there is no situation where you cannot change the way you talk about what happened. You can always find a more hopeful and positive slant.

Our story is the vehicle through which we communicate to others and ourselves a piece of our life. Our story is how we put events into perspective and assign meaning to what happened. Stories offer a range of responses to hurt that go from presenting events as a challenge to presenting them as an unmitigated disaster. As we tell our story, too often we forget we are offering a perspective as well as reciting the facts. We forget that the perspective and meaning we create from hurtful situations determine the effect these events will have on our life.

Dana, introduced in chapter 1, who was upset because she was passed over for a job promotion, responded to this slight by telling all her friends her grievance story, and she told it from a number of unintended perspectives. Dana said that life is unfair, that she never gets a break, and that it is too difficult for her either to change jobs or work harder to get a promotion. Dana did not understand that putting forth these perspectives was disabling. Her oft-told tale of woe made it extremely difficult for her to take any positive steps in her life.

If Dana's story line is true and her life is unfair, why should she try at all to make it better? Why make an effort if it will go without reward? With hope, one expects good things to happen at least occasionally. Without hope, Dana feels listless and depressed. And if Dana continues to feel that it is too difficult to work for another promotion or to look for a new job, then she is guaranteeing her fate in her current job.

I felt sad when I saw that Dana did not realize the effect her story had on her mood and behavior. If asked, Dana would tell me that she was just giving an objective reporting of the facts, and the facts were clear: she was wronged. She did not see how she crafted her story to present a certain interpretation. She did not understand the power of her tale and how it influenced her feelings and actions. She was fully into playing the blame game and suffered the inevitable yet unintended consequences.

Then Dana attended one of my class series. Although her failed promotion effort had occurred almost eighteen months earlier, her saga of the unfair bosses was so fresh that you would have thought the misfortune occurred within the last month. To Dana's credit, she decided that as long as she had paid for the forgiveness class she would give the techniques a try. She practiced PERT and studiously challenged her unenforceable rules.

She reported that these practices did not make her resentment completely go away. She felt less anger, but she noticed that she still felt upset with her bosses. However, to Dana's surprise, she reported two changes she had not anticipated. The first was the growing sense of power she felt through the practice of challenging her unenforceable rules. She recognized that if she did not have power over her bosses, she at least could have power over her thoughts. She soon realized the confidence that comes from practice and was delighted with her new sense of power.

She also noticed that her grievance story was changing. What she found was that for the first time she was tired of telling the same old story. This was because the forgiveness practices were changing how she saw the situation. Dana reported that she understood that telling her grievance story gave her bosses unlimited power to hurt her. Now that she understood how her grievance was formed and had techniques to practice, she no longer felt helpless, and as a result she had to change her story. Her story now included the desire to practice and gain control of her thinking. Dana found that through the telling of a new kind of story she felt energetic and saw a variety of choices in how to respond.

Dana is far from an isolated case. The success she feels is common. Practice allows you to help yourself, sometimes in unexpected ways.

One of the benefits people find from practicing the techniques in chapters 9 and 10 is the change they see in their grievance story.

Before I go further I want to emphasize one point. Simply by practicing new ways of thinking, you are breaking the vicious cycle and taking a brave step in the forgiveness process. Through practice, we make the effort to feel better and heal ourselves. We are saying that life may have been difficult, but it is not going to crush us. As we practice, our story changes to reflect our effort, increased self-confidence, and the evolving perspective peace and clear thinking provide. Practicing forgiveness techniques is a bold statement of belief in ourselves.

As I mentioned in the last chapter, the techniques I offer work. The scientific results prove that my method helps people to learn how to forgive for the good of their emotional and physical health. Many have used these techniques and forgiven those who have hurt them. There are countless stories that attest to the power of these practices. Chapters 9 and 10 have helped to prepare for our next challenge. That is working to change our grievance story.

Let's look at Sarah. Sarah is the woman we met in the introduction and chapter 5 whose husband, Jim, became a substance abuser and left her with a baby and a host of unpaid bills. Sarah talked endlessly about her ex-husband and his problems with substance abuse. She gave too much attention to her problems and not enough to what she was going to do about them. Listening to her, one would have thought that her ex-husband, Jim, was eight feet tall and that she was about four-feet-six. Her grievance story was strangling her.

I often ask people to consider who is the central character in their grievance story. When I asked this question Sarah perked up. She responded that Jim was the main character in her story. Jim's problems and the damage they caused were at the heart of how she talked about her life. Even though their relationship was brief, Sarah loved Jim and depended on him. She loved the thought of being married and of being part of a couple. I responded that this might make sense if Jim were a good husband. However, by now Jim was halfway across the United States, and she had a child to raise alone. How did making Jim her central character help her heal and get on with her life?

Sarah did not like that question. Agreeing with me meant that she would have to acknowledge the end of her dream. She would have to admit that Jim was gone, that he was never coming back, and that he was a bad choice for a mate. She would have to admit that her decision to marry Jim was a hasty one and that her parents and friends were right. As long as Jim was at the center of her story, he was a part of her life. If Sarah put herself at the center of her story, then she might have to grieve her loss and move on. Sarah found this a scary thought.

Sarah's confusion is one with which many people struggle. Sarah resisted changing her story in part because it would acknowledge her tremendous loss. Sarah's grievance story was as much the expression of a dream as a statement of fact. Sarah was making a common mistake. In her unwillingness to admit the end of her relationship with Jim, she forgot there were many other fish in the sea. By resisting mourning her marriage, Sarah made it difficult to have a successful relationship with someone else.

Sarah confused her small dream with her big dream. Her small dream was to create a successful relationship with Jim. Her big dream was to create a successful relationship. Sarah forgot that failing at one did not mean she would fail at the other. Her relationship with Jim ended, but that did not mean the end of all relationships. It did not mean she was a failure. Her big and small dreams were not one and the same, even though Sarah thought they were. I reminded Sarah of this distinction, and for the first time in a long while she smiled. For a moment she understood that Jim was not the only chance she had for a good relationship. As Sarah smiled I told her that she felt good because she was now connected to her **positive intention.**

POSITIVE INTENTION

Positive intention is a central concept in my forgiveness process, and I will teach you to find your positive intention. Positive intention is an unparalleled way to reconnect with your big dreams. Positive intention also helps us to resist depression when a small dream is stifled. It reminds us of our deepest hopes and allows us to mourn our losses.

I have a hypothesis that one of the things we find most difficult about hurts is how we lose sight of our positive intention. When some-

one is hurt they focus their attention on their pain. They create grievance stories and tell them to others. By doing this, we lose sight of the
big picture and of the goals we have for our life. I see time and again
that when hurt people reconnect with their noblest goals they gain an
immediate burst of power. Finding your positive intention reconnects
you with your goals. The sad truth is, your grievances separated you from
your most positive goals through your excessive focus on what went
wrong.

Connecting to your positive intention is the quickest and most
direct way to change your grievance story. As soon as Sarah changed her
story to reflect her positive intention, her forgiveness accelerated. Her
mood improved, and her energy returned. Instead of focusing on the
past, it now reflected her desire for a loving relationship with Jim. She
talked about Jim as an obstacle to her goal, not as the goal itself. As
Sarah changed her story to reflect her positive intention, her grievance
lost much of its power. Sarah did not stop feeling sad and hurt immediately, but the change in her story altered the way she thought and
reacted to her situation.

In the rest of this chapter I will demonstrate how to find your positive intention and skillfully use it to change a grievance story. You
will find this process both helpful and healing. Our positive intention
reminds us of the life goals that dwelling on painful experience has
shifted aside.

The biggest drawback to telling grievance stories is they keep us
connected in a powerless way with people who have hurt us. When we
mull over our past wounds and hurts, we remind ourselves of a part of
our life that did not work. Reconnecting with our positive intention
reminds us of our goals and enables us to move forward.

Positive intention can be defined as the strongest positive motivation we had for being in the grievance situation in the first place. In
chapter 1 I said that all grievances start with a situation that did not
work out. We had an experience where either we did not get what we
wanted or we got something we did not want. In either case, we wanted
something for our well-being. Our positive intention is remembering
what that something was and expressing it in the most beneficial terms
we can find.

Sarah wanted a loving relationship with her spouse. Her positive intention was to create a loving partnership. A positive intention refers to the broader success—in this case for a loving relationship—rather than the specific instance of that success. She tried her utmost to make her positive intention happen with Jim, but she could not succeed. Yet her goal was not limited to a marriage with Jim; her lack of success in relationship with Jim did not mean that her goal was not worthy. Unfortunately, not all love relationships work out. Does that mean we all give up on love?

The fact that a relationship did not work does not have to keep Sarah from her goal of developing a good relationship. To develop a good relationship, Sarah may have to enter counseling, read books on relationships, or talk to people who have been successful. She may have to ask friends and lovers to give her honest feedback or critique new partners she brings home. There are many ways to make her next relationship better, and they can happen most easily when she is connected to her positive intention. When we are connected to our positive intention, our story reflects our goal and what we have to do to obtain that goal.

In any grievance story, someone does not get what he or she wants. Unacknowledged is that behind each painful situation is a positive intention. Once found and reclaimed, the positive intention alters the grievance story. The story is no longer just about the person and or situation that caused pain but about the goal that was not quite reached. Suddenly, instead of just recycling pain, the grievance story becomes a vehicle for learning how to change to attain that goal. The grievance story becomes a part of the positive intention story.

The person or event that hurt us is important insofar as we can learn from the situation. In no way, though, do we allow our grievance to distract us from our goal. If we continue to pursue our goal, we exact the greatest revenge on someone who has hurt us. We move on. We find peace.

YOUR POSITIVE INTENTION: KEEPING YOU ON THE ROAD

I like to use the following image to help people understand positive intention. Imagine that your positive intentions are long and winding roads that take you from the beginning of your life to the end. Many of us have positive intentions such as a loving family, a long-term and loving partnership, intimacy, supportive friends, meaningful work, good health, creating beauty, or personal growth. Each of these goals will be more or less important at different times of our life. For example, family may take up most of your time when you are in your thirties. At that time you may have less energy for your personal growth. At other times of your life circumstances may force you to change the way you approach your goals, such as when you become ill, your partner dies, or you retire.

If you imagine each positive intention as a road, then the next step is to see yourself driving on that road toward your goals. When you are young you may be riding a bicycle on the road and then as you age you may drive progressively more expensive cars. Now, say you are forty-five and your teenage son leaves home under a cloud. Or, say you are forty-five and your wife leaves you for another man. Or, say you are forty-five and your business fails and you were cheated. Your positive intention of a loving family or business success has taken a hit. For the sake of this exercise picture your loss as a tire blowout on the road of intimacy. I know when this happens many of us would more readily picture this as a head-on collision, but remember we can recover from the loss of a spouse, business, or relationship with a child.

In this image you find yourself on the side of the highway trying to change a flat tire. Remember, it is common for obstacles to emerge. Maybe no one has ever taught you how to change a tire and you stand there confused and scared. Alternatively, you let your spare tire get flat and you are struggling to use an underinflated tire. You are then trying to figure out when the next highway patrol officer will come by. Throughout this experience you are likely muttering under your breath that you do not have time for this, that you are late for an important meeting.

This metaphorical flat tire can derail us on the road to intimacy. Often we do not know how to fix the hole in our heart. Many of us will not have prepared for the possibility of deep loss. Many people let their friendships wither and their resilience remain dormant. Some will craft a story to tell everyone in their life how terrible it was to be stuck. Many will stay stuck on the side of the road complaining about how unfair this is. Too many will get used to a grievance story and forget there are other ways to describe what happened.

Now, shift your visualization to remember that life often forces us to modify our plans. Visualize reminding yourself you always have the choice of how long you take to get back on the road. No one really wants to be one of those people who stay on the side of the road for years afraid to trust their car again. We can always ask ourselves, "What happens if I get another flat tire?" Dangers do lurk and we are never certain of safety. Nevertheless, life always goes on.

Observe in the visualization that you make peace with the truth that life always goes on. Picture yourself fixing the tire, patting yourself on the back for taking care of yourself, and without impatience starting out again. Picture yourself connecting to your positive intention. Your positive intention is the time it takes you to fix your tire, make peace with the disruption, and to the best of your ability move forward again on the road. Picture yourself checking your spare from time to time and doing your best to remain safe.

As we connect to our positive intention we begin to find forgiveness. Forgiveness is the peace we feel as we cease resentment toward our car. Forgiveness is the peace that comes from understanding we are responsible for whether or not we feel okay. Forgiveness is the compassion we experience as we remind ourselves that by driving a car we run the risk of a breakdown. Forgiveness is the power we get as we assert that we have a deep well of resilience to draw upon. Forgiveness is the grace that helps us remember, while on the side of the road, we can look around and appreciate our beautiful surroundings.

Forgiveness is the positive feeling we have as we review the myriad of times our car ran perfectly. Forgiveness offers us peace as we remember the problem could have been worse. Forgiveness is the power we feel as we create a hero's story where we overcome difficulties. In our hero's story we talk about how well we coped and how little need we had to blame. In that story we remind others and ourselves that we are a survivor.

To do this we tell the story from the point of view of our positive intention, not from the grievance. The positive intention may come in the form of the auto club that comes to fix the tire. The positive intention may be our willingness to walk and get help. The positive intention is that part of each of us that works hard to get our car up and running and watches out that we do not go over any potholes as we drive away.

FINDING YOUR POSITIVE INTENTION

To find your positive intention, ask the following question: In general terms, how would I describe the good effect on my life if my grievance situation had worked out perfectly? Other ways of asking this are, What was my reason for being in this situation in the first place? What was my long-term dream? What was my goal, expressed in the most positive terms? Follow these easy steps:

1. Find a quiet place where you can be undisturbed for about ten minutes.
2. Practice PERT once or twice to get yourself into a relaxed frame of mind.
3. Ask yourself, What was my reason for being in the grievance situation in the first place? What was my goal, expressed in positive terms?
4. Think about your response until you have a one- or two-sentence positive intention.
5. Promise yourself you will not tell the grievance story any longer.
6. Practice telling the positive intention story to a handful of trusted people.

Jill complained to almost anyone who would listen. She was still incensed about her ex-husband, Stan, because he had run away with one of her closest friends. At the drop of a hat she would grimace and tell nasty stories about Stan and her friend Debbie. She spent so much time on images of them together or planning revenge that she literally ached all of the time. One day while she was in midstory, I asked, "Why do you care so much about what they are doing?" When she started to repeat the same old story, I replied, "If you put so much energy into him and his life with Debbie, how will you have any energy left to develop your own loving relationship?"

Jill had a difficult time learning to find a positive intention. She was so devastated by the loss of a husband and a friend that she had lost faith in relationships. She did not want to think about another relationship and found both men and women to be a threat. I asked her if she had ever had a relationship end poorly before. She said yes, and I asked if she was able to trust again. Jill said she was and that she still hoped for a good relationship with a man. She responded in the same way about her friends.

Jill was in a lot of pain. Her loss was serious and getting over it was no easy task. Finding her positive intention was a crucial part of her healing. Jill's task was to develop enough trust to risk a loving relationship with a new man and new friends.

I asked her to tell her grievance story from the point of view of her positive intention. She would start the story from the beginning, which was her intention to create a loving partnership, and talk about the relationships that did not work out as things to learn from if she wanted to get her positive intention met. I asked her to consciously use *I* at the beginning of each sentence and to remind herself that her story should center on her and what she wanted and not on her ex.

Jill's positive intention led her to talk about her lifelong desire to develop strong and supportive relationships. She highlighted her best friend from childhood with whom she was still close. She mentioned the numerous supportive and warm relationships she had with the people with whom she worked. Jill brought up two love affairs from her past she had ended and how that had hurt them. She talked with understanding that some relationships work out while others do not. The loss of her marriage and friendship caused Jill to think long and hard about her expectations of people. She saw that while her goal of relationship was true for her, it was also clear that the desire for relationship and the guarantee that a certain one will endure is different. Her story turned into a story of trust and how that is a struggle for her. Ultimately her positive intention story turned from Stan and Debbie and squarely onto Jill. And that is where her story belongs and that is how she cleared the space for forgiveness.

FINDING POSITIVE INTENTION IN SITUATIONS OF DEVASTATING LOSS

I have used positive intention with people who have suffered extreme tragedies such as the men and women from Northern Ireland. Their positive intention was to have a loving family. Losing a family member is an enormous and devastating loss. It shakes the survivors' sense of safety and destroys family cohesiveness. However, even an event like this does not have to permanently detour one's positive intention. Whatever the hurt may be, in order to heal, we must answer a central question: How do I tell a story that helps me move on from the past and meet my goals?

If your positive intention was to create a loving family and a family member dies or is murdered, the family story does not end. Many times life forces us to change direction and figure out how to adapt as best we can. In a terrible situation such as this, we can take our love and give it to our remaining family members. Another possibility is to do work that serves as a memorial to the person who was murdered. The positive intention story starts with the desire for a loving family. It covers the pain and tragedy; it does not deny pain and suffering. The positive intention story does not imagine a world filled only with beauty and goodness; it does put the hurt into a perspective that promotes healing.

With a devastating loss, the positive intention story reflects the struggle of integrating the loss with your long-term goal. Your story focuses on how best to manifest your positive intention within the limitations that life imposes. Your grievance is taken off center stage and moved to the side, where it belongs.

One of the things I enjoy about my work is how many people are surprised at what they find when they look for their positive intention. Many were in difficult situations that resolved when they discovered what their true goals were. In one instance a man was struggling with his mother-in-law. In another situation a woman was struggling with a difficult boss. In each of these examples discovering the positive intention was crucial to forgiveness.

Over the course of his marriage, Andy had a difficult relationship with his in-laws. To his way of thinking his mother-in-law was always nasty to him. She was cold and critical with Andy yet greeted the rest of his family with warmth and affection. Andy remembers a time when he was ill and his mother-in-law was indifferent to his suffering. She had strict standards for cleanliness in her home, and Andy was not the neatest of people. She would yell at him and accuse him of deliberately messing up her home. Andy and his wife fought every time they visited her parents, and by the time he came to my class, Andy was sick of the situation.

When Andy looked for his positive intention, he was surprised to see that he could find no tangible goals regarding his mother-in-law. Of course he wanted her to mellow out and treat him better, but if he was honest with himself she was unimportant to him. The only reason he visited her was to support his wife and help her stay in touch with her family. His positive intention, therefore, was to be kind and considerate toward his wife.

Andy realized each time he reacted with anger toward his mother-in-law that he was hurting his wife. He dearly loved his wife and valued their marriage and her feelings. If his behavior caused his wife to suffer, Andy understood he was not living his positive intention. Each time he told a grievance story about his mother-in-law, he was giving power to a woman who was relatively unimportant to him. Realizing this, he changed his story to reflect his desire to remain kind to his wife. As he told his positive intention story, the power his mother-in-law had over him diminished. Needless to say, his relationship with his wife improved, their visits to her parents became much less stressful, and Andy's reactions to his mother-in-law mellowed.

Sharon was a nurse at a local hospital. She worked long hours and had a difficult commute. She was a single parent to two teenage boys and had a lot of stress in her life. She came to see me because she hated her boss. He was new at his job and was engaging in a power struggle with the older nurses for control. Sharon was a veteran nurse who was very proud of her skills and years of service. Sharon resented being treated like a kid and therefore was constantly butting heads with her boss.

When Sharon connected with her positive intention, she found her deepest desire was to help her patients. She had made her boss the central character in a grievance story, and in that story her boss stood between her and her job. Sharon used the PERT practice to reduce her stress and began to tell a positive intention story. In this story she was a hero working hard to help sick people. In her positive intention story there was little time to obsess about a boss undermining her authority. She had patients to care for and was an excellent nurse. Sharon became the hero rather than the victim in her story.

FINDING POSITIVE INTENTION WITH RANDOM ACTS OF VIOLENCE

In some situations finding a positive intention may not be as easy as the examples presented. This does not change the fact that in each situation someone was denied something they wanted. For example, many people have been the victim of random acts of cruelty. Rapes, accidents, robberies, and muggings are sadly a part of life.

Cindy and Joan are examples of people I worked with who were the victims of random acts of violence. Cindy was hurt in a hit-and-run car accident. She was on her way home from work one day when a driver passed too close to her and forced her car off the road. She slammed into the guardrail with a forceful hit. Cindy suffered numerous broken bones and a concussion, and she endured a lengthy recovery. In her situation it was tricky to find Cindy's strongest positive intention related to the accident or the driver of the other car.

Cindy did not have any desire to meet the driver who hit her, and she was not motivated by recovering from a car accident. She did remember that when the accident occurred she had been thinking of her children. She had to reflect a while before she realized that her overwhelming desire to protect and raise her children was her positive intention. Following this discovery, she used the power of her care for her children to motivate her healing. Cindy learned to talk about her passionate struggle to overcome the difficulties of a car accident as a heroic effort to successfully mother her sons.

Joan was a different story. Directly accessing her positive intention was difficult. The question that connected Joan to her positive intention was: How have I been harmed by this experience? When Joan became clear about what she lost she was free to find what she had wanted.

Joan loved walking and often walked to work. On weekends she often took long walks in the hills with her friends. One day a car came out of nowhere and hit her from behind. She was thrown into the air and landed on the side of the road. She woke in the hospital to discover she had three broken ribs and a smashed pelvis. She had a long recovery and walked with a limp for years.

I saw Joan about nine months after the accident. She struggled with her loss of mobility and independence. She missed walking tremendously and was quite resentful about her loss. When describing her positive intention, she at first thought that her goal was to walk freely again. That was excellent motivation, but I worried that this goal might take her a long time to obtain and lead to frustration. Therefore, I asked her what was the worst thing the accident took from her. She immediately replied, "My independence. I cannot do what I want to do without help."

I suggested that she tell her story as a struggle for independence. She was to describe herself as the hero in a struggle to take care of herself. Her positive intention was to become independent again as this was what was taken from her. In her story Joan achieved small successes all of the time. She made many small steps to independence. Ultimately her goal was to resume walking. Walking symbolized independence and connecting with her desire for independence helped Joan develop a compelling positive intention story.

In the instances where you or someone you love is the victim of random acts that cause injury, often independence, safety, or physical health has been compromised. One of these can serve as the positive intention. Again, the goal is to tell a story in a way that the grievance becomes part of a larger picture. The healing story thus does not focus on the offender or what has been lost but on the positive intention to regain health, safety, or independence.

PERSONAL GROWTH AS A POSITIVE INTENTION

The final goal of this chapter is to provide you a choice in how you can find your positive intention. I already showed you how to create your positive intention and gave examples of the strongest approach. I defined positive intention as a focus on the big goal that the grievance thwarted.

I have found that some people choose desire for personal growth as their positive intention. They talk about the need to learn from difficulty and become stronger people. Personal growth, therefore, is an alternative positive intention that has proven useful to many people.

Personal growth is a helpful goal for dealing with grievances when you have a hard time finding your positive intention for the situation. Moreover, personal growth works well as a positive intention when you have a grievance that causes so much hurt or anger that you cannot see any good that could come of it.

Personal growth worked with a woman whose business partner cheated her out of money. Natalie lost eighty thousand dollars and was in no mood to think about her positive intention. So I asked her to focus instead on her hope to grow as a human being who can cope with adversity. She agreed to give that a try and came up with the following: "I want to become a stronger person." In this way personal growth became Natalie's goal, and her business partner's actions were only catalysts to that goal. As Natalie started to affirm her positive intention, she returned to graduate school, a process that was impossible when she was dwelling on the misdeeds of her partner.

Each of us interprets personal growth differently. Alex wanted to prove to his parents that he was not a loser. Therefore, his goal was to show his parents that he would not complain over a business failure. Others, such as Julie, wish to develop greater emotional competence. She wanted to be able to deal with rejection without eating a pint of ice cream each evening. Still others wish simply to suffer less and are willing to change to meet that goal. Sally could think of no greater ambition than not hurting so damn much, and her story reflected her desire to feel better.

There is no one perfect way to construct a positive intention. I have provided guidelines that I know will work. What is critical is how you change your story to center on a larger goal and not on the grievance. You do this by reminding yourself that your small goals are not the same as your big goals. You take the hurt off center stage in your life and put your healing there instead. When you start to tell yourself and other people your positive intention story, you facilitate healing that you may not have thought possible.

FORGIVENESS EMERGING

When we talk about our positive intention, take responsibility for our feelings, and take the hurt less personally, what we find is the emergence of forgiveness. Joan found her will to recover her health and independence, and she discovered that the person who hit her was unimportant to that end. She forgave him but did not condone his actions. She forgave him but still jumped every time a car came too close. She forgave him but got angry every time her children did not buckle their seat belts. She took control of her feelings and her life. She ended her grievance.

You will discover as you tell your positive intention story that you feel better. One reason is that you are closer to telling a balanced story. This is because each of us has many experiences. Negative ones are not more important than positive ones. A grievance freezes a hurtful experience into an unchangeable solid. Then it rents too much space in our mind and leads to feelings of helplessness. The truth is that wounds hurt, but they do not have to be crippling.

Each of us can forgive those who have hurt us. When we put our grievances into the perspective of challenges to our goals, we are giving an accurate account. Everything that hurts us is a challenge to our happiness. It is a challenge to be happy in this world. Wounds can cripple the happiness only of those who do not know how to cope and forgive. Finding our positive intention helps us connect with the big picture. Telling a positive intention story reminds everyone who hears us that we are a hero and not a victim. We deserve the best, and forgiveness helps us find it.

CHAPTER 12

The HEAL Method

He that cannot forgive others breaks the bridge over which he must pass himself, for every man has need to be forgiven.

LORD HERBERT

In the previous three chapters I guided you through my basic forgiveness techniques for learning how to forgive. We have seen how forgiveness eases emotional distress, allows people to think more clearly, and helps end the vicious cycle of a grievance story. We have learned about the three parts of a grievance and the corresponding components of forgiveness. I related stories of people who have used my methods to forgive a host of difficulties and hurts. I have seen my forgiveness process work time and time again to help people hurt less. And I have used these methods in my own life.

My first two research projects did not include the concept of positive intention, and yet these projects were highly successful. Knowing I was going to work with the people from Northern Ireland compelled me to make sure my methods were as strong as possible. Toward that end, I expanded on the idea of positive intention and created the HEAL method. It acts as a simple mnemonic device to help participants grasp the essentials of forgiveness. Integrating all that has been covered in the previous chapters, the HEAL method provides a simple and quick response to any hurtful experience.

The HEAL method will be covered in the next two chapters. Please read both chapters before you begin to practice. I want to remind you again that you can forgive those who have hurt you without using this method. You have the forgiveness tools, and they are proven to work.

The HEAL method is designed as a kind of advanced practice of Heart Focus, challenging unenforceable rules, and PERT.

HEAL is designed for people who have already learned the basics of Forgive for Good and have practiced the forgiveness tools. The HEAL method is not simply an add-on; it is a powerful way to reinforce and practice forgiveness.

The HEAL method can be practiced in two different ways. It can be used in both a long and short practice, and I have seen terrific results from both. The HEAL method is the strongest technique I know for healing situations where the experience of hurt goes particularly deep. This is why the longer form of HEAL is so valuable.

In certain cases people report the hurt is so profound and so present that it feels like a part of them. The grievance becomes as real as anything else in their life. Often these people have experienced unkindnesses that anyone would find difficult to bear. I will use a couple of stories as examples.

Charlie's mother abandoned him at birth. Charlie grew up in foster families, and it was not until he was nine that he had a stable home. At that time he was adopted by a family that raised him until he went away to college. He graduated from college and later married and had two children. However, Charlie spent much of his life feeling alienated and rejected, and his marriage and family suffered. Charlie blamed his mother for all of his difficulties. He blamed his mother for his inability to make friends and create a successful marriage. He blamed his mother for his employment difficulties and his general malaise.

Charlie referred to himself as a person abandoned at birth who never got over it. He talked about his mother with anger and hurt. He was adamant that his adult unhappiness was caused by his abandonment by his mother almost fifty years earlier. When I listened to Charlie I wondered where the family who took him in and raised him fit into his story. I also wondered where the attempts his wife and children made to love him were acknowledged. Chiefly, I wondered about the practicality of giving a woman he had never met so much power to hurt him. Charlie was a man who had practiced his story of abandonment so many times that any other approach to his life appeared impossible.

Charlie went through my class series and did not appear to get much out of it. He asked a couple of questions and clearly struggled with his unenforceable rules. He appeared to be saying, "Of course a mother should not abandon her child. Do not try to convince me otherwise. Of course my life is ruined when my mother did not even love me." It was only when we got to guided practice of the HEAL method that I could see any change in Charlie's demeanor. In this and the next chapter I will show how Charlie was able to move on and how HEAL helped facilitate his change.

Elana is a good example of someone for whom the HEAL method was instrumental in bringing peace to her life. Elana was a woman in her midsixties who had endured a long and difficult marriage with a workaholic husband. Her husband, Jesse, had a successful business career and spent little time at home. When home, he was usually working or tired and had almost no energy for Elana. Jesse promised that when he retired things would be different and that the two of them would finally do things together.

Jesse retired when he was sixty-five and for the first year of his retirement was miserable. He missed his work, developed few friends, and was lost without an office to go to. He spent most of that first year depressed and irritable. After a year or so his mood improved, and he and Elana became closer than at any other time in their marriage. She was anticipating more of the same when Jesse came home one day from playing golf and said he felt sick and dizzy.

When his symptoms did not improve Elana drove him to the hospital, only to find out he had had a stroke. While in the hospital he had another. While not crippled by the strokes, Jesse has been deeply affected by them. He lost some of his memory, and his speech has been impaired. He also became moody and easily fatigued. Daily Elana confronts reminders of Jesse's illness.

To Elana the time they spent happy together seems a fleeting memory. It was too little too late. She was just getting used to having a husband when he was taken from her again. Elana came to my forgiveness class because a year later she was still mad at her husband for waiting so long to join his life with hers. She felt cheated out of their time together and frustrated by her years of waiting. She too was helped by her practice of the HEAL method.

Both Charlie and Elana had to deal with an intense experience. Abandonment at birth and the disability of a long-absent spouse are painful at best. However, for each person, complaining about the past and feeling like a victim only made their lives more difficult. Each found greater peace, as they were able to forgive.

In addition to helping people forgive difficult, embedded, hurtful experiences, the HEAL method works in another important way. It represents an advanced form of PERT, the best quick balm to feelings when you are faced with a reminder of a past hurt. I recommend that people practice PERT for a while and then move on to the HEAL method. The difference is that the HEAL method is designed to work with a specific hurtful experience, while PERT is for general emotional soothing and refocusing.

The HEAL practice focuses attention in your heart to transform hurt feelings at the moment you feel emotionally upset. To get the most out of the HEAL method, you need to have practiced the Heart Focus and PERT techniques taught in chapter 9. When you feel comfortable with those, you are ready to learn the HEAL method.

When first practicing the HEAL method it is beneficial to set aside about fifteen minutes. It is also useful to have privacy and some quiet. After practicing on a specific grievance, you can use the HEAL method in the same way you do PERT—quickly and immediately.

I designed HEAL so that each letter corresponds to a specific aspect of my teaching. Each letter is an integral part of the process and must be practiced. Each letter will be described separately for teaching purposes but when we practice the HEAL method the steps are to be combined. The letters of the HEAL method stand for *Hope*, *Educate*, *Affirm*, and *Long-Term*. Please practice each element in exactly that order.

H IS FOR HOPE

The H in HEAL stands for *Hope*. The first component of HEAL is to make a strong *Hope* statement. The *Hope* statement represents the specific positive outcome that you desired in the hurtful situation. In the previous chapter, I described this as the small goal and showed you how to keep it separate from your large goal, or positive intention. The small goal is related to one specific hurtful experience. The small goal is to be expressed as a wish, preference, or hope. The *Hope* statement is a desire for a specific outcome in a specific situation.

For Sharon, consumed by a love affair that went bad, learning to say to herself, "I wanted my relationship with Keith to last," helped keep her goal in focus. Before this practice Sharon was in a lot of pain. She was not thinking of what she wanted. She was obsessed with what she had lost. In fact, she was remembering at all times what she did *not* want: the end of her relationship with Keith. The *H* in HEAL helped her remember what she would have liked to happen.

I chose the word *hope* deliberately. In chapter 10 we saw how people often confuse what they hope will happen with what has to happen. This confusion results in the creation of unenforceable rules. These are at the root of our suffering and lay the groundwork for grievances to form. When we create a *Hope* statement we are reminding ourselves that we wished or hoped for something to go our way. We hoped to be loved, to make money, to get a job or promotion, to have caring parents, to be safe, to be healthy, to have a faithful spouse or lover, or to have people treat us with respect or honesty.

Making *Hope* statements is a way to remind ourselves of the goal that lies just under the hurt. Telling ourselves that all we can ever do is hope things go our way is a good reminder of life's uncertainty. Asserting our hopes is a statement of pride and power when we understand that all our hopes do not manifest. Pride and power result from accepting the vulnerability in hoping for things. We couple our vulnerability with an assertion that we will not be stopped from strongly hoping for good things to happen. With this approach we make every reasonable effort to get our hopes realized.

The *Hope* statement must be worded in positive terms. This is critical to the practice of the HEAL method. The *H* focuses on what you wanted to happen in this situation instead of what you did not want to occur. Many people find this difficult; often they say they wanted bad things not to happen to them. They have a hard time remembering they once wanted something good.

Remember, it is not the same to say "I wanted my husband not to cheat on me" as "I wanted a strong and lasting marriage." The first response is worded in the negative, the second in the positive. For example, Sharon used to say, "I hoped Keith would not leave me." However, that was not her real hope. Her positive hope was for a stable, loving relationship with Keith. Sometimes finding your *Hope* statement can take effort. Yet numerous testimonials have proven to me that it is well worth the time.

Sarah was a woman who had a hard time making positive *Hope* statements. Her refrain was she wished Jim had not taken drugs. She wished that he had not gone away and left her alone with her child. She wished her marriage had not broken up. These *H* statements, while true, did not address Sarah's real goal. Her positive hope was to establish and maintain a successful marriage with Jim. It took some effort on her part, but Sarah finally arrived at the realization that her specific goal in this situation was, "I wanted a happy marriage with Jim."

I want to belabor the obvious. Not all of our small goals will be the best goals. Sarah could have made a better choice of husband. They had a very short courtship, and she had been cautioned by her family and friends not to get involved with Jim. In addition, Jim had a history of alcohol problems. These things do not affect the *Hope* statement. When you are crafting a good *H* statement you take the goal you had at face value. Later in this process you can examine whether the specific small goal was optimal for meeting your positive intention.

The second condition for a successful HOPE statement is that we make it personal. We are making an *H* statement for us and no one else. To do this we make an assertive statement of our goal not just that something good happen. In an *H* statement we are not just wishing for happiness but that a personal goal be met. We are not just wishing for love, but love in a particular relationship. We are not wishing for world peace but that we experience peace. To this end the *Hope* statement usually begins with the word *I* and focuses on our personal goal. In this way it is different from your positive intention, your large goal.

Charlie, who had spent his life lamenting his abandonment by his mother, at first could not imagine connecting with his positive goal. He wished for a loving parent, but he was afraid that putting his wish into words would be an act of futility. It is true that he would get nowhere if he wanted his mother to miraculously emerge from the grave and love him. However, the act of acknowledging his wish while at the same time making peace with not getting that wish had the potential to be healing for Charlie. His *H* statement turned out to be: "I hoped for a mother who treated me with love."

The final condition for crafting a good *Hope* statement is to make it *specific*. This means that your *Hope* statement not only is phrased in positive terms and reflects a personal goal but also reflects your specific hope. For example, a good *Hope* statement is not "I prefer that my work be pleasant" or "I wanted to be in business with a partner who would not steal." A useful *Hope* statement is "I hoped Sidney would be an honest and reliable business partner."

When one is upset over an act of infidelity that ruined a marriage, the *Hope* statement concerns that specific relationship, not relationships in general. When you are distressed by the uncaring attitude of a friend, you refer to the specific quality you wanted your friend to develop. When you are upset because your children did not call when they promised, your *Hope* statement refers specifically to what you wanted from your children. Again, this is a reminder to craft your *Hope* statement around your small, specific goal rather than your larger positive intention.

The *Hope* in HEAL is never your desire to change another person's character. Needing to change someone else is the principal ingredient in an unenforceable rule. Remember, trying to change the unchangeable is at the root of the grievance process. Changing another person's personality traits is a waste of time even though many of us spend years in this useless process. When our attempts to change others do not bear fruit, we feel angry and resentful.

The upset we feel when others do not change in the way we want them to is what forgiveness resolves. Forgiveness helps us stop wasting our time trying to change people who do not want to change. Forgiveness allows us to regain control of our lives as we try less to control the lives of others. Forgiveness allows us to manage the effect of other people's hurtful actions in our lives.

Not only is it futile to create an *H* statement that is about changing how someone acts, it is also fruitless to craft an *H* statement about another person's character. This is because we can never forgive something as vague as a person's traits, temperament, or personality. At best, we can forgive specific behavior that we hypothesize reveals the person's character. This is an important distinction, and one that can save us a lot of pain. We can see behavior, but we can only guess at character. Criticizing someone's character is not the best way to spend our limited resources of energy and time. To forgive, we need to focus on the behaviors, such as harsh speech and unkind action, that were at variance with what we wanted.

I suggested to Dana that an appropriate hope did not include her boss becoming a more compassionate person. She had no idea what kind of human being her boss really was. All Dana knew was that she did not get a promotion she felt she deserved. Charlie too would not be able to get a mother who was a better person. Charlie had no idea what kind of person his mother was apart from his outrage that she abandoned him. That is really all he knew of his mother and this limited information dominated his life for years.

Remember, to become ready to forgive someone you have to know exactly what the action was that offended you and how it affected your feelings. In chapter 6 we learned these were two of the preconditions for forgiveness. To say you hoped your husband was nicer to you does not provide detail about the hoped-for behavior. To say that you hoped your husband would speak to you with tenderness is closer to what you wanted.

I want to leave you with a gentle reminder. There is no perfect *Hope* statement. *H* statements work, but there is wiggle room when you create them. Your task is to think of exactly what you wanted in a situation that hurt. You are to phrase it in positive terms, make it personal, and be as specific as you can. Limit the vague generalizations about someone's character, and above all be patient with yourself as you learn how to do this. Remember, you are learning to forgive, find peace, and heal.

E IS FOR EDUCATE

The *E* in HEAL stands for *Educate*. In a nutshell, *E* reminds you about the way things work: there are limits to your control over other people, yourself, or life events. We *Educate* ourselves about the way the world really operates. *Educate* means that each specific hope you have exists with the awareness that you may not get what you want. *Educate* also means you are aware that every hope you have has several possible outcomes: it may turn out better, worse, or exactly how you anticipated. You do not know in any specific situation whether or not you will get what you want. Therefore, you hope, do your best, and await the results.

We make our difficulties worse when we forget that all we could ever do was hope or wish for the results we wanted. We create grievances when we forget we have limited control to make our wishes come true. Limited control is a reality for every one of us, and it can be difficult for humans to accept. We create unenforceable rules when we insist that what we want to happen must happen. To educate yourself is to understand, as the Rolling Stones used to say, "You can't always get what you want."

For example, we might need to forgive love relationships that went sour. Or we have failed marriages and love affairs that ended with infidelity and anger. Life doesn't always go the way we planned. Unfortunately, relationships that end poorly are a fact of life and a common experience.

In the *Educate* statement we both acknowledge the possibility of not getting what we want and fully accept that reality. For Sharon, an appropriate *E* statement must reflect the inherent instability in relationships. Her *E* statement could be something like, "Even though I really wanted the relationship with Keith to work, I understand and accept the fact that not all relationships work out." While *Hope* gets one in touch with a legitimate desire for a positive outcome, *Educate* reminds us that there are always forces that resist our control. The good news is that with practice we can see our unenforceable rules melt away in the presence of a realistic outlook.

The *H* statement represents a personal wish or desire. The *E* statement tunes in to the impersonal nature of not getting what we want. We focus on the personal in *Hope* statements and move to the impersonal in *Educate* statements. The best *E* statement reflects a personal desire yet accepts factors that are beyond our control. *Educate* statements are helpful because when we generalize the cause of a grievance, we take the personal sting away.

Sharon's first response when asked to construct an *E* statement was to say, "I will never find a good man, and I just have to live with it." But this statement is not about learning the limits on her ability to control events; it's instead about self-pity. Her mistake is a common one. She has confused uncertainty with negativity. Sharon does not know what the future will hold; she doesn't know whether or not she will find a good man. She only knows that her last attempt failed. There is a world of difference between negative certainty and uncertainty. It can mean the difference between healing and depression.

With this response, Sharon gave up hope. She substituted hopelessness for the uncertainty of trying again to make a relationship work. Sharon, in her hurt and confusion, thought she was accepting reality. In fact, she was making up a reality. She was stating as fact something that was pure conjecture.

The truth is, there is no certainty with relationships. Some relationships work, some do not. Some people remain married until death, others divorce in six months. Some long-term marriages are rich and intimate, some are living hells. After some reflection, Sharon changed her *E* statement to "I accept that many love affairs do not work out."

A second difficulty people face when crafting *Educate* statements involves accepting uncertainty. I urge people to begin their *E* statement like this: "I understand and accept that . . ." However, some find the word *accept* too strong. If that is the case for you, simply use the word *understand.* I urge you to remember one thing: you take a risk every time you want something, because you may not get what you want. So much of my training in forgiveness involves accepting this simple fact of life. "You can't always get what you want . . . but if you try sometimes you just might find you get what you need."

When making the *E* statement, understand it has two parts. The first part is the general statement acknowledging that every hope carries with it the possibility of failure. Examples of this are: some friends are disloyal, some relationships end, some parents are bad, some business arrangements do not work. It is common to be disappointed.

The second part of the *E* statement says you accept life's uncertainty. By no means does your *E* statement mean that you condone any specific hurtful action. We can disagree with what someone did and understand that what they did was common and that we cannot control their behavior. We can also disagree with what someone did and see at the same time how it helps us to move on. The important thing is to focus our attention on what we can do to heal. What we are saying in the E statement is that we accept that hurtful things are a part of the vulnerability inherent in hoping. On the positive side, strongly wanting things to go well is how people create life's greatest triumphs.

For Charlie, the first part of his E statement meant acknowledging the reality that many parents do not care for their children. He did not struggle with this part. However, Charlie could not use the word *accept*. He found this to be too strong. His severe upset was in the way. The E statement he created was "I understand that many parents do not care for their children." He was able to say he understood, but he was not able to say he accepted this reality. Through this process Charlie, for the first time, could see his mother's abandonment with an impersonal eye.

Elana's E statement focused on the inevitability that people we love could become ill. She too was unable to say she accepted the uncertainty but was willing to say she understood. The difference between accepting and understanding is not big. I urge you to experiment with *accept*, but do not feel bad if that is too strong for you. Elana's H and E statements were: "After years of neglect, I hoped for a number of loving years with Jesse. However, I understand that even with the best of intentions people become ill."

Elana's H and E statements reflect the parts of the HEAL method that can elicit feelings of sadness and loss. These parts of the HEAL method focus on the past. They focus on a past where something went wrong. They focus on a past where we were hurt or mistreated. By clearly articulating the *Hope*, you are acknowledging that something you wanted did not happen. By learning to *Educate* yourself about uncertainty, you soften your demand that things turn out the way you want. For some people this leads to an awareness of loss, which can make them sad. I refer to these two parts of HEAL as the grieving steps of the process. However, feelings of sadness are not inevitable with HEAL practice. I find that the closer in time people are to the hurt, the more likely it is that sadness will emerge.

There is nothing wrong with feeling sad. Sadness is a natural response to loss. We all feel sad when we lose something important. Losing a dream, such as the dream of a good love affair, of a job promotion, or of a loyal best friend, can hurt profoundly. Yet feeling sad is not the same as feeling hopeless or depressed. These feelings usually emerge from holding unenforceable rules. They rarely emerge from the simple act of admitting that you were unable to get something you wanted. Depression usually accompanies negative statements like Sharon's, in which she was asserting she would never again have a good relationship. Despair and sadness are different experiences and arise from different kinds of thinking.

Asserting "never again" is very different from accepting that many relationships end poorly. Hope always carries with it the possibility of loss. The power of HEAL is when we focus our attention in our heart and we minimize these negative feelings. However, it is important to acknowledge that loss is a part of most grievances and that some sadness is inevitable.

USING THE *H* AND *E* STATEMENTS IN PRACTICE

We will discuss the last two steps of HEAL, the A and L statements, in the next chapter. But first a word on how to use what you have already learned.

To begin practice of the HEAL method, start with three to five minutes of practicing Heart Focus then hold your attention in the area around your heart. This area should feel warm and peaceful because during your Heart Focus practice, you have thought of someone you love or something that leaves you feeling positive. Continue to breathe slowly and deeply into and out of your stomach. Then craft an appropriate *Hope* statement. This statement should be positive, personal, and specific. Remember to keep breathing slowly and deeply into and out of your belly and to center your attention in the area around your heart.

Then release the *Hope* statement into the impersonality of the *Educate* statement. The E acknowledges the uncertainty inherent in wanting anything. Keep breathing slowly and deeply.

Now attach the *E* statement to the end of the *H* statement. The two statements are best joined with a "however, and I understand and accept . . ." Here is an example of H and E statements. H statement: "I hoped my business partner Sarah would remain a trusted colleague." E statement: "However, I understand and accept that not all business partnerships work out the way I want."

Practice the H and E parts of this process until you are comfortable with your statements. Then resolve to leave your hurtful past behind and move on. When you do this, you are ready to learn and practice the A and L components of the HEAL method.

CHAPTER 13

The HEAL Method Part II:
Soothing the Hurt

One word frees us of all the weight and pain of life: That word is love.
SOPHOCLES

The first two stages of the HEAL method focus on the past and that which caused the grievance. The *Hope* and *Educate* statements help us to orient our pain and loss and allow us to put them into a healing perspective. *H* reminds us that there was always something positive we wanted. *E* reminds us that no matter how positive the goal, we may not get what we want.

The *H* and *E* statements also help us to see what thoughts caused us pain. This is important, and we have covered this in detail. Unenforceable rules, the release of stress chemicals, and the lack of understanding of the commonness of suffering are all examples of how we create grievances. However, no matter how well we understand what lay behind our hurt, too many of us remain stuck in pain. Understanding where the hurt comes from and doing something to soothe it are two different tasks.

We all need to learn how to move on and hurt less. I designed the final two steps of the HEAL method, the *A* and *L*, specifically for this purpose. These two steps offer the opportunity to leave the hurt behind and direct the ship of your life forward.

LETTING GO OF HURTS

Before moving on to the final two steps, though, let's consider one point. Some people find it difficult to let go of their hurts and move from the *E* of the HEAL method to the *A*. They get stuck after completing the *H* and *E* parts because their thinking ruts cause them to repeatedly upset themselves.

Darlene is a case in point. Darlene tried the HEAL method and reported that after practicing *H* and *E* she felt too sad to continue. The minute she thought of Jack, the fiancé who jilted her, she felt sad. She got lost in her experience of sadness and loss. It became clear that Darlene did not know how to handle her hurt feelings. Darlene's pain stopped her from proper practice of the HEAL method. Darlene's feelings were so strong that she did not practice my HEAL method but her own painful version of the process.

Darlene started her practice with good intentions. Her *H* statement said, "I hoped to marry Jack and have a good and long relationship." This was a fine *Hope* statement. It was personal, specific, and positive. She acknowledged that she hoped for a sound relationship instead of creating an unenforceable rule about having to have a sound relationship. Darlene then started on her *E* statement, but she ran into trouble. Instead of reminding herself, "I understand and accept that some relationships fail even with the best intentions of the partners," she crafted an unenforceable rule that said, "I know that some relationships may end, but it is not okay that mine failed. My fiancé was wrong, wrong."

I told Darlene there was nothing wrong with feeling sad. Her sadness was a normal response to loss, and ending an engagement is a huge loss. I suggested to Darlene she could learn to bear her sadness. This would happen when she noticed that sadness, like all her feelings, would pass. I asked her if, even now, she always was sad. She said no. She said that when she snuggles with her children she feels good.

I asked her if she always feels good, and the answer was no. I asked her if she ever feels happy and sad in the same day, and she said yes. I asked her to remember something sad from her past and then something happy. Did each of these feelings change and go away? She admitted that yes, they had gone away. Therefore, these feelings too would change and go away someday.

When people look they see that their feelings often change from day to day and even hour to hour. This is because what we pay attention to is always shifting. When we pay attention to losses we tend to feel sadness. When we pay attention to our blessings we tend to feel happier.

Interestingly, the fact that all our feelings eventually change and pass means that it is possible to gain control of them. Our feelings are directly related to how we think and what we pay attention to. When we pay attention to losses, we tend to feel sadness. When we pay attention to our blessings, we tend to feel happier. We can change what we pay attention to. Unfortunately, many people imagine their feelings control them and not the other way around.

I suggested to Darlene that she practice the HEAL method even when she felt sad. I suggested she pay more attention to her practice than how she felt. This is an important point. In some ways practicing the HEAL method is like taking medicine. You need to take your medicine sometimes even when you do not feel like it. That is the only way you can know if the medicine actually works. I reminded Darlene that proper practice of HEAL would in time help her feel better.

I suggested that Darlene practice an appropriate *E* statement even if at first she did not believe in it. I reminded her to practice PERT and the Breath of Thanks. PERT reminded her of the calm to be gained through slow and deep belly breathing. It also gave her a reason to think of her children in a loving and appreciative way. In time, Darlene found that her sad feelings were not to be feared and did not last forever.

I offered Darlene one strong caveat: if her sad feelings proved overwhelming, interfered with her normal activities, such as eating and sleeping, kept her isolated, or led her to feel suicidal, she should speak to a trained counselor. At that point how to forgive would not be her first concern. I make that same suggestion to anyone reading this book. *Forgive for Good* is not meant to substitute for psychotherapy or the need for medication. If you suffer disturbing physical symptoms or disabling emotional pain, please find an appropriate therapist or medical doctor for a consultation.

I also made sure Darlene's pain was not new; her boyfriend had not left that day, that week, or even that month. When wounds are new, we simply need to be patient. At times like those we should do our best to treat ourselves with kindness and experience the hurt and sadness that come with loss.

Previously I mentioned that forgiveness is often not the best initial response to hurt. First, make sure that you clearly know what happened and how you feel and that you have told a couple of trusted people. This process can take time. Do not bypass hurt feelings. They provide us with valuable information, showing us what we value and what needs attention. However, when we tune in hurt feelings and tune out gratitude, beauty, and love, we struggle to remember that other points of view are also possible.

Our hurt feelings are important, but we help ourselves to remember they will pass. I work with many people who struggle to trust their good feelings. They are more comfortable when their painful feelings come to visit, like annoying relatives who do not know when to leave. These people's remote controls are stuck, and they do not know how to bring them in to the shop to be fixed. Being stuck in a cycle of pain makes it easy to forget that negative feelings are no more real than positive ones.

Love, feelings of appreciation and gratitude, and the ability to notice beauty all are real. They are important. They are deep expressions of the human experience. Unfortunately, many disappointed and hurt people develop the bad habit of focusing more on their hurts than their blessings. This keeps them stuck in a cycle of pain and the sense that lasting peace and love are out of their grasp. Even good feelings will change and pass on. Some days we see the cup as half full and some days as half empty. To have a deep and full life, we need to be able to experience all of our emotions appropriately. The problem is we cannot find the full range of human experience when our remote is stuck on the grievance channel.

Remember, at some point both your good and bad feelings will come and go. That is why your remote needs to be ready to change the channel. Remember, when stuck on your hurt or grievance channels, you can change your experience by gently reminding yourself there are other channels. You can practice PERT, challenge your unenforceable rules, or practice the HEAL method. In particular, the HEAL method will help you find peace from painful or difficult events.

Once we pinpoint the source of our pain from the practice of our H and E statements, we are ready to move on to the remaining two steps of the HEAL method.

THE HEAL METHOD: *A* IS FOR AFFIRM

As a reminder, you begin the HEAL method with a brief practice of the Heart Focus. While keeping your attention on the area around your heart, continue to breathe slowly and deeply into and out of your belly, then craft good *H* and *E* statements.

The next step in the HEAL method is *A*, to *Affirm* your positive intention. I showed you how to find positive intention in chapter 11. Positive intention reminds us of the life goals that our focus on a hurtful experience has shifted aside. Alternatively, positive intention reminds us that we can grow from any hurtful experience.

A drawback to holding grievances is that they keep us connected in a powerless way with people who have hurt us. When you mull over in your mind past wounds and hurts you remind yourself of a part of your life that did not work out well. To affirm your positive intention reconnects you with your goals that allow you to move forward.

Rachel came into the forgiveness training incensed about her mother because she had been abandoned at birth. In her life she had a habit of grimacing and telling nasty stories about her mother and all of the things that had been taken from her. She spent so much time on images of her mother that she lost sight of the possibilities in her life. In midstory, dwelling on how awful this was, she was asked, "Why do you care so much about your mother?" When she started to repeat the same old story, I asked, "Why do you rent so much space in your mind to someone who did not care for you? How will that help you? Isn't what you really want a way to survive this abandonment, not dwell on it?"

Rachel was startled and taken aback. She had heard about positive intention but had never thought to apply the concept to her life. When I asked Rachel to construct a helpful *Affirm* statement she had a tough time. She was so devastated by her loss that it was hard for her to come up with anything. I suggested as an alternative that she focus on a positive intention to grow as a human being. Rachel came up with the following *A* statement: "My positive intention is to use my experiences to become a stronger person."

I told Rachel her goal was to practice the HEAL method every day for a week. First, I told her to do the full HEAL practice two times per day. This required about twenty-five minutes a day to practice. Then, with practice she could repeat the HEAL statements to herself more quickly and ten brief practice attempts could be done in ten minutes. Rachel accepted the assignment and after a couple of days noticed that her story started to shift. She found that affirming her positive intention helped her to first develop and then carry out better life plans.

Prior to forgiveness training, Rachel had started and stopped various college programs. She had a rocky employment history and a history of short-term jobs. In addition, her marriage was a constant struggle because whatever her husband offered was never enough. When she connected with her positive intention, Rachel went back to graduate school and became a nurse. She and her husband entered marriage counseling, a request her husband had made for years but that she had rebuffed by saying no counselor could understand what she had been through. In addition, Rachel, of all people, started a gratitude journal.

Like Rachel, when you craft a strong A statement you shift attention to your future. In the HEAL method the H and E statements were focused on the past. The A and L statements are for the present and future. When you make a strong positive intention, you motivate yourself. Your story changes, and your true goals emerge. Finally, we move to the L statement, in which you offer your commitment to live the life you have chosen as fully as possible.

L IS FOR LONG-TERM

The L in HEAL stands for making a *Long-Term Commitment* to your long-range well-being. The L statement emphasizes the importance of practice. A strong L statement commits you both to practice the HEAL method whenever you feel upset over a past hurt and to tell your story from your positive intention even when your habits are telling you to dwell on the hurt. The L statement is the final part of the HEAL method.

Every L statement includes the following: "I make the long-term commitment to follow my positive intention and use the HEAL method."

For many of you this will be sufficient. However, some people find that in order to manifest their positive intention they have to learn new skills. Then to their L statement they add the following: "I make a long-term commitment to learn the specific new skills I need to prosper." Some of the training and supportive services I have seen people benefit from are assertiveness training, stress management, nutrition classes, continued education, public speaking, twelve-step programs, and individual or family counseling. In addition, a few simple techniques will help almost everyone follow their positive intention.

The first technique is to look for people who have successfully healed from a similar grievance Since all of our grievances arise from common experiences, we can find people who have moved past their pain. Listen to what they say, and determine how you can incorporate their positive lessons in your life. Try to model your behavior after the successful behavior of others. One man I know took this advice to heart.

Victor is the clergyman who struggled with his superiors' seeming indifference to his health problems at his current location. When Victor understood he had to change, he searched for people who demonstrated reasonable responses to uncaring superiors. He found someone who struggled with similar situation and spent time discussing his difficulty with that man. Victor felt heard and supported and was reminded he had some difficult choices to make. What this man offered Victor was help in asserting himself and the understanding that even in difficult situations Victor still has a choice to make.

The second technique is to ask a friend or family member to let you know when you are overdoing your grievance story. Choose someone you trust, and ask this person to remind you gently when you slip back into bad habits. The friend needs to do nothing more than say she or he hears a grievance story. You can then choose to refocus on your positive intention. Alan had a friend stop him whenever he complained about his ex-wife.

A third simple technique is to give yourself permission to mull over the grievance for a short period each day. When Dana remembered how she was cheated out of a promotion, she told herself that she would dwell on it only at 7:00 P.M. each evening. She gave herself fifteen minutes a day to think about how she was wronged. Each night for about a week she sat down at the kitchen table and asked herself if she needed to vent. Many times she did not, but if she did she wrote her feelings down. Then she practiced PERT or found something to watch on her gratitude or beauty channels before getting up to have dinner. In this way she spared the rest of her day and learned information about how she was coping with her perceived injustice.

The final technique is to reward yourself for your practice of the techniques offered in this book. Michael kept count every day of the times he practiced the HEAL method. On every day that he practiced more than five times he purchased a special dessert. At the end of the week, if he practiced more than forty times he rewarded himself with a massage.

Rachel decided that she and her husband needed counseling to make their marriage work. Her first L statement was a simple reaffirmation to practice HEAL and remain focused on her positive intention. Since her positive intention was personal growth, she realized that because she had spent so many years being bitter, she lacked personal growth skills. In addition to counseling, Rachel committed herself to daily practice of the Breath of Thanks and took a meditation class. When she practiced the HEAL method she did so with a new L statement. This L statement committed her to experiment with and learn a variety of personal growth skills.

Elana, whom we met in the previous chapter, made the commitment to practice the HEAL method every day for three weeks. At the beginning of her practice the results were fleeting, but by the end of the first week she started to see changes in her mood and temperament. By the end of two weeks of practice, she was convinced that her present relationship with her husband, even after the stroke, was more important than what she had lost. She saw she could never recover the past. Elana saw also that it was love that kept her in her marriage. She could accept errors she had made that were grounded in love. Elana saw clearly that love was her positive intention.

Elana also saw that she had a lifelong difficulty with confrontation. She had been afraid all those years to really request more from her husband, and she saw this was a pattern in all her relationships. She decided to take an assertiveness class to learn how to ask for what she wanted. Whether or not assertiveness training helped her marriage, Elana knew it would help her.

After three weeks, she forgave her husband the excessive attention he had placed on his work, his lack of attention, his humanness, and the hurt that came from knowing the time she had left with him was fleeting. She made peace, as she understood that each of them did the best they could. As she forgave him she noticed an awakening in her heart and a renewed tenderness toward her husband, diminished capacity and all. She found that the practice of HEAL allowed her to appreciate whatever time she had left with her husband and learn ways to grow as a person. Forgiveness had opened both new and old doors that she had never even considered.

GUIDED PRACTICE OF THE HEAL METHOD (FULL VERSION)

1. Think of an unresolved grievance in your life. Pick one where you can at least imagine you could feel different.
2. Practice Heart Focus for three to five minutes. Focus your attention in the area around your heart. Ensure that you are breathing slowly and deeply into and out of your belly.
3. Reflect for a moment on what you would have preferred to happen in this specific situation. Make an *H* statement to reflect your *Hope* that is personal, specific, and positive.
4. Hold in your heart your *H* statement: "I hoped . . ."
5. When the *H* statement is clear, then *Educate* yourself about the limitations in demanding things always work out the way you want. Make your *E* statement broad, and in your heart understand and accept that you are okay even though all your hopes cannot be gratified.
6. *Affirm* your positive intention (A), the positive long-term goal underneath the hope you had for this specific situation.
7. With determination, hold your *A* statement in the warm feelings in your heart. Repeat your positive intention a couple of times.

8. Make an *L* statement, which stands for a *Long-Term Commitment* to
   * Practice the HEAL method—both the full and brief versions;
   * Follow your positive intention even when difficult;
   * Learn the skills you need to manifest your positive intention;
   * Practice each letter in order at least twice.
9. Then continue to breathe slowly and deeply into and out of your belly for another thirty seconds to a minute.

GUIDED PRACTICE OF THE HEAL METHOD (BRIEF VERSION)

At any time you feel hurt or anger over an unresolved grievance:

1. Bring your attention fully to your stomach as you slowly draw in and out two slow and deep breaths.
2. On the third inhalation bring to your mind's eye an image of someone you love or of a beautiful scene in nature that fills you with awe and peace. Often people have a stronger response when they imagine their positive feelings are centered in the area around their heart. Continue to breathe slowly into and out of your belly.
3. Reflect on what you would have preferred to happen in this specific situation. Make a *Hope* statement that is personal, specific, and positive.
4. Then *Educate* yourself about the limitations in demanding things always work out the way you want.
5. *Affirm* your positive intention—the positive, long-term goal underneath the hope you had for this specific grievance.
6. Make a *Long-Term Commitment* to practice the HEAL method and follow your positive intention.

To get optimal benefit from the HEAL method, practice the full version at least once each day. The benefits are great if at first you practice twice each day. I advise all people to practice the full method at least once every day for a week. After a couple of days you will have sufficient practice to also employ the brief version as needed.

Through the HEAL method you reduce the power of your grievance. You heal yourself, and you allow yourself to recover that loving, positive direction that lay behind much of your actions. The HEAL method is particularly useful whenever a disturbing memory or painful feeling emerges. At other times you many find it helpful to repeat silently to yourself the following: *Hope*, *Educate*, *Affirm*, and *Long-Term*. Allow those words to circulate in the area around your heart. Remember, through *Hope*, *Educate*, *Affirm*, and *Long-Term*, you are working hard to heal your wounds and make peace your reality.

CHAPTER 14

The Four Stages of Becoming a Forgiving Person

Doing an injury puts you below your enemy;
Revenging one makes you but even with him;
Forgiving it sets you above him.

BENJAMIN FRANKLIN, *Poor Richard's Almanac*

I hope you have taken the opportunity to practice these powerful and proven forgiveness techniques. If so, you now have the skills to make peace with the unresolved issues in your life. You have the tools to end the power old hurts hold over you and to forgive those who have hurt you.

In this chapter I suggest other ways we can bring the power of forgiveness into our life. These possibilities emerge as I examine the four stages people go through as they learn to forgive. In a nutshell, besides helping to heal past hurts, forgiveness can help minimize the possibility of creating present and future hurts. Another way of putting this is we can use forgiveness to inoculate ourselves against being hurt again.

You have heard true stories and seen statistics that show how the choice to forgive past hurts can help improve health and heal relationships. A useful way to think about these benefits is possible only because we have the ability to make choices. Other people can hurt us, but only we choose how to react. Each of us has the choice to forgive or not to forgive, and no one can force us to do either. If I want to forgive someone, no one can stop me, no matter how poorly the offender may have acted. This choice of whether or not to forgive is an example of the power we have to heal the wounds in our life and move on.

Because we can choose to forgive, we have a choice also about whether or not to take offense in the first place. My understanding of forgiveness suggests the radical notion that life would improve if we rarely or never used the power of choice to take offense. Since we have choice, wouldn't it make sense to limit the amount of times we are hurt or offended?

When you have practiced forgiveness on a couple of hurtful situations, you soon find that you have become a more forgiving person. You may notice you are less inclined to get angry or that you feel more patient with people. Forgiveness—the ability to live life without taking offense, without giving blame when hurt, and by telling stories that reflect peace and understanding—is a choice that can be practiced in a host of situations. Forgiveness, while not the only choice, is a skillful way to deal with the "slings and arrows of outrageous fortune."

In this chapter I describe the four stages people go through as they learn to becoming more forgiving. The first of these stages starts with the offender controlling you through their power to hurt you. As people pass from stage to stage, they gain the power to control the degree of anger they feel. As they follow the steps outlined in these pages, they see that learning to forgive can be more than just a way to resolve past hurts and grievances. People learn to use forgiveness to minimize their chance of getting hurt in the present as well as limit the amount of time they remain hurt from the past.

We have seen that forgiveness can heal the past and provide a more peaceful present. Forgiveness allows us to think more clearly, problem-solve wisely, and have greater access to loving feelings. After learning the HEAL forgiveness method, we have an understanding of how to forgive someone who has hurt us. We have seen the steps to take and read stories of people like ourselves who have learned to forgive. Now I will show us how to extend the use of forgiveness in ways we may not have anticipated.

FOUR STAGES OF BECOMING A FORGIVING PERSON

It is my hypothesis that there are four stages on the journey to becoming a forgiving person. One way of thinking about this is to compare forgiveness to the process of tuning in a radio to a favorite station. To make this analogy work you have to imagine an analog and not a digital dial on the radio. The first step one takes to tune the radio is to find a particular station out of the static. You may get the station you want at first by accident. Maybe you were going through all the stations on the dial and heard a snippet of a song you liked. Finding that station again can be hard if the signal is not strong.

To find the particular station you want you have go back to where you heard the music you liked and adjust your dial. At first the station may be hard to distinguish but with practice you can find it. It may take some time for fine-tuning, but when you are certain you have the proper station you leave the dial set. This station then becomes the one you hear when you turn on your radio.

We know that starting with this station does not stop us from finding other stations. There will be times when the music is better higher up on the dial. We will have times when we are in the mood for something different. Learning to forgive is like fine-tuning the forgiveness station on the radio. As you fine-tune the forgiveness channel less and less static and interference get in the way.

Yet as with your favorite radio station, you are not forced to listen to forgiveness when you wish to change the channel. Once you have tuned into forgiveness you can find it again when you need it. If you do not tune forgiveness in you cannot know what it feels like. If you do not tune forgiveness in you cannot make a good choice on whether or not to choose it again in the future.

TOWARD FORGIVING REGULARLY: STAGES ONE TO THREE

In the first stage of becoming a forgiving person, people experience a loss in their life, feel angry or hurt, and tend to justify their negative emotions. Any of the hurt or angry people whose stories are presented in this book demonstrate this first stage of forgiveness. Darlene, whom we met in chapter 6, was very angry at being jilted by her fiancé, Jack. In her mind his actions were wrong, she was relatively blameless, and his abandonment caused her emotional distress. Darlene told many people a story of how awful she felt and how poorly Jack behaved.

At this stage of forgiveness you are filled with self-justified anger or hurt. At some point in your life you were wounded, and you still feel mad at or hurt by the person who wronged you. You blame the person committing the wrong for how you are feeling. It is their action and not your choice of response that you determine to be the cause of your distress. You have forgotten that you have choices about how you can react, or you are so wounded that you are convinced that it would not be right to forgive the offense. At the first stage there is usually both active and submerged anger as well as a great deal of pain.

The second stage emerges when after feeling upset with someone for a while we realize that our hurt and anger do not feel good. We become concerned about our emotional balance as well as our physical health. We begin to see the consequences of our grievance on our happiness and well-being. Some, after feeling upset for a while, begin to think about how to repair the damage to the relationship. Others simply decide that they have thought about a past grievance enough and it is time to move on.

Whatever the motivation at the second stage, we take steps to lessen the impact the grievance has on our life and relationships. We may try to see the problem from the other person's point of view, or we can decide to minimize the problem by saying it was no big deal. Another strategy is to look for a way to soothe upset feelings. In any case, after an extended period, the offended person is no longer actively aggrieved. At this stage, we tell our friends that we have let go of much of the hurt and anger toward the person who hurt us.

In the second stage of forgiveness we notice that our bad feelings are not helping us, so we take steps to see things differently. When we take steps to soothe our emotional and physical distress, we naturally disentangle ourselves from the offender. Susan demonstrated second-stage forgiveness. She complained regularly about her terrible childhood, and eventually her husband got tired of hearing about it and told her so. At first she got angry with him. Her initial response was to label Barry a jerk and to immediately call her friend Donna for affirmation.

When Susan calmed down she asked Barry why he had said that to her. He responded that she obsessed about her parents way too much. Barry said it did not make sense to struggle that much when she saw her parents only twice a year. This confrontation with her husband led

Susan to begin forgiveness training. She learned the forgiveness methods that allowed her to agree with Barry. Susan was able to manifest her positive intention and fully appreciate the care and mentoring she received from the older women friends whom she saw often.

In the third stage of becoming a forgiving person, we remember how good it felt the last time we were able to forgive. That forgiveness experience could have taken place fifteen minutes ago, when we felt peaceful after practicing the HEAL method, or two years ago. In the third stage, when we notice a grievance forming we practice PERT or HEAL immediately. We challenge our unenforceable rules on the spot. We do this so that the problem does not rent a lot of space in our mind. The third stage comes after we have seen the results of forgiveness in action and we choose to let go of a new interpersonal grievance quickly.

In the third stage, when we are offended we deliberately choose to feel the hurt for a shorter period. We have learned that the negative feeling will pass. We turn our attention either to repairing the relationship or to letting go of seeing the situation as a problem. We learn to rent not the grievance space but the solution space. We decide to forgive because we have practiced and see the clear benefit of forgiveness in our lives. This stage can emerge in a relationship damaged by an affair, in an ongoing office situation, or in a long-term conflict with a sibling.

In the third stage we are more in control. We are aware that the length of time we experience a situation as a grievance is primarily up to us. Susan is an excellent example of a person at this stage. She made the decision that the next time someone hurt her she was going to work hard not to let it become a grievance. She decided to herself that if her mother or anyone else pushed her buttons she was not going to let it trigger a depression. In this stage of forgiveness the time spent angry and hurt became Susan's to control. She made the decision to minimize her time spent upset, and with practice she was successful.

BECOMING A FORGIVING PERSON: STAGE FOUR

The fourth stage of becoming a forgiving person is the most difficult and possibly the most powerful. At this stage you simply become a forgiving person. This stage comes as you make the decision to forgive first and let many troubling things go. As a forgiving person, you become resistant to taking offense. Your skin becomes tougher. You take less personal offense, you are convinced that you are responsible for how you feel, and you tell stories that show you and other people in the light of your positive intention.

The fourth stage of forgiveness involves the choice to rarely if ever take offense. This does not mean that we condone unkindness. It does not mean we become a doormat. It means we save being upset only for situations where getting upset helps us. We do not take hurtful actions so personally, and we do not blame the offender for how we are feeling. At this stage we understand that people are not perfect and that we can expect them to hurt us at times. Stage four usually emerges at the same time as some or all of the following ways of thinking about offenses.

The fourth stage usually emerges when we think in the following ways about being offended:

- I want to waste as little of my life as possible in the discomfort caused by anger or hurt. I want to react well when things do not go the way I want. This decision allows me to forgive myself, forgive others, and even forgive life itself when necessary.
- Life comes with positive and unpleasant experiences. Can I reasonably expect to have only good experiences come my way? I hope for the good and know I can forgive the bad.
- Dealing with life is a challenge. I want to be a survivor and not a victim. Each hurtful situation challenges my determination to live as fully and lovingly as possible. I accept the challenges that life sends my way.
- I know it hurts when people do not forgive me. I do not want to hurt others in this way, so I will perceive the problem in a way that I can either deal with successfully or let it go.
- Life is filled with beauty and incredible marvels. I am missing these experiences if I am stuck in the remembrance of old hurts or wounds. I forgive myself for getting sidetracked.
- People do the best they can. When they err, the best way to help them is by offering understanding. The first step in this process is to forgive whatever constituted the specific offense.

- I am not perfect. How can I expect anyone else to be?
- I understand that everyone, including me, operates primarily out of self-interest. I expect that sometimes I, in my self-interest, will be hurt by someone else's expression of their self-interest. When I understand this is an ordinary part of life, what is there to be upset about? When I grasp that self-interest is my guiding principle, how can I not offer forgiveness to everyone, including myself, for behaving that way?

This kind of thinking serves as examples of stage four forgiveness. These are not the only ways one can think to become a forgiving person. Each of you will develop your own way of thinking about forgiveness. It is likely you already have thoughts like these in your best relationships. Many of you have successful marriages that are at stage four of forgiveness. These marriages allow your partner to make mistakes and you put your energy into working out the problems rather than taking offense, blaming, and creating grievance stories.

One key aspect of stage four forgiveness is learning to think like a forgiving person. Another is learning to practice forgiveness every day. To practice forgiveness we do not have to wait for someone to hurt us badly. Practicing forgiveness allows us to develop forgiveness muscles in the same way that going to the gym develops physical muscles. As with muscles in your arm, in order to grow stronger your forgiveness muscles must be regularly worked.

I suggest that people looking to grow to stage four forgiveness practice on the small slights and injustices we face daily. For example, imagine you are in the express checkout line (limit of ten items) at your local supermarket. You see two people ahead of you with fourteen items in their carts. Now picture yourself as you come to the counter. Ask yourself how will you respond. Notice that you have a range of choices.

One possible response is to get mad at the people who have too many items. You can insult them and the checkout person for letting them in the line. Another response is to ignore the situation and read a magazine. Alternatively, you can gossip with the person next to you about the huge number of selfish people spoiling the area in which you live. Or you can use this situation as an opportunity to forgive the people who are in line with extra items. You can use your supermarket check-out as forgiveness practice. When you practice in this way, forgiveness is there when you really need it.

Another powerful way to practice forgiveness is to remind yourself that other people do not always have your best interest at heart. When you explore this idea you realize that you also do not always act in the best interest of others. Soon from this perspective, it is inevitable that people hurt one another. Therefore, there will be many opportunities to practice forgiveness.

For example, Harry's boss has been uptight and nasty all week because he is worried about his sick wife. He is short with Harry and does not notice Harry's efforts at all. In one sense Harry is justified in his frustration with his boss. His boss has been rude and is a poor manager. From another point of view, Harry could ask what's the big deal. The boss's mind has been on his wife, his fears, and his struggles and not on Harry's feelings.

To Harry's boss, his wife is more important than how Harry feels. Harry makes a problem out of this because to Harry how he feels is more important than the health of his boss's wife. Harry can choose to forgive his boss for his poor conduct by understanding his own self-interest for what it is. He cares more about himself and expects his boss to do the same. His boss cares more about his wife and little about Harry's feel-ings. Forgiveness provides a balm for hurt feelings when what is impor-tant to you collides with what is important to another.

Another way to use the inevitability of differing self-interest is to remember that disappointments, hurts, and wounds occur in all rela-tionships. They occur in all stable long-term marriages, in loving fami-lies, and among good friends. Every relationship has its good and bad points in the same way that every person does. Because of this truth, all relationships give us an almost unlimited opportunity to practice for-giveness, to take less offense, and prevent conflicts from escalating.

Sometimes people hurt us because they want to do what they want to do and not what we want them to do. Most of the time we call that selfish, but sometimes it is simply people making their own decisions.

Anna was hurt when her younger brother, Dave, decided to go skiing with his friends rather than visit their parents. Anna regularly paid more attention to her parents than to her brother.

This time Anna had to drive the six hours to her parents' house alone. On the way her car broke down, and she was stranded for about three hours. She waited first for the tow truck and then for the repair shop to get the part her car needed. You can imagine she was pissed at her brother. She thought he was selfish and inconsiderate. When I heard the story I wondered, Why does her brother have to do what Anna wants and not what he wants? They are both adults. They are both independent.

What would Anna's experience be like if she forgave her brother even before she left on her trip? When her car broke down, she would have already taken responsibility for her own feelings and saved herself a lot of grief and possibly a nasty showdown with her brother. She could forgive the fact that Dave made a different choice about how to spend his free time. She could use this situation to practice forgiveness.

Forgiving Dave in no way has to deter Anna from asking Dave to join her on trips. Neither does forgiving Dave mean Anna has to like the choices her brother makes. Forgiveness means that Anna stops blaming her brother for her feelings, and it allows her to understand she visits her parents because it is important to her. Visiting her parents does not have to be of the same importance for Dave for them to remain loving siblings. Then Anna realizes that she visits her parents because she wants to. Dave is not a bad person because he makes different choices. When you allow people to be different, you can forgive them. Through forgiveness, you understand that what is right for you will not be right for everybody.

Sometimes we feel hurt when people do not care for us in the way or at the time that we want them to. Steve regularly felt hurt when his wife fell asleep at 9:00 P.M. each night. To him the night was young, and he wanted a companion. He wanted to have sex with her, and he took her tiredness personally. Steve left late in the morning and was a night owl. He did not need a lot of sleep. Marjorie, on the other hand, cared for the couple's three young children and had to get up early with the kids. She was home all day with the two youngest children and did work for Steve's business. Marjorie was not a night owl and needed at least seven hours of sleep each night. By nine each evening she could not keep her eyes open.

Each time Marjorie fell asleep, Steve felt hurt and rejected. His hurt feelings caused a major strain in their marriage. Marjorie tried hard to give Steve what she could within the limitations of their schedules. Imagine the difference it would make if Steve forgave Marjorie's tiredness, her different sleep cycle, and her exhausting care for their three small children instead of pouting each evening as Marjorie falls asleep.

Sometimes a grievance is the result of someone's deliberate attempt to wound us. Often the person doing the hurting justifies wounding us as a response to a hurt we have inflicted on them. Steve and Marjorie's relationship is an example of this pattern of hurt. Marjorie often went upstairs to bed just to hurt her husband. She rejected him on purpose because he was so unforgiving of her tiredness. At other times she would keep their children up late just so she would be unavailable. In Marjorie's mind Steve deserved this treatment because of how insensitive and unkind he was to her.

Steve ragged on his wife relentlessly. He would gripe at her in the morning and again when he got home. He complained to his friends and family that Marjorie was uncaring, cold, and unresponsive. In particular, Steve was sarcastic to his wife, and sometimes he would wake Marjorie up just to start trouble. Steve justified his harsh treatment of Marjorie as a natural response to her inability to meet his needs. Both Marjorie and Steve justified their unkind responses as the result of their partner's actions. They gave themselves permission to be hurtful as responses to their partner's actions.

I like to imagine what would happen if either Steve or Marjorie regularly forgave the other. Imagine if both Steve and Marjorie understood that hurt people tend to do unkind things, and they heard in their partner's unkindness a cry of pain. Then, when they saw their partner acting from pain, they would understand the other was hurt and would not take the actions personally. Imagine if Steve and Marjorie's unkindness triggered in their partner a desire to be kind and to spare each other further pain. Then, instead of responding with cruelty, either or both partners could respond with renewed affection arising out of their forgiveness. In this situation there are so many opportunities to practice forgiveness.

Finally, some of our wounds come about as the result of poor dumb luck. Sometimes we may just be in the wrong place at the wrong time. Anna's car broke down hours from home while attempting to visit her parents. She was two hundred miles from home with a broken car, even though she'd had her car checked out before she left. Anna made a difficult situation worse by blaming her brother for not joining her. She forgot that accidents and breakdowns can happen at any time and that getting a car checked does not guarantee it will remain working. Imagine if Anna forgave her brother, forgave her car, and simply enjoyed the experience as best she could. What an ideal opportunity to practice forgiveness!

Clark was to board a plane in Denver to visit his girlfriend in Los Angeles. He was supposed to arrive at 6:00 P.M. on Friday evening. He and Colette had been a couple for eight months and Clark was a regular visitor. Clark arrived at the Denver airport and was able to board a plane that had been delayed. He ran to the gate and got on a plane leaving two hours before his was scheduled to depart. The earlier plane got him to Colette's house at 4:00 P.M. instead of 6:00. Clark tried to call from the Denver airport, but her phone was busy.

When Clark arrived Colette was not entirely happy to see him. She was surprised that he was there early. Colette worked at home and was not finished with her work. Clark was hurt and his first response was to wonder why he bothered to come see her. Colette felt guilty and was mad at Clark for disturbing her work. Colette was the kind of person who put her full attention on her work. She worked hard and played hard.

Colette was caught between a rock and a hard place. She had work to do and a deadline to meet. She also wanted to see her boyfriend. She knew that Clark was demanding and required a lot of attention. Clark's demanding nature was one of the reasons Colette asked him to arrive at 6:00. She wanted to have time to complete her work, take a shower, and sit down for a moment before he arrived. Clark meant no harm when he boarded the earlier plane. He simply had the opportunity to take an earlier plane. This innocent action led to bad feelings on both sides. All because of dumb luck and two people who were not practiced enough in forgiveness.

Step four of forgiveness means we take the opportunity to forgive whenever we can. We understand how common it is to be hurt. We look to make peace. We look to give people the benefit of the doubt. We do not become a doormat. We become a person who actively understands the power of forgiveness and the tendency of people to hurt each other.

You understand that each person sees the world a little differently. You understand the limitations of your point of view. You understand that we all want slightly different things because we have had different experiences. The way I teach this is by reminding you that we are each watching our own particular movie. You are the star of that movie and there are an infinite number of possible plot lines. Your movie comes from your past and your experiences that are filled with your hopes and dreams.

I like to imagine the world to be a huge multiplex theater. In that complex I notice there are an enormous number of movies available. These theaters play all sorts of different films. Some people spend their time watching horror movies while others prefer love stories. If John just watched a double feature of Westerns he would have a hard time conversing with Jennie who watched the *Star Wars* trilogy. This is an example of how we struggle with people who did not watch the same movie we did.

Darlene was furious at her fiancé for leaving her. The movie *Betrayal* had a long run in her movie theater. Each time she watched the movie she hated the other leading character, her fiancé. Unfortunately, Darlene's fiancé was not watching *Betrayal* but *Love Story*. Darlene's fiancé left her for a new relationship with another woman. He was enjoying endless repeats of *Love Story* and did not even know *Betrayal* was playing in Darlene's theater down the street.

I have suggested that people forgive others for watching different movies. I have said to people like Darlene, Which movie would you like to watch four hundred times, *Betrayal* or *Love Story*? If your fiancé is enjoying his film he sure isn't going to stop at your cinema anytime soon. At stage four you expect other people to be watching different movies. Instead of being angry you save your attention for those who sit down next to you at your theater and offer to share their popcorn.

In addition, we want to be able to talk to people who have watched different movies. It can take effort to listen well enough to hear the plot of their movie. We usually want them to listen to the plot of our movie. Too often we simply criticize people for going to a different film. However, if we are in a relationship we want to know not only the plot of their movie but a review. In that way we show them that we care and avoid creating grievances.

Amanda and Joe had been married for twenty-five years. Joe was thinking of slowing down and working less. Amanda had raised children and was feeling bored working part-time at a low-wage job. At fifty, each was watching entirely different films. Joe's was a travelogue that had them in Hawaii for an extended vacation. Amanda wanted a demanding full-time job with the opportunity to make a sizable chunk of her own money. She was watching *Working Girl*. However, neither of them was forgiving the other. Both claimed to feel misunderstood and hurt and wondered if the marriage could be saved.

Through forgiveness they learned to expect that they might be at different developmental stages. Through forgiveness they learned to ask if they were watching the same movie and if not, could the other please fill them in. Through forgiveness they realized their positive intentions were very much in line. However, they both understood they might have to wait to get everything they wanted. As a first step Amanda and Joe decided to take a long trip and then to switch roles. Joe worked part-time, and Amanda went back to the career she had left long ago. They agreed to revisit their decision every year with the understanding their marriage must be preserved.

The fourth stage of forgiveness is a sign that we understand the power we have over our feelings and the inevitability of conflict. Please do not feel that you have to be at the same stage of forgiveness with all people and in all relationships. Toward some people we feel such love that we are easily at the fourth stage: openhearted and ready to forgive. Many of us feel that way toward our children or spouses. Forgiving them does not mean we approve of all they do; it means that we acknowledge our hurts but do not make our child or spouse the enemy. We have a reservoir of love to draw upon that allows us access to forgiveness. The forgiveness allows us to let the insult go and work together to solve the problem.

There are other people who have hurt you, and you have no reservoir of goodwill to draw upon. With these folks you can stay stuck at stage one for years. At this stage your well of goodwill for them is dry, and you cannot imagine feeling openhearted toward them. I wrote this book to help you with those people. You now have the forgiveness tools you need to move forward. With these and all people, remember that you have the choice to forgive. At the second stage you choose forgiveness once in order to hurt less. At the third you choose it daily to hurt less. At the fourth stage you become forgiving so your choice is already made. At all stages you choose forgiveness to experience more peace and healing.

When I began my first forgiveness experiment five years ago I had two goals. One was to teach people how to forgive those who had hurt them. The other goal was to use forgiveness to prevent problems as well as heal hurts. I saw that my clients, friends, and family sometimes thought about forgiveness for their big hurts. Usually when they thought about forgiveness it was too late. They talked about how hard it was to forgive. They had failed to adequately practice forgiveness and so their forgiveness muscles were flabby.

I wanted a training that could heal the little as well as big hurts. I wanted to teach people to become more forgiving, not just to forgive someone who had hurt him or her. I have that same wish for you. That you try out what I teach and realize the power you now have to live a life of greater peace and harmony. I want you to practice forgiveness so that when you need it you are ready. I hope you become a forgiving person so that you can lead a life where you rarely feel the need to take offense.

This book teaches you how to change your hurt and angry reactions so that the unkindness of life no longer leaves you feeling upset for long periods. If you expect things to go wrong sometimes and you are ready with forgiveness, then you become a more powerful person. As you forgive you begin to tell stories of heroic understanding and unruffled self-acceptance.

Samantha forgave her husband for driving her and their car into a tree. They had been arguing, screaming at each other actually, before he lost control of the wheel. She was upset with him because of an affair and his inability to hold a job. Because Samantha could forgive her husband for their car accident, and the resulting chronic pain and medical bills, she knew she could forgive anything. Moreover, if she can forgive anything, then why bother holding grudges and staying upset in the first place? That is the fourth stage of forgiveness in action. That is the full power of forgiveness.

Lest you think I am encouraging you to become passive, just forgiving everyone because they are human, I want to end this chapter with a teaching story. This story is to remind you that you have to take good care of yourself. Even if you forgive people, you still have to deal with difficult individuals and situations.

A long time ago a village had a saint living near it. That saint walked among the hills and one day came upon a rattlesnake lying in the grass. The snake lunged with its fangs bared and made to bite the holy man. The saint smiled, and the snake was stopped by his kindness and love. The saint spoke to the rattler and asked the snake to give up biting the village's children. He said in that way the snake would be better liked and cause less harm.

Because of the power the holy man possessed, the snake agreed to stop biting. The next week the saint walked by the same spot and saw the snake on the ground lying in a pool of its own blood. The snake used what little strength it had to admonish the saint for almost killing him. "Look what happened to me when I took your advice. I am a bloody mess. Look what happened to me when I tried to be nice and not bite, and now everyone is trying to hurt me." The saint looked at the snake, smiled, and said, "I never told you not to hiss."

CHAPTER 15

Forgive Yourself

Reversing your treatment of the man you have wronged is better than asking his forgiveness.

ELBERT HUBBARD

In my forgiveness research projects I taught people how to forgive another person who had injured them. Whether it was college students, middle-aged working people, or Catholics and Protestants from Northern Ireland, each of the participants came to learn how to forgive someone else. I have shown you the how and why of their success. In addition to my research, about three years ago I started to teach public classes. These classes were open to anyone in the community who wished to learn my forgiveness process. In these classes I also focused on teaching people to forgive someone else.

One of the things I noticed was there were a number of people in each class who also wanted to know how to forgive themselves. These folks would always tentatively raise their hands and hesitatingly ask a question about forgiving themselves. They would say something along the lines of "It is hard to forgive my (mother, friend, business partner, lover, husband, etc.) but even harder to forgive myself. Do your methods work for self-forgiveness as well?"

For a long time I did not know the answer to that question. As I listened to people talk I learned there were a variety of things for which people need to forgive themselves. I listened to people talk about the many kinds of upsets they struggled with, and I learned that they were interested in forgiving things they had done both to other people and to themselves. The theme running through the myriad of stories was that their own behavior was unacceptable in some way and could not be forgiven.

It soon became apparent that implicit in learning how to forgive is an understanding of how to cope with the way we react to being hurt. Understanding that holding grudges and creating a grievance story are not the best approaches to letting go of anger and frustration is in essence a type of self-forgiveness. In order to forgive others, we need to first come to terms with how and why we reacted the way we did and what we can do to ensure that we do not repeat the same behavior in the future. Self-forgiveness is both a beneficial part of the forgiveness process and a necessary skill in learning to overcome being upset with ourselves. In the rest of the chapter, I will show you how to use forgiveness methods to forgive yourself for good.

FOUR CATEGORIES OF SELF-FORGIVENESS

After listening to the many ways people can be upset with themselves, I have broken these down into four categories of self-forgiveness. The first category contains people who are upset with themselves for failing at one of life's important tasks. The tasks could be developmental such as graduating from college or social such as getting married or having children. These people felt at least in part of their lives they had been a failure. The second category holds people who are upset with themselves for not taking action when they thought it necessary, to help either themselves or someone else. The third category contains people who were upset that they hurt someone else. These were usually people who had cheated on lovers or spouses, behaved terribly as parents, or behaved poorly in business. The fourth category was filled with people who were upset with themselves for self-destructive acts such as alcohol abuse or an unwillingness to work hard.

These categories help to give us an idea of the most common ways people become upset with themselves. These categories are not mutually exclusive. That is, someone could be upset at themselves for their alcohol abuse and the way in which it led to hurting someone else. Or someone could be upset at themselves for not being able to maintain a healthy relationship and how that hampered them in making a crucial decision.

Terri was a woman in her late forties whose self-forgiveness issue was how she ended up in a painful financial status. Terri was upset at herself for failing at an important life task. Terri literally loathed herself for the economic choices she made as an adult. Terri worked for many years as a preschool teacher. She loved her job, appreciated the small children, and felt she was contributing to the world through her work. Her husband had challenged her career choice in terms of its financial opportunities many times during their marriage. Every discussion ended because Terri was unwilling to give up a career she liked so much.

Terri had been married to Stan for fifteen years, and they had two children. Stan died after a lengthy illness and left the family in financial difficulty. Terri had never considered the necessity of making a lot of money and always assumed she would have enough. When Stan died her career choice of teacher no longer provided enough income for her and her children. Terry's forgiveness issue was the tremendous resentment she felt toward herself for not anticipating her future needs.

Ned did not feel that he did what was necessary to protect his wife from his father, and so he falls into the second category. Ned's wife and father hated each other. Ned had been married for nine years, and for the entire time Ned's father insulted Nora every time he saw her. Dad regularly told Ned he married the wrong woman, and Ned, for reasons of his own, allowed his father do this.

Nora traded insults with Dad and regularly told Ned how much she detested his father. Ned was sick of his father's insults. He did not like the way Nora responded but knew that if his father stopped attacking, Nora would stop as well. Ned was sick of his dad's behavior but bitterly disappointed in his inability to confront and stop his father. When I met him, Ned said he could forgive his father for being such an asshole but could not forgive himself for not protecting his wife.

Donna is a woman who had difficulty forgiving herself for doing an act that hurt someone else and so belongs in the third category of self-forgiveness offenses. Donna ended a seventeen-year marriage by having an affair with a friend of her ex-husband's. Donna knew for a number of years that her marriage was in bad shape. She and her husband had not had sex for the last two years of their marriage, and before that the sex was lethargic and sporadic.

For a number of years Donna's husband barely noticed her. Jeff, a successful businessman, worked all the time and made a lot of money. He loved his work and spent many nights in the office. He also traveled a lot, leaving Donna alone for nights on end. Donna was also entering midlife and struggled with getting older and the fact that her two teenage children would soon be moving out.

In her confusion and pain, Donna initiated an affair with a family friend who had lost his wife to cancer. She stayed in the affair for just three months, but the passion she felt in the affair and its contrast to her feelings for her husband told her that her marriage was over. Donna ended the affair and her marriage at the same time. Her husband moved out of the house, and her children spent every other weekend with him.

Donna dated a bit, but stopped when she realized she was racked with guilt. She felt guilty about the affair. Because of the affair she felt guilty about ending her marriage. Because of the affair she felt guilty about hurting her children. Donna felt that having an affair meant that the end of the marriage was her fault. In particular she regretted that she and her husband did not go into counseling. Donna's guilt over the affair paralyzed her even though there were other causes of the marital breakup.

Erica is a woman who at the age of thirty-one decided she had to clean up her life. Erica's mother died, and Erica did not want her life to end up the way her mother's did. Erica found changing her behavior and forgiving herself to be a more difficult task than she anticipated.

Erica's mom was a single mother who never had either a steady job or a steady relationship. She loved her daughter and always treated her with as much kindness as she was able. But she had a drinking problem and never developed the skills necessary for long-term employment. Starting at fifteen, Erica became a heavy user of marijuana. She also drank every weekend and had brief sexual relationships with a large number of men. At the age of thirty-one, Erica saw that if she did not change her ways she would end up like her mother. One of the factors making it hard for Erica to change was her inability to forgive herself for her self-destructive behavior.

When concerns about self-forgiveness came from people such as these I was at first uncertain what to say. My research showed that my forgiveness method worked with interpersonal forgiveness, but I had done no research on self-forgiveness. I was interested to find that no one else had either. Self-forgiveness was an aspect of forgiveness that science had not yet gotten to. I felt uncertain as to how to help these people and had to tell them so. As I was telling people this I was not satisfied with my response. I knew I was missing something, but I was not sure what to do about it.

After thinking about self-forgiveness for some months, I realized that with modification all that I teach could be applied to self-forgiveness. I saw that the basic grievance process was the same and that all grievances emerged from a negative response to not getting what one wanted. I realized that PERT was a powerful way to change feelings whether about self or another. I realized that "unenforceable rules" played a major role in creating a grievance applied to self as well as to interpersonal forgiveness. I saw that the HEAL method would work with self-forgiveness as well as interpersonal forgiveness. I saw that changing the channels was an important tool for self-forgiveness.

When I started to explore self-forgiving I saw how common it was for people to not know how to do this. As I started to listen to the people who came to forgiveness classes I saw how important self-forgiveness was. So many people spend their lives trapped in guilt and shame over their past actions. So many people feel paralyzed because they have never forgiven themselves for failures of one kind or another. Many people told me they had a harder time forgiving themselves than other people.

I saw that often self-forgiveness is an aspect of interpersonal forgiveness. Sarah was upset with herself for letting her husband destroy their lives. Dana was upset with herself for missing the signs that showed she was not going to get the promotion and for, as she put it, taking a job at the wrong company. Darlene felt that her fiancé jilted her because she was not sexy enough.

I came to see one interesting fact about self-forgiveness. When looked at properly it is easier than forgiving someone else. This is because we have more power over our actions than we do over the actions of others. Interpersonal forgiveness is difficult precisely because we cannot change the way other people act. The vulnerability caused by our limited control is at the heart of many of the unenforceable rules we create. We want people to treat us a certain way, and unfortunately they often choose to treat us the way they want to.

Darlene wants her spouse to love her and instead he cheats on her. Mary wants her mother to help with the children and instead she shows up at her home drunk. Jonathan wants his neighbors to have quiet parties and instead he has to call the police every time they hold a party. Lorraine wants her son to succeed in school and instead he drops out of high school at the age of seventeen. None of these people can control the actions of others in their lives. No matter how hard they huffed or puffed, there was no way they could change someone who did not want to change.

The bottom line is we have more control over our own actions than over the actions of others. We can always learn new ways to do old things. We have the freedom to experiment with acting in different ways until we find one that works. We can talk to people who are successful and find out how they do what they do. In many ways we can change our own behavior.

As a result, self-forgiveness is a powerful tool in learning how to become a forgiving person. In life, we all make bad decisions, make mistakes, and act from poor information, and learning how to forgive ourselves will help us when the time comes to forgive others. By practicing the forgiveness methods in this book, you can learn the tools to forgive both yourself and others. Both are crucial in learning to become a forgiving person.

FORGIVING OURSELVES

Forgiveness of self emerges when we understand that even with our own actions we do not have total control. Nobody is perfect. Everybody makes mistakes. We all make bad decisions and act from poor information. Being human means you and I will fail at some things and cause other people harm. Needing to be perfect is an unenforceable rule. Wanting never to hurt anyone else is an unenforceable rule. Needing to be successful is always an unenforceable rule. Being human allows us to offer forgiveness to ourselves, never forgetting that we have resources at our disposal to improve ourselves and help others.

The major block to both self-forgiveness and establishing new behaviors is habit. Each of us has habits that are difficult to change. Ned is a good example. Whenever Ned's dad insulted him or his wife, Ned shut down inside. He felt afraid to say anything to his dad and then hated himself for letting his dad get away with bad behavior. Ned's self-forgiveness hinged on his ability to take charge of his assertiveness and at the same time forgive the ways that he did not adequately assert himself.

In one important way it might be easier for Ned to forgive himself than his dad. He has the ability to change a behavior that he does not like. He does not have that power over his father. Simply, he can choose to act differently. His father had brutalized Ned as a kid and now brutalized Nora as an adult, and Ned had never fought back with his words. Thirty-five years later Ned finally learned how to speak assertively to his father. Part of Ned's forgiveness journey was to learn to tell his dad each time his boundary was crossed.

The second advantage you have when you attempt self-forgiveness is you can make amends for your actions. When you need to forgive someone else you cannot guarantee they will apologize or care. After the affair Donna apologized to her husband on a number of occasions. Donna made it a point to support the way Jeff parented their children. Ned also apologized to Nora and learned to take her side when she complained about his father.

To make amends you look for a way to be kind to those you have hurt. Erica joined a twelve-step program and embraced the steps where atonement was highlighted. In cases where the people you have hurt are dead or otherwise unavailable, you can provide a symbolic kindness to someone else. You can work in a nursing home instead of helping your own dead parents. You can tutor in a school when you want to make amends to your grown children. You can give money to a charity for financial misdeeds.

At a minimum, everyone can begin by offering a sincere apology for bad behavior. If the person you hurt is yourself, you can learn to talk about yourself with kindness. You can highlight your good points and articulate your strengths. You can reward your positive changes and forgive the ways you fail.

After contemplating self-forgiveness for quite a while I introduce these ideas through an advanced class. In this class, I explored how to use my forgiveness methods to forgive yourself. The follow-up class was only for people who had already completed one of my interpersonal forgiveness classes. I showed how to apply my forgiveness methods to self-forgiveness with a group of people who already knew about interpersonal forgiveness. I teach self-forgiveness to people who have learned my forgiveness training. Therefore, I suggest you practice these methods first in your dealings with other people. Start with interpersonal forgiveness. When there is some degree of success then try the forgiveness process in the quest to forgive yourself.

This is not to say that self-forgiveness is radically different from interpersonal forgiveness. One of the great benefits of my work and research is the understanding that forgiveness of one offense does not differ from forgiveness of another. In most ways self-forgiveness follows the same process as interpersonal forgiveness. The overriding goal with forgiveness—to experience peace—is the same. We want to be able to accept our mistakes and correct them as necessary. We do not need to suffer endlessly. We can forgive ourselves for failing, make the necessary changes and move on to honor our positive intention.

Ned and Donna showed me that a long-standing grievance against oneself can hurt as much or more than a grievance held against someone else.

Ned may think he should have stopped his father's insults long ago. The truth is, Ned could not stop his father until he was ready. Equally clear is that Ned's continued frustration with himself did not help him take constructive action. Or Erica may hate the way she lived a part of her life, but again, Erica could not change her life until she had proper training and sufficient motivation. She needed the self-care that came through forgiveness lessons.

In some ways Terri was faced with a more difficult struggle. She had done nothing wrong except poor financial planning. Terri had a job that did not pay her enough, and with her husband's death she faced drastically changed life circumstances. Terri faced the demanding task of learning new job skills and letting go of a job she loved. These were difficult transitions, and at first she beat herself up for getting herself into this predicament. Terri needed to forgive herself.

The three components of interpersonal forgiveness can be used in a similar manner for self-forgiveness. The three key components of forgiveness are

1. taking something less personally
2. taking responsibility for your feelings
3. telling a positive intention story

I demonstrated in chapter 1 how taking something too personally begins the process of creating a grievance. Donna had an affair. Erica used too many drugs. Ned did not stand up to his father. Terri stuck with the wrong job. Forgiveness begins when we realize we are not alone in whatever we did wrong. Remember, every mistake you make has been done thousands of times by other people. You created no new evil or managed no new failure. What you did was react in a common way to human difficulties. While you may have done things that were unkind or unskillful, they are in the past, and through forgiveness we can learn and practice better ways to act.

We can learn to take things less personally through understanding we are human and will make mistakes. Each of us has the potential to be unkind or fail at certain things. No one is immune from that aspect of being human. Every mistake is a common one and has been made before. We can forgive, learn, and grow rather than continue to beat ourselves up and stay stuck. Shame, embarrassment, and guilt are emotions that do little to help us grow. Forgiveness is easy when we understand that we all make mistakes.

The second step in forgiving ourselves occurs as people stop blaming their past actions for how they feel. Ned constantly beat himself up for not standing up to his father. Terri blasted herself for not seeing the future clearly and for holding on to a job that did not pay enough. Donna became paralyzed because she had an affair. Erica hated herself for acting like her mother. Each of these people became a victim of both their actions and the way they reacted to what they did.

I taught each of them the PERT technique and asked them each to practice in the same way as if their grievance were with their parents or spouse. I taught each of these people to create enforceable rules in the same way as if their grievance were with their neighbor or boss. I reminded them that they could forgive themselves. I reminded them each that they could feel peaceful again.

My goal was to help Donna, Ned, Terri, and Erica take responsibility for how they feel. It pained me to see how their past actions held them in pain. My goal was to help them become more peaceful so their grievance would rent less space in their mind. My goal was not to help Donna, Ned, Terri, and Erica ignore their mistakes or to condone their actions, but rather to teach them to forgive themselves so they could learn and practice better ways of acting.

The third step in forgiving ourselves occurs as we change our grievance story into a forgiveness story by reconnecting with our positive intention. We can do this just as well when we are upset with ourselves as with our best friend. The grievance story focuses on the offense and how bad we feel about it. It rents a good deal of space in our mind as we tell ourselves and others the bad things that happened and our inability to cope.

Even though Ned was a successful businessperson and had a stable marriage, he thought of himself as a failure because he did not stand up to his father. His grievance about standing up to his father colored his opinion of himself. Ned would perceive any praise he received as a joke, since, if the person giving him a compliment only knew what a wimp he was they would never praise him. Donna's affair dominated her self-talk for a long time after she ended the affair. She condemned herself for ending a marriage that had been broken for years and referred to herself as a bad person rather than as a woman who, under stress, made a poor decision.

Terri was depressed over the loss of her husband, the loss of her job, and her sense of failure. Losing a spouse and job is bad enough, but Terri made it much worse by condemning herself. She thought that death was out of her control but a better-paying job was not. Terri was correct except for one huge error in thinking. Nothing in your past can be changed. Only the present is under your current control. Only the present could be changed.

After her mother died Erica looked in the mirror and did not like what she saw. She saw a failure—a woman dependent on drugs, a loser in love. By blaming herself, she missed the effect her mother's parenting had on her development. Most important, she missed the part of her that was aching to change.

All of these four people wanted to make changes in their lives. All of them saw that something needed to be done to improve their lives. Unfortunately, they created more pain by creating a grievance story rather than grieving their losses and making the changes that were necessary. All were able to forgive themselves in large part because they changed their grievance stories to reflect their positive intention.

Terri, Erica, Donna, and Larry were each able to change their grievance story into a new story that reflected hope and positive intention. For Terri, the positive intention was to take good care of her children. She saw that this loving goal lay behind her frustration and sense of failure. She was mainly upset at herself for putting her children at risk. When Terri went back to school to learn computer technology she reminded herself of the love she felt for her children, and that love sustained her.

Erica saw that a loving part of herself wanted to rescue her from a difficult life. The death of her mother triggered that loving part into taking action. She changed her grievance story to reflect this loving aspect, focusing on her dreams and future goals rather than on her painful past.

Donna's positive intention was to create a successful long-term relationship. She did not want to give up on marriage just because her first had ended badly. Donna saw that she had to learn better communication skills to avoid the problems that occurred in her marriage to Jeff. She understood that she was not assertive enough with Jeff and that she had fooled herself into thinking things would magically get better.

After her divorce Donna decided that a new relationship would have to wait. She saw with some chagrin that she was capable of unkind actions such as having an affair. Therefore, she took it upon herself to develop new parts of herself with a therapist. She wanted to learn about herself and thereby grow in the hope of creating a stronger relationship with another man.

Ned's positive intention was to do what he could to support and honor his marriage. This meant that he would side with Nora and not his father. He would evaluate the success of his behavior not by its effect on either him or his dad but by the quality of his marriage. When he did this Nora became an ally and provided Ned with guidance and support. Ned learned that as long as he was renting out so much space to his dad there was insufficient room for Nora. As he followed his positive intention, the reactions of his father became less important to him. Nora's support became fundamental, and they united and learned together how to talk assertively to Ned's father.

FORGIVING YOURSELF USING THE HEAL METHOD

I have distilled the three components of my forgiveness training into a simple guided imagery practice that I call the HEAL method. The HEAL method is covered fully in chapters 12 and 13. With some simple modification you can use the HEAL method for forgiving yourself.

The *H* in HEAL stands for *Hope*. When you create a *Hope* statement you are reminding yourself that you wished or hoped that you would behave in a certain way. You hoped to be a good spouse, to make money, to get a job or promotion, to be a caring parent, to keep the people you love safe, to be healthy, or to treat people with respect or honesty. Ned wanted to maintain a loving relationship with Nora even under the provocation of a difficult parent. He wanted to protect her from the insults of his father. His *Hope* statement began with the word *I* and was focused on his specific goal: "I wanted to stand up to my father when he criticized my wife." Donna's *Hope* statement was, "I hoped to end my relationship with Jeff in a perfect manner maintaining both his and my dignity." Both *H* statements are positive, personal, and specific.

The *E* in HEAL stands for *Educate*. In an *E* statement we *Educate* ourselves to the possibility of things not turning out the way we would like. Erica's *E* statement says, "I hoped by thirty-one to be sober and competent." Erica commits to change, does her best, and awaits the results. She makes every good attempt to reclaim her life but still might experience moments of despair or the desire for drugs. These do not make her a failure. They make her human. She reminds herself that many people take two steps forward and one step backward. For Donna an appropriate *E* statement might reflect the inherent limitations of human relationship. She hoped for a dignified end to her marriage yet now realizes that perfect endings are not always possible. Her *E* statement is, "I understand and accept that many relationships, even with the best of intentions, end in hurt."

When making your *E* statement, remember it has two parts. The first part is the general statement acknowledging that every hope carries with it the possibility of failure. Examples of this are: I can only do my best; many good love affairs end in a messy way; often parents have a hard time showing their love properly; people are commonly disappointed in other people's behavior; I will not return everybody's love in the way they want. The second part of your *E* statement asserts that you understand and accept the uncertainty.

I want to emphasize one point. Making an *E* statement does not mean you condone your hurtful actions. You may no more approve of your own affair than of your spouse's. You can disagree with what you did and understand that what you did was common. You can disagree with what you did and work hard to change your behavior. You can disagree with what you did and work hard to make amends. You can apologize and hope you are forgiven. What you are saying with your *E* statement is you accept that doing hurtful things and feeling pain are normal parts of being human.

The next step in the HEAL method, *A*, means you *Affirm* your positive intention. For developing self-forgiveness, a useful positive intention is the desire to experience greater happiness. You can learn to talk about your mistakes or poor choices as failed attempts to find happiness. You then describe your positive intention as learning better ways to make yourself happy.

Often, people beat themselves up over mistakes they made. Erica dwelled on her failures and focused on her addiction. Eventually she saw that by taking drugs she was trying to make herself happy. Happiness was a good goal for Erica, but in the past she had used unskillful methods to meet that goal. Her positive intention story went on to say that drugs proved a poor choice for happiness. She asserted that her own happiness was important and that she was going to try more productive ways to make herself feel good. Her *A* statement was, "I commit to lasting and skillful ways to feel happy.

The last step in HEAL, *L*, stands for making a *Long-Term Commitment* to your well-being. Every *L* statement includes the following: "I make the long-term commitment to follow my positive intention and use the HEAL method." Some of you may find that in order to manifest your positive intention you have to learn new skills. Then your *L* statement can add the following: "I make a long-term commitment to learn whatever new skills I need to prosper."

For self-forgiveness, your *L* statement can also include your commitment to make amends to those you have hurt. Donna reminded herself how much she wanted to treat Jeff with kindness. She encouraged her children to visit him and spoke highly of him to them. Ned reminded himself of his desire to stay connected to his wife. He practiced daily gratitude reminders of how lucky he was to be Nora's husband. He did this so he would never take her affection for granted. In that way he would never allow his father to get between him and Nora again.

To help develop self-forgiveness we must make a powerful resolve to stop our destructive behaviors. Terri was adamant that she would never give up on her desire to get a job that paid more. She made a long-term commitment to financial well-being. Her positive intention was the loving care of her children, and her long-term commitment included her commitment to attend computer school regularly, cut down on expenses, and to take classes in financial management.

Erica's long-term commitment was to sobriety and the development of good work habits. Erica attended twelve-step programs regularly, started therapy, and looked for a mentor who would help her develop good work habits. These actions arose out of her positive intention that focused on her desire for greater happiness. She practiced the HEAL method regularly for a while until her anger with herself lessened. She forgave herself and her mother and moved on with her life. Forgiving herself was the key aspect in leading to the positive changes Erica made in her life.

Self-forgiveness has much in common with forgiving others. Both involve taking less offense, taking more responsibility for how we feel, and changing the story to reflect a positive intention. The impetus for both is to heal—to create the best life we can for ourselves, the people we love, and the communities in which we live. When we suffer less and focus on our positive intention, we do our best.

No one is perfect. Everyone has flaws. Forgiving yourself is just another way to Forgive for Good. Here are the 9 steps to self-forgiveness:

1. Know exactly how you feel about what you did. Be able to articulate the specific wrong you have committed and the harm it caused. Tell a couple of trusted people about your experience.
2. Understand your goal. Forgiveness is to enable you to feel at peace even though you did things you wished you had not. You do not have to reconcile with the person you have hurt.
3. Self-forgiveness can be defined as the recognition that everyone including yourself makes mistakes, that blame and shame can be replaced by making amends and developing better ways to behave, and that your grievance story can be changed and relinquished.
4. Recognize that your primary distress is coming from the hurt feelings, thoughts, and physical upset you are experiencing right now, not what you did two minutes or ten years ago.
5. At each moment that you feel upset practice stress management techniques to soothe your body's fight or flight response.
6. Recognize the unenforceable rules you have that demand you be lovable and competent at all times. Remind yourself that every single human being makes mistakes and has much to learn. Remind yourself that no one is a failure: Each of us is only someone who was unable to successfully accomplish something at a particular place and time.
7. Learn to do good rather than feel bad. If you have hurt others or yourself, instead of mentally replaying the hurt, look for ways to apologize, make amends and, when necessary, develop new skills so you won't make the same mistake again.
8. Appreciate your good points. Take time out of each day to keep track of the kind and loving things you do.
9. Amend your grievance story to reflect your heroic choice to learn, grow, and forgive.

CHAPTER 16

Above and Beyond

Doing an injury puts you below your enemy;
Revenging one makes you but even with him;
Forgiving it sets you above him.

BENJAMIN FRANKLIN, *Poor Richard's Almanac*

Each of us has experienced hurt caused by friends, lovers, family members, or business partners. In every situation where a grievance was created, we responded unskillfully to not getting what we wanted. *Forgive for Good* has shown you how to respond more skillfully to the hurts you experience and has given you scientifically proven tools for healing those hurts and moving on.

You have learned that forgiveness is not the same as approving of unkindness. Forgiveness does not mean you have to reconcile with someone who mistreated you. You do not have to forget what happened. Forgiveness does not mean you lie down and become a doormat when you are hurt.

Forgiveness means we find peace even though we were in pain and mistreated. Forgiveness means we move on in our life after an abandonment or affair. It means we become responsible for how we feel. Forgiveness means we learn to take painful events less personally. Forgiveness means we reconnect with our positive intention. Forgiveness means we change our grievance story. Forgiveness means that we do not stop smelling the roses simply because we are hurt. Forgiveness means we make better decisions for guiding our lives and forgiveness means we feel better.

Jeremy made peace with having a boss who lied to him. Sarah made peace with having had a husband who mistreated her. Dana forgave not getting a deserved promotion. Suzanne forgave her husband for wrecking their car and causing her enduring physical pain. People whose family members were murdered felt physically and emotionally better after learning to forgive. This book has given you the keys to experiencing the same kind of healing and peace.

The grievance and forgiveness process is like a solar eclipse. In an eclipse the sun appears to be gone. But it has not disappeared; it has just been covered over by the moon. When we create a grievance the warmth of the sun of friendship, love, and beauty recede from our view. Grievances become the moon that blocks the sun. To forgive, we remember the eclipse is only temporary. We remember that people in other parts of the earth have a clear view of the sun. With forgiveness we understand that as we change our perspective the sun reappears in its luminous radiance.

Many of you remember the game show *Let's Make a Deal*. On that show contestants were asked whether they wanted to trade a trinket they brought to the show for one or more prizes. The contestants would be offered brightly colored boxes and money or asked to choose what was behind one of the curtains. None of the contestants knew what they were trading for. The object of the game was for each contestant to trade for the best prize they could. There was an element of risk because once a contestant received something on the next trade they had something to lose. Most of the prizes were good ones, but sometimes a contestant made a trade and got junk in return.

The object of the game was for each contestant to trade for the best prize possible. At the end of the show the two contestants who had won the most valuable prizes were asked if they wished to bid on the Big Deal of the Day. In the Big Deal the contestants got to choose the prize behind one of three doors. Sometimes the prizes were worth a good deal of money, such as cars or home entertainment centers, living room furniture or expensive vacations. Most of the Big Deal prizes were valuable, but sometimes the contestant got a donkey or a shelf full of old newspapers or a bunch of old car tires. These worthless prizes were referred to as "clunkers" and they came up periodically. The "clunker" was the booby prize.

I was always intrigued by the reaction of the contestants who got the clunker. I found it fascinating to see how they handled the disappointment of getting onto a game show and instead of coming home with a home entertainment center became the proud owners of old tires. Some contestants were notably upset and looked either angry or about to cry. However, others smiled, laughed, and thanked the host for letting them play the game. They seemed to understand that when they play a game they do not always emerge the winner.

I now see that the contestants who lost but did not forget that it was only a game were actually quite forgiving. Clearly, they wanted to win a big prize. Clearly, they did not get what they wanted. However, these folks did not take the loss personally, and they did not blame the game show for ruining their day. The story they told about their experience would certainly not be a grievance story, even though they were disappointed. They walked away from the show, and even though they lost they had a good time.

I often think of *Let's Make a Deal* when I listen to people who have been mistreated or hurt. Often these people forget that in the game of life clunkers appear on a regular basis. In fact, the rule book of life contains innumerable references to loss, pain, and disappointment. Having clunkers written in makes it possible to lose the game. It is this possibility that makes winning even more rewarding.

To play the game of life means we had better prepare for the clunkers that come our way. Our real opportunity is the gift of being in the game at all. We are lucky to be alive, and we have the opportunity to learn the rules of the game and play as best we can.

At this the book's end, I offer you a summary of the forgiveness process. This summary is not intended to be a substitute for reading the book but a reminder of the steps to take in getting over your hurts and wounds. These nine steps to forgiveness are a good but not complete summary of my methods. They distill the process of how to forgive either yourself or someone else.

NINE STEPS TO FORGIVENESS

1. Know exactly how you feel about what happened, and be able to articulate what about the situation is not okay. Then tell a couple of trusted people about your experience.

2. Make a commitment to yourself to do what you have to do to feel better. Forgiveness is for you and not for anyone else. No one else even has to know about your decision.

3. Understand your goal. Forgiveness does not necessarily mean reconciling with the person who upset you or condoning their action. What you are after is peace. Forgiveness can be defined as the peace and understanding that come from blaming less that which has hurt you, taking the experience less personally, and changing your grievance story.

4. Get the right perspective on what is happening. Recognize that your primary distress is coming from the hurt feelings, thoughts, and physical upset you are suffering now, not what offended you or hurt you two minutes—or ten years—ago.

5. At the moment you feel upset, practice the Positive Emotion Refocusing Technique (PERT) to soothe your body's flight-or-fight response.

6. Give up expecting things from other people, or life, that they do not choose to give you. Recognize the unenforceable rules you have for your health or how you or other people must behave. Remind yourself that you can hope for health, love, friendship, and prosperity and work hard to get them. However, you will suffer if you demand that these things occur when you do not have the power to make them happen.

7. Put your energy into looking for another way to get your positive goals met than through the experience that has hurt you. In other words, find your positive intention. Instead of mentally replaying your hurt, seek out new ways to get what you want.

8. Remember that a life well lived is your best revenge. Instead of focusing on your wounded feelings, and thereby giving the person who hurt you power over you, learn to look for the love, beauty, and kindness around you.

9. Amend your grievance story to remind yourself of the heroic choice to forgive.

To review these nine steps and apply them to a specific story, let's look at Mallory. Mallory was an attractive and sweet young woman of twenty-five. She reported that her mother was cold and rejecting while her father was quiet and stayed in the background. She grew up feeling unattractive and uncared for and struggled to create good relationships. Her parents were successful in business, and Mallory was raised in an upper-middle-class neighborhood.

Mallory came to a forgiveness class because her fiancé, Skip, decided he was more interested in sleeping with a local cocktail waitress than in remaining faithful to her. Mallory described this betrayal as an example of how rejecting and unfair the world was. It showed how she never got a break. Mallory felt angry, hurt, confused, scared, and lonely. Skip had moved out, but Mallory considered begging him to return.

When the class met Mallory, we could see the hurt in her eyes and the sorrow in the way she held herself. It was difficult to have a conversation without her bringing up one or more of the many people who had done her wrong. She had innumerable grievance stories—a long list from her parents' actions and now a repertoire of adult betrayals.

Mallory had satisfied the first step in the forgiveness process like a professional. She determined what she did not like about her fiancé's behavior and knew in gruesome detail how she felt about it. She told anyone willing to listen what a louse Skip was. Clearly, step one was not a problem for her.

Learning the second and third steps of forgiveness, however, were a challenge for Mallory. She was in so much pain that she could not think straight. She thought Skip was the reason she suffered. To her it was a foreign concept that she might want to heal just for her own well-being. She thought that healing meant only one thing: that the relationship with Skip would become okay. She even considered taking him back because she did not think other men would ever find her attractive.

Mallory's misunderstanding of forgiveness was an impediment to her healing. She thought forgiving Skip meant she had to be a doormat her entire life, that she had to stay with Skip and feel his cheating was okay. She confused forgiveness with condoning and reconciling with Skip. Eventually she learned that forgiveness meant she could feel peaceful when thinking of Skip and that he was not responsible for her pain. She also learned that forgiveness freed her to make the best decisions she could for her life.

The fourth step also presented challenges. Mallory struggled to understand how controlling the way she felt in the present was more important than reviewing what happened to her in the past. She had trained herself to talk relentlessly of her past and of how her parents and poor relationships limited her options and happiness. It was hard for her to believe that focusing on the past again and again was the reason for her current distress. The insight that forgiveness starts in the present was a challenge.

I emphasized to Mallory that we cannot change the past, but we can change how much space we rent in our mind to the hurtful parts of the past. I showed Mallory that she cannot change the past but she can change the amount of blame she gives the past for how she feels today. I explained to Mallory that she could do these things when she practices the Forgive for Good techniques. I then taught Mallory the PERT technique, the fifth step. When she first practiced it a lightbulb began to glimmer in her mind. She saw for an instant that breathing slowly and deeply affected how she felt. By practicing PERT she gained a brief measure of control over her hurt and anger. When she did not practice PERT, she remained in a state of upset and continually blamed her former fiancé for how she felt. Pain, anger, and frustration leading to blame and as a result more pain, anger, and frustration. As Mallory practiced PERT she saw she was in control of how much space to give her ex-fiancé.

Mallory simultaneously experimented with challenging her unenforceable rules, the sixth step. While she wanted Skip to love and be faithful to her, it was clearly impossible to make him act in this way. His behavior was a constant reminder to Mallory that he did what he wanted and she had limited power over him. Mallory also started to examine her theory that her parents had ruined her life. She noticed that she had an unenforceable rule that her parents must love her and treat her with kindness. Her parents had showed Mallory some love and care but also some cruelty and lack of care. Her parents' behavior was a reminder that no matter how much Mallory wanted things to go her way, she did not have the power to control other people's behavior. Mallory, by continuing to insist that her past change, was dooming herself to endless cycles of blame, offense, and suffering.

As the forgiveness training progressed Mallory got in the habit of practicing the HEAL Method. She began to look at her suffering and started to ask herself what unenforceable rule she was trying to enforce. I emphasized to her that she would not be so upset unless she was trying to change something she could not change. Mallory saw that trying to change her ex-fiancé's behavior would always lead to pain and helplessness. She became able to comprehend that just because she hoped for something, it did not have to come true. She also understood that she would not be so upset if her rules were more reasonable. Therefore, Mallory took it upon herself to create more enforceable rules. The consequence of this practice was her realization that she was more in control of how she felt than she was of other people's actions.

Due to her effort Mallory was able to finally ask herself the revealing question, "What do I really want." Through asking she saw that Skip and her parents were not in control of her life. She realized that if they were not in control of her life then she must be. Emerging from this insight she started to work on her positive intention, the seventh step. Mallory realized that her positive intention was to learn how to value herself and her actions; it had little to do with getting married. She saw it was more important for her to feel good about herself than it was for other people to feel good about her. Finding her positive intention helped Mallory focus on creating her future and not lamenting her past. Out of her reflection a powerful positive intention was born along with the commitment to learn new skills.

Connecting to her positive intention pushed Mallory to make changes in her life, the eighth step. She changed her story to reflect her goal of finding things about herself to approve of. She told a new story of learning about herself and how hard it is for her to approve of herself. She talked about blaming other people and of holding on to the past as impediments to her goal of healing. She told about entering counseling, looking for male friends and not lovers, and appreciating her good qualities. She did not gloss over the difficulties she faced. She moved her past difficulties off center stage and her positive goals into the limelight.

Mallory found her positive intention helped her free up space so she could uncover other ways to get her needs met. She realized that neither Skip nor her parents were ever going to approve of her in the way she wanted. She was going to have to find that in herself. Mallory undertook the difficult task of learning a new habit. Her old habit had been to see her glass as half empty. She undertook the task of retraining her mind to see where her cup might be already full.

Mallory looked at her life and saw that she was a good student and was capable of making excellent grades in school. She found appreciation for her parent's business acumen and the freedom that granted her to attend college full-time. She looked to appreciate the beautiful area in which she lived and she gave herself credit for her excellent exercise routine.

Mallory also practiced the Breath of Thanks when she was driving and watching TV. She made it a point when shopping to marvel at the opportunities she had to purchase a stupendous array of items. She learned to stop for a minute at the local shopping mall and say thanks to all of the people working there. She would walk into her local supermarket and for a moment would appreciate the abundance of food choices in front of her.

Her parents were financially successful and provided her with ongoing financial help. Mallory had known that financial success did not predict emotional caring, and she had experienced the pain of parents who were more interested in their business than parenting. She had dwelled for years on what she had lost. Now she saw that her parents' financial success was also a blessing, since it granted her freedom to attend college full-time. Mallory practiced and saw the value of the old adage that a life well lived is the best revenge.

When I bumped into Mallory a year after the forgiveness classes ended I was delighted at the changes in her. She was filled with energy and showed a lovely smile. When I asked her about Skip, she almost responded, "Skip who?" Instead of talking about Skip, she wanted to talk about how much she had learned about herself. When I asked her about her parents she mentioned the relationship with them had improved. Mallory accepted what they could offer and realized their enormous emotional limitations. As an adult, she understood she was the only one who could create a good life for herself. She was learning to let her parents off the hook. She forgave them their mistakes.

The biggest change in Mallory was the way she told what used to be her grievance stories. She talked about her ongoing struggles, and she did so by reflecting her positive intention. She talked with pride of forgiving Skip and learning how to take care of herself. She asserted that because she forgave Skip the next person who hurt her would be easier to forgive. Mallory was a woman who took her forgiveness training to heart. She completed the full nine steps and now presented herself as a hero and not a victim.

Mallory, of course, did not always have it easy. She still longed for an *Ozzie and Harriet* family. When she found the longing overpowering, she practiced the HEAL method and cut the longing down to size. When she found the longing overpowering she told herself to make the best of what she had or she would take a walk and remind herself of the blessings of a beautiful day or the possibilities the future might bring.

This book has been a lesson on how to make peace when the curtain you choose or the one that life chooses for you has a clunker behind it. As you practice the HEAL method, you come to understand the full power that forgiveness has to heal your life. I hope you will make the decision to simply become a forgiving person, to accept that in life you will have bad experiences as well as good. It develops great confidence to be able to handle what comes your way without getting lost in blame and suffering. We do not know what life has in store, but we do know that forgiveness provides the strength to get back in the game and resume playing.

To become a forgiving person, we first have to practice forgiving smaller grievances. Then when a bigger insult comes we are ready and able to deal with it. Alternatively, like Mallory, once we learn to forgive a major grievance, we can understand the value of limiting the power the pain and anger hold over us the next time we are hurt. None of us can make the people in our life behave kindly, fairly, or honestly at all times. We cannot end the cruelty that exists. What we can do is forgive the unkindness that comes our way and put energy into manifesting our positive intention. Then we can help others to do the same.

Forgiveness is above all a choice. It is a choice to find peace and live life fully. We can choose either to remain stuck in the pain and frustration of the past or to move on to the potential of the future. It is a choice we can all make, and it is a choice that will lead us to a healthier and happier life. Research has shown us the health benefits of learning to forgive. The personal stories throughout the book demonstrate that these forgiveness methods work. The choice to practice forgiveness is now yours.

When you look you will see that the world we live in is a complex and miraculous place. No one knows what will happen tomorrow. Each of us has lives filled with some success and failure, some suffering and happiness. Everywhere we look we can find love and beauty as well as brutal selfishness and unkindness.

Forgiveness, like other positive emotions such as hope, compassion, and appreciation, are natural expressions of being human. They exist within a deep part of each of us. Like many things, they require practice to perfect. When you practice these positive feelings they become stronger and easier to find. When I held a grievance against my friend Sam I felt only anger and helplessness. Now I feel love and a strong connection with him. I feel lucky to be his friend. I have forgiven him, and my memories of the past are good ones. Forgiveness has opened me to wonderful parts of myself. While it did not come easily, it was well worth the effort.

Forgiveness can be as natural a response to hurt as are anger and pain. Before reading this book many of you had not learned how to look for the forgiveness inside of you. I have shown you how to uncover the part of yourself where forgiveness is hidden. I believe each of you can and will Forgive for Good. I hope I have convinced you of the power of forgiveness to improve your life.

I have shown you how to rent less space in your mind to your hurts and grievances. I hope you are enjoying your beauty, love, and forgiveness channels. Remember that you control the remote. In time, I am convinced that each of you will Forgive for Good and that your mind, body, relationships, community, and spirit will benefit.

Acknowledgments

I want to thank my two children Anna and Danny who were patient with my many days spent writing and listening to Yankee games on the computer.

I want to thank my wife Jan who showed me love, encouragement, and care. Jan is one of those people who does not need a forgiveness book because she almost never takes offense and holds no grudges. I have learned of forgiveness from watching her skillful reactions to experience and I often consider myself someone who puts into words the gentle way she lives her life.

Dr. Kenneth R. Pelletier and Dr. William Haskell at the Stanford Center for Research in Disease Prevention provided first rate kindness, guidance, and support. They both found a way to make forgiveness projects in strife torn Northern Ireland a responsible way to spend time in a world class medical school and for that I am grateful. Dr. Carl Thoresen showed me that good research can be conducted in areas of the heart and spirit and his encouragement and support were invaluable. In addition he is a kind, visionary, and collaborative research partner who demonstrates a palpable belief in the goodness of human beings. Dr. Stephanie Evans was the coordinator for the Stanford Forgiveness Project and treated the project as if it were her own. Her dedication, delightful and caring way with study participants, and her vision were as important to the success of the project as anything I did. Alex Harris, Samuel Standard, Sonya Benisovich, and Jennifer Bruning were all graduate students whose hard work and positive outlook made the Stanford Forgiveness Project succeed. Shira Neuberger helped me when I did not know what I was doing and through her labors I completed a Ph.D. dissertation on time and with a good number of participants. Andrew

Winzelberg, Ph.D. generously provided statistics help and is a first-rate running partner.

I owe my work in Northern Ireland to the ideas and inspiration of the Reverend Byron Bland. Bryon's innate compassion for people who suffer and his long standing belief in peaceful conflict resolution were the underpinnings for our Northern Ireland HOPE projects. He is also a remarkably easy man with whom to collaborate and I anticipate more HOPE projects in the future.

In addition I thank Norma McConville and all the courageous people I met from Northern Ireland whose willingness to grow continues to inspire me.

Jillian Manus, my agent, had the idea for this book before I did. I would not be here without her leadership and vision. Jeremy Katz gave me the first hints of how to organize a forgiveness book. His help was given freely and generously and I thank him for that. Gideon Weil is a delightful and supportive editor. He is generous with praise, answers all questions with patience and respect and I felt he was entirely in my corner.

And finally thank you to all the people who came to my classes. I want you to know the appreciative wonder I feel every time you listen, ask questions, often change for the better, and through it all help me create this work.